NPR's Podcast Start Up Guide

GLEN WELDON

NPR's Podcast Start Up Guide

Create, Launch, and Grow a Podcast on Any Budget

TEN SPEED PRESS
California | New York

CONTENTS

PART 1
IMAGINE

PART 2
PLAN

At NPR, we think of ourselves as storytellers.

That might surprise you, if you equate the word *story* with "fiction." We don't.

Humans have used stories to convey information for hundreds of thousands of years. Storytelling is programmed into our DNA (quite literally, as DNA is essentially the story the body tells itself to make us who we are).

There's a very simple reason for that. Information, in and of itself, is inert—many discrete sets of data points that just...sit there.

Stories bring information to life. They're the dynamic infrastructure we construct to transform those inert data points into a series of moving moments that take our audience on a journey. Some of those journeys inform and educate. Some delight and surprise. Some spur action. Some offer comfort and companionship.

NPR has been in the business of storytelling since our first broadcast on April 20, 1971, and we've never stopped. What we *have* done—and continue to do—is adapt. That's where this book comes in.

NPR's legacy of broadcasting news, telling stories, and starting conversations over the airwaves has made our transition into podcasts an organic one, since so many principles of audio journalism and storytelling are also critical principles of podcasting. Over time, we've found new stories and new ways to tell them, which has resulted in some of the most beloved, critically acclaimed, and listened-to podcasts in the world.

At NPR we talk a lot about "driveway moments"—the X factor that keeps listeners sitting in their idling cars, amid the gathering dark, after they arrive home from work, so they can hear the end of the story or feature—their companion on the last few miles of their commute. As podcasting has grown over the past half-decade, and as the field's competitiveness has intensified, it's this way of thinking that has led more and more people to ask us about how we create our shows.

This book will walk you through a certain amount of nerdy-but-necessary audiophilic technical detail—mics and mixers, WAV files and room tone. Mostly, though, it will provide a practical guide to how we at NPR approach storytelling by always foregrounding the listener's experience.

You'll learn how and why our award-winning podcasts sound like they do—the best practices we've adopted, the hard-won knowledge we've earned over the decades. And yet, even if you follow the guidelines in this book to the letter, the podcast you make won't sound like NPR.

Because ultimately, your podcast must, should—and will—sound like you. This book is about storytelling, and your podcast is the story only you can tell.

Good luck!

—Anya Grundmann, senior vice president for programming and audience development, NPR

Podcasting with a Plan

Whoever you are, whatever you love, there's a podcast for you. More every day. Sports fan, knitting obsessive, culture vulture, armchair psychologist, political junkie, science nerd, foodie, left-handed Bolivian dental hygienist[1]—you name it, there's a podcast about it.

Podcasting's growth has been nuts, and it's continuing. In 2019, the *New York Times* counted more than seven hundred thousand podcasts in existence,[2] with two to three thousand new shows appearing every dang *month*. That same year, podcasting reached a major milestone when an Infinite Dial Study by Edison Research and Triton Digital found that more than 50 percent of Americans ages twelve and over said they had ever listened to a podcast.

Podcasts are booming because they speak to our collective obsession with wanting to know stuff (the faster the better; we're busy!) and to enjoy stuff (being busy can be stressful; we need downtime!). Podcasts make these leaps in knowledge and pleasure available in the time it takes to tuck in earbuds—while freeing our eyeballs and hands to do other things. We listen while we commute, work out, walk the dog, cook, or drift to sleep.

But there's another growth curve. Hundreds of thousands of us are transforming our love of listening to podcasts into creating them.

Maybe you picked up this book because you've got an idea or a message that's important to you. Maybe friends or family have said, "You should do a podcast!" Maybe you want to explore audio storytelling. Or maybe you heard that podcasts can help your business.[3]

Most of us who love podcasts haven't thought too much about what goes into making them. They're just there for us. We wake up,

1 Give it time!

2 According to podcast hosting service Blubrry—which lik so many onlin srvics, has no us whatsovr for th lttr *e*, which is how you know it's got its FINGR ON TH PULS!

3 Read: Maybe your boss called you into their office and said, "You know *Serial*? Why can't we do that, but, you know, for restaurant supply sales? *We've got to move these salt shakers, Jenkins!*" Or, um, words to that effect.

open our phone, and our favorite podcasts are downloaded and waiting. But a *lot* of steps happen between the seed of an idea and that polished, finished[4] product.

With so many people getting into podcasting, quality varies hugely. Too hugely. Sure, the barrier to entry in podcasting is low—like, *very* low. So low it's making a divot in the carpet: If you've got a mic and a laptop, you can create a successful podcast, right?

Wrong. Execution matters. Poor sound quality, sloppy or non-existent editing, undercooked storytelling, and a host of other issues render many—okay, most—podcasts unsustainable and unlistenable.

The barrier to entry may be low, but the learning curve is steep.

Sit down with any podcaster and you'll hear stories from the trenches, from forgetting to hit the Record button to learning—with slow-dawning horror—that the one interview subject they've built an episode around dried up somewhere between the juicy preinterview and the guarded, dull-as-dishwater recording session. While any project worth undertaking has challenges, many of the most common stumbling blocks, blind alleys, rabbit holes, and curve balls are avoidable, if you know the questions to ask yourself first.

That's what this book's about. Setting your sights on quality is crucial in a crowded marketplace where audiences will move on if they aren't instantly hooked by a story. And every podcast out there is jostling for attention—for listeners clicking, downloading, and sharing—in the merciless algorithmic mosh pit called the internet.

Consider this: Typically, 20 to 35 percent of a podcast episode's audience drops out in the first five minutes. Getting and keeping audience attention is serious business. You have to give this podcasting thing your best shot to avoid the dreaded, all-too-common petering-out phenomenon that some have labeled "podfade."[5]

I'm here to help. I want to share what we at NPR know about keeping people listening.

This book is the definitive, go-to guide on how to podcast, powered by NPR's decades of experience, expertise, and acclaim in the audio space.[6] I'll share proven strategies, from nurturing the glimmerings of an idea to getting your audience to hit Play. You'll learn how to figure out the best structure and format for your podcast; storytelling techniques that hook listeners; important fundamentals on scheduling, budgeting, and legalities;[7] the dos and don'ts for recording and editing; and the nuts and bolts for the launch and distribution of the final product.

4 Or unpolished! Unfinished! That's kind of the charm, sometimes! As we'll discuss!

5 You and I, however, will not be calling it "podfade." Because come on.

6 Yeah, I know. "Audio space." Last time. Promise.

7 NO NODDING OFF! IT'S IMPORTANT!

Some of this book's information has been adapted from materials developed by the NPR Training team—which includes our wide-ranging catalog of tips and tricks for audio journalism and storytelling. But you'll get much more than that. How do the pros open a story in a compelling way that makes listeners stick around? What advice do they have for aspiring podcasters? You'll find insights from some of the most respected names in the NPR and podcasting universe, plus wisdom from our producers, writers, editors, sound technicians, and project managers, who know what it takes to get a podcast done and *done*.

To be clear: The goal isn't for you to sound like NPR. It's to outfit you with the questions to ask yourself—based on the hard-won lessons we've learned over the years—that will make you sound like *you*.

Because that, at the end of the (very long!) day, is what your podcast must and should be: *your* voice, *your* passion.

Your story.

Your Intrepid Guide for This Podcast Odyssey

That would be me, Glen Weldon. I'm an editor at the NPR Arts Desk; I've written a lot of film, television, and book criticism; I'm the author of two exceedingly nerdy cultural histories—and I'm a podcaster myself. For over ten years I've been a panelist on NPR's *Pop Culture Happy Hour*, a lively roundtable discussion podcast about the latest television, movies, books, games, and comics.

Like NPR, I was an early adopter of podcasts, but on the listening side. Nearly from the moment of their inception, you could find me, earbuds in, listening to *The Ricky Gervais Show*; *Jordan, Jesse, Go!*; *You Look Nice Today*; *Uhh Yeah Dude*; and a host of others. I'm currently following 123 podcasts—comedy, news, narrative, trivia, and more. In this book, I offer you my perspective from both sides of the mic—as someone who creates podcasts and as a fan from the get-go.

When we started *Pop Culture Happy Hour* at NPR, we hoped to channel our enthusiasm for pop culture into a show that would help people curate their movies, books, television, music, comics—and, increasingly, podcasts. We put it together on the fly in our spare time.

Translation: We didn't have a clue.

Further translation: We screwed up—a lot—as we found the show's voice, tone, and shape.

I've learned a tremendous amount watching our producers over the years assembling each episode—booking guests, monitoring audio levels, inserting clips, tracking conversations, editing the whole thing together with an ear for clarity and concision—and then listening to feedback, in a constant attempt to make the show the best it can be.

I *love* yammering about podcasts. If you ever see me out and about and say hi, I'll kick off our conversation by asking you what your favorite podcasts are, and then I'll proselytize to you about mine.[8] Think of this book as me cornering you in a bar to talk about everything that this fascinating and (nearly) limitless medium can do.

What to Expect from This Book

This book is a series of if/then statements, basically.

Let me explain: Well before we launch any new podcast, we at NPR ask ourselves a long series of questions that hit on every aspect of what the podcast will be—format, length, tone, intent, originality, audience, sound design, budget, staff, and so on.

These questions get asked and answered over months[9] in meetings, over Slack, and in email threads filled with charts of audience metrics and words like *verticals* and *platform* and, yes, *audio space*.[10]

But you? Instead of a metric ton of meetings, you get this book.

Understand: NPR is a national network dedicated to audio journalism, entertainment, and storytelling. We have staff and resources that you, as a new podcaster, won't—at least, not at first. Maybe not ever. Which is okay. Because those *questions* that we ask ourselves? They're key, whether you're a one-person band, a gaggle, a herd, or a frickin' juggernaut. They're the same ones you need to ask yourself before, during, and after hitting Record.

You can answer *no* to some, most, even all of them. And given your resources—how much time, money, and passion you've got at your disposal—you may answer no to a bunch. But you'll be doing so from a position of knowledge.

Winging it is always an option, of course. But you're reading this book because you, or at least a significant part of you, don't want to do that. You want to tap into the knowledge of folks who make podcasts for a living and have years of experience answering those if/then statements—some obvious; many not. For example:

IF you name your podcast without checking whether another podcast has beaten you to that name, THEN your audience won't easily find it.[11]

IF you don't take steps to keep your specific audience in mind while making it, THEN your podcast risks growing shapeless and unfocused.

8 They change daily. Hourly, sometimes.

9 Years! In more than one case! Ask me about it when you meet me!

10 I lied. Sue me.

11 Lawyers, though? They'll find it. And their cease-and-desist letters will find you, too.

IF you decide to listen to the jerks complaining about your vocal fry and speak differently to avoid it, THEN you risk upsetting those nonjerk listeners who expect your podcast to sound like . . . you.

This book follows the four general life stages of a podcast:

Part 1: Imagine. This helps you drill down to the core idea and purpose of your podcast, drawing on how we at NPR brainstorm and evaluate new podcast ideas.

Part 2: Plan. This covers planning essentials that any podcast will benefit from: finding your voice, getting your gear, learning about legal stuff, and the all-important fundamentals of audio storytelling and mapping out your idea before you hit Record.

Part 3: Create. This section helps you navigate the fun, complex process of actually *making* an audio project, from first recording to final cut.

Part 4: Share. This final section dives into launching and growing a podcast, from understanding the technical details to soliciting constructive feedback to spreading the word.

In addition to sidebars, lists, explanatory text, and anecdotes from NPR podcasting pros, there's an interactive component. You'll find exercises, questions to consider, and suggested charts for keeping track of your podcasting process. You might want to keep a notebook to write in or a document open on your computer, building your own personal podcast road map as you move through the book. Or feel free to just read, ponder, and wrap your head around the whole dang idea of doing a podcast. Consider this your handbook for thinking through each stage and making a podcast that's entirely yours, whether you're a solo host bootstrapping it or you're spearheading a series for a business with a big budget. We at NPR have your back: We want you to be *you*, launching a podcast that reflects your best work—a podcast you can be proud of.

 If you've got a great idea, if at all possible: Don't wait too long to execute it. Do it, do it again, and keep getting better at it until it's great.

—Stephen Thompson, writer/editor, NPR Music, cohost, *Pop Culture Happy Hour*

IMAGINE

Questions to Ask Yourself

This largely interactive section will help you ask and answer fundamental—and, trust me, too often overlooked—questions about your podcast. That's why the chapter titles in part 1 each ask a question—and chapter 2 is *made of* questions! You'll learn about the ceaseless churn going on in podcasting, figure out your central idea and purpose, define your audience, think about format, consider who might be on your team, and start figuring out schedule and budget.

Some of what you'll do here is blue-sky conceptual; some is gunmetal-gray nuts-and-bolts. You'll find yourself wearing two hats— the Pointy, Stars-and-Moons-Covered Wizard Hat of Imagination, and the, um ... Whatever-Kind-of-Hat-Bean-Counters-Wear[1] of Logistics. That's because you're easing yourself into the dual roles of Podcast Chief Visioneer and Chief Executive. As with any creative endeavor that you aim to share with others,[2] you'll often experience ecstatic bouts of creative fizz—"*That's it!!!*"—followed closely and inevitably by, "Okay, so how do I get there?"

Let's start getting there.

[1] I'm thinking a beanie? Stands to reason, right?

[2] As in, *real* others. Outside your circle of family and friends, who love you unconditionally and who will tell you they think it's great—because you cannot make your podcast better if it is built upon a *thin tiss-you of lies.*

CHAPTER 1

Wait. What *Is* a Podcast?

Of all the questions you will be asked in this book, "What is a podcast?" might be the hardest to answer.

Kidding.

Sort of.

Today, millions upon millions of people listen to podcasts, more all the time. And if you ask one of those millions what a podcast is, they'll probably say, "A show I listen to."[1]

They're basically right. But to *make* a podcast, you need to know more than that. Because you'll be using technology that's changing. And a distribution system that's changing. And trying to reach an audience that's changing and expecting more and more from podcasts.

In short, everything's in flux and is likely to remain . . . fluxing. Since the podcast was born, it's boomed, faded, reboomed, crashed, and re-reboomed—and it's technically not even hit drinking age yet. The technology for creating and distributing podcasts has morphed and mutated right alongside. All this makes the definition of a podcast something of a moving target. But try to hit it you must, in order to make informed creative decisions and to give your podcast the best odds of survival amid all the rockin' and rollin'.

Podcast Defined

Podcasts are an on-demand,[2] on-the-go medium ideally suited to the speed of now, allowing us to absorb information, insight, and/ or diversion through our ears while we do other things. The narrow, conventional definition of a podcast is that it's a downloadable audio file, found in an online podcast directory, searched out by listeners who may sign up to receive it on a regular basis via RSS (Really Simple Syndication) feed.

[1] "Duh," they will conclude. To themselves, probably, unless they're your older brother.

[2] Spoiler: This is the crucial bit. Or at least, it was. Keep reading.

Some people listen via a podcast's website. More often, though, they download episodes into their smartphones via a podcasting app and listen without being tethered to internet connectivity. Increasingly, they listen in cars and at home through smart speakers.

Importantly—historically, anyway—your audience *chooses* your podcast. That's the on-demand part. This makes podcasts different from terrestrial radio and other broadcast media that push out their programming, casting a wide net for a passive audience.

Podcasting is narrowcasting. Active-casting. Niche-casting, if you will. It's an experience that listeners deliberately seek out. It doesn't have to be everything to everyone. In fact, if it tries to be, it's breaking an implicit contract with the person who deliberately sought it out.

Podcasts allow for an infinite range of topics and ideas. In broadcasting, there's obviously a limit to what you can put on in a 24-hour period. And that means that there are gatekeepers who determine what is worthy of those time constraints. In podcasting, there are no constraints. You can focus on things that would probably never make it to terrestrial radio because terrestrial radio was and is designed to appeal to the greatest numbers of people listening at that given moment. That is the key difference between what podcasting does and what terrestrial broadcasting does.

—Guy Raz, creator, *How I Built This with Guy Raz*,
  cocreator, *TED Radio Hour* and *Wow in the World*

See, podcasts thrive on a feeling of intimacy. Intellectually, listeners know that hundreds, thousands, even millions of others might be listening to the same episode they are. But if you're doing your job, they don't feel it.

That's because the podcast is speaking to them—often *from inside their own dang heads*, via earbuds—about a topic they specifically selected, that's being delivered to them by people they feel familiarity with, if not affection for. This combination of choice and comfort transforms the act of listening from passive and idle to active and engaged.

This process of choosing still happens a lot. But it's changing. In addition to searching in directories, people now encounter podcasts through audio streaming services like Pandora, Spotify,

Stitcher, and NPR One. These services gradually "learn" what listeners like through what they click on, and then they serve up options presumably relevant to those interests. More and more people are finding podcasts on Facebook and YouTube, too.

These changes in where people can find podcasts have brought changes in how people consume them. Streaming podcast audiences are getting more casual, more spontaneous—some might say more capricious.

The traditional model was that people searched for, selected, and (ideally) followed podcasts, maybe based on friends' recommendations. Now, there's an endless array of possibilities to sort through. Think of the difference between search/follow and streaming as the difference between dining at a restaurant that serves the particular cuisine you want versus cruising an all-you-can-eat buffet and sampling all the luscious options competing for your taste buds. Listeners on streaming platforms are grazing at the podcast buffet, with a plethora of podcasts competing for their attention.

What does this mean for podcasters? You gotta be *goooood*. NPR's listener data shows that if you don't grab followers' attention in the first few minutes, they skip the episode. With streaming audiences, the window is *seconds*.

Does this change the foundational definition of a podcast as a downloadable audio file? Nope. But pretty much everything else is changing. Bottom line: There are more ways than ever for you to reach your audience, but you've got to work harder to get noticed, attract them, and keep them.

The Podcast Landscape from Thirty Thousand Feet

Podcasts can last minutes to hours; be published daily, weekly, or on whatever schedule is decided; and be divided into "seasons" à la TV. They span the world, with Spanish-language podcasts being particularly robust. As for topics, well. A cynic (hi!) might peruse the shows topping the Apple Podcasts chart and conclude that the most successful are about everything from true crime to nonfiction murder investigations. But there's actually a healthy mix of topics in the top one hundred: news analysis/opinion, money management, comedy, trivia, cooking, and . . . okay, yeah, lots of true crime. Growth areas also include podcasting for kids and religion/spirituality podcasts.

Who's listening? The male-to-female mix was approximately two-thirds male and one-third female when Edison Research

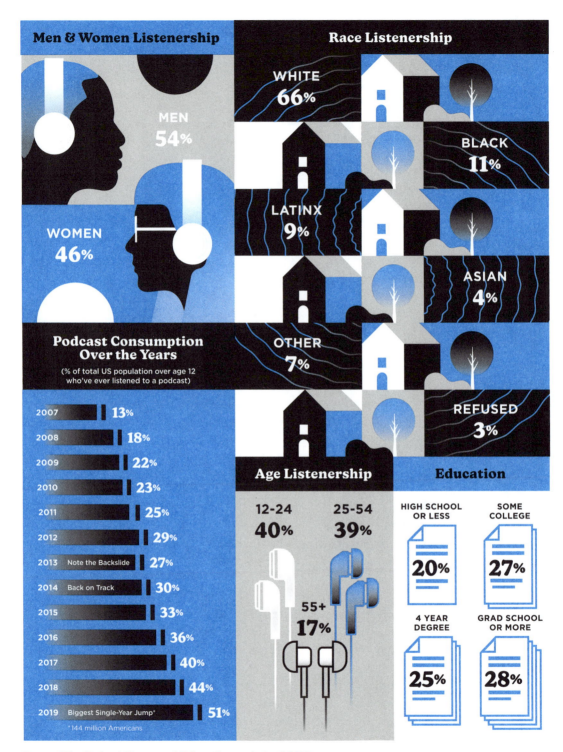

Men & Women Listenership

MEN
54%

WOMEN
46%

Race Listenership

WHITE
66%

BLACK
11%

LATINX
9%

ASIAN
4%

OTHER
7%

REFUSED
3%

Podcast Consumption Over the Years

(% of total US population over age 12 who've ever listened to a podcast)

Year		%
2007		13%
2008		18%
2009		22%
2010		23%
2011		25%
2012		29%
2013	Note the Backslide	27%
2014	Back on Track	30%
2015		33%
2016		36%
2017		40%
2018		44%
2019	Biggest Single-Year Jump*	51%

*144 million Americans

Age Listenership

12-24
40%

25-54
39%

55+
17%

Education

HIGH SCHOOL OR LESS
20%

SOME COLLEGE
27%

4 YEAR DEGREE
25%

GRAD SCHOOL OR MORE
28%

Source: "The Podcast Consumer," Edison Research, April 2019.

started following this stat in 2006. These days, women comprise almost half of podcast listeners.

Making money with podcasts is, well, a thing. As in: a really difficult thing. Podcasts are, at least for now, for the most part free. For more about the challenges of and options for funding/profiting from podcasts, see chapter 16.

On an industry level, there's a concerted effort to put podcasts behind a paywall. It'll be interesting to see how well this works, given that listeners aren't accustomed to paying for podcasts.

The funding model that seems to be taking off is one that splits the difference: You offer your listeners an extra show or two every week that they can access only if they shell out a few bucks every month. On an episode of the podcast *Inside Voices*, comedian Jon Gabrus candidly discussed how he hosts one podcast that reaches thousands and thousands of listeners, and he hosts another podcast available only to Patreon subscribers, which reaches only several hundred. But those few hundred listeners feel more deeply engaged . . . and provide him with a steady income that his free podcast does not.

A Brief History of Podcasting

Podcast is a mashup of two words: *iPod* and *broadcast*. Coined in 2004 by Ben Hammersley in an article for the *Guardian*, the name nails podcasting's parentage in all its blended fabulousness.

And really, it is a fabulous blend. Back then, millions of us were walking around with chunky MP3 players tucked into our pockets feeding music to our ears—the music carefully curated by us into personalized playlists from our online archive—a toggle-laden labor of love, though this was far less painstaking than when we had to juggle them together from towering stacks of CDs or (in days of yore) tote zippered packets of custom-burned CDs to play on our Walkman or boom box.

This streamlined, user-friendly technology arose alongside affordable (even free) digital recording and editing tools that put audio production into the hands of anyone who wanted to "sound [their] barbaric yawp over the roofs of the world."[3] Suddenly, said yawpers could be you or me.

3 Look it up.

But this tech coupling was actually a threesome because into that cozy bed jumped a growing public acceptance, thanks to blogs, of the power of individuals—regular schmoes!—to capture attention and build lively communities and conversations around ideas and stories well told.

Podcasting was the love child of these three, bootstrapping us into a new way to communicate. Indeed, so ready was the world for this birth that just a year after the term was coined, the *New Oxford American Dictionary* selected *podcast* as word of the year, and George W. Bush became the first president to deliver his weekly address in podcast form.

Podcasts started as a way anyone with an idea could put it out there in search of connection and community. And early on, podcasting grew nice and steady. It survived the Great Recession in 2008 and plateaued for a while after 2010, though by 2013 Apple had one billion podcast subscribers—not too shabby.

Then, in 2014, came *Serial*. The Pod That Changed Everything. Indeed, some divide podcasting history into BS (before *Serial*) and PS (post-*Serial*). Bringing the tone and approach of *This American Life* to true crime, this gripping, human, and palpably empathetic investigative podcast raised both public awareness of podcasts and the bar for what the medium could deliver.

After that the floodgates opened. These days, everyone and their pet iguana has a podcast. The big players (iHeartRadio, Earwolf, Gimlet, Stitcher, Wondery, and yes, NPR) are in it, too, looking to capture ears beyond the "gee, sure hope you're listening" mode of traditional broadcast. Streaming services that were once music-only have put podcasts in their lineup. Hollywood's looking at podcasts as a place to scout and test-drive ideas. Bean counters and analysts are involved. Which means listener data is being collected. Leading to more advertising dollars being spent. Leading to more stakeholders, higher expectations, endless discussion about "where this relationship is going," and blah blah blah.

Okay, But What Does It All Mean?

Let's keep our eye on why all of this economic hoo-ha matters to you as an aspiring podcaster.

Podcast rhymes with *broadcast*, but there the resemblance ends. Podcasting coincided with the rise of on-demand TV, movies, music, and hardy microcultures—people with specialized (read: obscure-to-wackadoodle) interests who once were isolated but now are able to find one another and ecstatically commune—and all of this was enabled and pushed to warp speed by the everything-is-available-all-the-time-so-why-not-have-it-right-now internet.

On Starting (and Growing) a Start-Up

Linda Holmes, cohost, *Pop Culture Happy Hour*

The best—and worst—thing about starting *Pop Culture Happy Hour* was that it was very informal. No budget, no meetings, very little formal planning; just people who liked and trusted one another starting something we were passionate about that we really hoped would work. Being so far under the radar gave us time to experiment, to learn, and to make the show according to our very particular philosophy, which was silly and positive but also analytical and committed. We tried out different segments, we added and subtracted pieces from the opening and closing patter, and we developed guidelines for what we should talk about. One was our "Zaxxon rule," which said that we shouldn't make "What's Making Me Happy This Week" something so personal that nobody else can enjoy it, no matter how happy it's making us. The rule was named after our agreement that Stephen Thompson should probably not focus on the Zaxxon arcade machine he'd acquired for his house.

But being so far under the radar also meant we made the show with people we already knew, and that meant it had some of the limitations of our social circles. We were all white people of similar age, even though we had varied cultural interests and brought very different perspectives in some ways. Once we felt confident enough to invite more people, including more people we didn't know well, the show benefited enormously and the range of voices grew. It's probably the single most significant change to the show since it began—both in terms of audience and creative growth—and it was all for the good.

Our somewhat improvised beginnings also didn't set any expectations about production resources, and we had to work hard over time to demonstrate what it would actually take to produce *PCHH* as something other than a side project. As the show got more professional, it required more time to produce, and it couldn't stay quite so casual forever. We eventually worked with NPR to bring it into the fold of official projects with official targets and official expectations and official money. I still believe in the messy experimentation model—like the way we developed our bullet-point semiscripts on Google Docs over a period of years—as an important way to develop ideas, but I also think you have to consider what a path to stability would look like, and how long you'll be happy working without one. Maybe it's forever—maybe you just want to make your show as long as you can, and that's okay. But it can also be really helpful to make the leap to actually having meetings and making plans; it can provide structure and support. You can still be weird and idiosyncratic in what you make. You'll just be taking a few more notes.

The podcasting boom is basically an outgrowth of our increasing expectation that content be über-customized to us, available literally at our fingertips via our keyboards/touchpads/screens (or at our tongue tips as we yell commands to our well-meaning smart speaker), precisely when we want and need it. And not just *stuff* like moisture-wicking workout clothes—but information, ideas, and stories. No media "gatekeepers" controlling when we have to tune in to catch the show, where we need to be when we do, or even what that show will be (thanks to those aforementioned affordable and widely available production tools that put content creation in the hands of everyone and their pet iguana). We, the listeners, can select, download, stream, binge, delete, and skip through a universe of content that's vying for our attention like a few million terriers on steroids. We, the listeners, have the power to decide what is "interesting," "relevant," and "important."

Where all of this is headed is anyone's guess (which, of course, has encouraged boatloads of exactly that). But two things are certain:

1   Consumers are becoming curators, taking active control over selecting what media offerings they will and will not receive.
2   And the one thing in this changing landscape that you and I, as podcast creators, can and must control is the quality of our work—the fundamental, unchanging best practices in storytelling and audio production known to capture attention, captivate minds and hearts, and put us in a position to build a loyal audience.

Basically, if we want the direct, dynamic, interactive, and intimate relationship with listeners that podcasts can offer, then we've got to be worthy of the trust our listeners place in us. That begins and ends with giving them the best-quality content we can.

For over a decade, all of us at NPR have been mapping the many ways that podcasts engender an entirely different kind of intimacy with listeners than broadcast radio does. We look to develop podcasts that have unique identities and voices that speak to unique needs in listeners. But, as Linda Holmes notes (see page 15), we also apply what our decades in radio have taught us about proven best practices for audio quality, so our listeners experience unique and idiosyncratic work at its very best—a recipe for success no matter where podcasting is headed. "There are already a ton of podcasts out there—which may at first seem daunting or discouraging," says J. C. Howard, a producer of *TED Radio Hour* and *How I Built This with Guy Raz*. "But there are also a ton of books, movies, and songs. Just because there are a ton doesn't mean the world doesn't need yours. Tell your story and tell it well."

Hopefully, this book will help you achieve exactly that.

CHAPTER 2

So...How Do I Get Started?

If you're reading this book, odds are you're fired up with a podcast idea. You know what your podcast is gonna be about, and you've spent some time noodling about it, doodling about it,[1] and coming up with a grabby title.

Totally normal.

It's everyone's first instinct (mine, too). Plus, if you share your podcast dream with others, they tend to ask, "Ooh! What's it about?" And you've gotta say *something*, right?

But if you want to develop the most compelling podcast possible, "What's it about?" *isn't* the first question to ask.

Because a podcast, like a book, film, newspaper, or magazine (ask your parents), is, first, last, and always, a *communicative medium.*[2] Its sole aim is to convey something—information, entertainment, a sense of community—to someone else. It's a conversation with your audience. The hard truth is, it's not only about what *you* want to *say*. It's about anticipating and delivering what *others* want to *hear*. As NPR Training audio production specialist Argin Hutchins says, "Find something interesting to talk about, then see if there is a reasonably sized audience out there for that idea." Indeed, without others, a podcast is an empty exercise— words cast into the void. Voiding words: not fun.

Now, look. Some of your favorite podcasts didn't start this way. I follow dozens of comedy podcasts, for example, and I know those comics didn't carefully ponder who'd end up listening or whether they needed to "justify the existence" of their podcast—because they already had an audience. They just needed to figure out how to bring that audience to this new medium. That takes skill, sure, but

1 Filling your diary with "ME + PODCAST" inside little hearts with arrows through them, say.

2 Eventually, anyway. It'll start off as a monologue, but as you solicit, receive, and implement audience feedback, it'll become a lively conversation quickly.

these folks were already in the communication business. They'd been doing the research and development—asking themselves the same questions you need to ask yourself—on comedy stages for years before heading into an audio booth. Figuring out what other people think is funny is their job.

Very few podcasts start with a built-in audience.[3] This is why, to grow your own listenership, you must first imagine what *others* would find fascinating, intriguing, puzzling, motivating, or enlightening—and then provide that, so they want to stay in conversation with you.

You don't *have* to ask yourself the audience question. God knows most podcasters don't. As Danielle Kurtzleben, a politics reporter for NPR who has hosted many NPR podcasts (including *Planet Money* and *The Indicator from Planet Money*), says: "There are definitely some podcasts out there that fall into the let's-just-talk-at-each-other trap (especially in their early episodes), with the apparent idea being that, 'Hey—the conversations I have with my friends/colleagues are witty and exciting. I bet other people would like to listen to them on demand.' Which is a bummer! Because there are podcasts where the concept is imaginative and exciting—[but] it ends up as a few people jabbering at each other (often for a tiresome hour), with no editing and no apparent plan. It's just not listenable."

Which is why the biggest, gnarliest, most essential question we at NPR ask ourselves when deciding what our next podcast will be is this: Is there an audience for it, and what does it look like?

An added plus of putting this question first: When the time comes to pitch or market your idea, you'll be ahead of the game—because having a clear answer to this question is what you need to get other people interested in funding, reviewing, recommending, and otherwise spreading word about your podcast.

This chapter will help you figure out your podcast's core concept and purpose by first defining your audience, and then by asking some important questions you should consider before you invest serious time and resources.

Question #1: Who's It For?

A podcast needs a reason for being. For most podcasters, that's probably being heard by someone else. That starts with identifying your audience. So, grab your notebook or open your podcast planning file on your computer, and here we go.

3 The recent trend of A-list celebrities launching podcasts—and promptly zooming to the top of the download charts—worries a lot of podcasters who've been putting in time for years. But those Poddy-Come-Latelies still have to put out *good* episodes, consistently. Many don't. Buy me a drink sometime and I'll talk your fool ear off about this.

Notes from the Pros: Time Is Precious

Guy Raz, creator, *How I Built This with Guy Raz,*
    cocreator, *TED Radio Hour* and *Wow in the World*

I have a really simple approach to how I think about podcasts. We have
about fourteen or fewer waking hours of the day, right? Most are spent
working. A few are spent doing things you have to do, like taking care
of kids or running errands. You might have one or two hours that are
just for you. And that might mean chopping vegetables, taking a run,
or commuting. If I'm asking you to give me one of those precious hours,
I'd better give you something that is going to make that time worthwhile
for you. When I think about all the shows that I've started, the question
I ask myself is, "Is the person listening to this gonna walk away from
it having learned something and having been enriched in some way?"
If I'm gonna ask a lot of you, I've got to give you a lot. That is basically
how I think about starting shows. It's about serving the people who
are listening.

EXERCISE Know Thy Listener

First, a few questions.

— Are your listeners local, national, or a blend of the two?
   For example, a podcast about road trips could cover the entire
   United States or just Vermont (that is, mostly local, but some
   national appeal).

— People listen to podcasts while driving, exercising, walking
   the dog, folding laundry. Where is your audience, and what
   are they doing while listening to your podcast?

— How is your audience feeling? Stressed out and dying for diversion? Wrestling with a decision? Needing answers to a gnarly problem? Looking for book recs? Seeking support and a sense that they're not alone? Bored with chicken and wanting fabulous new ways to cook it?

Based on your answers to these questions, start a running list of every possible type of person who might be interested in your podcast. Get ridiculously granular and insanely optimistic. For example, for a podcast about craft beer you're calling *Gettin' Crafty*, possible audiences might be bar owners, foodies, college students, and more. In your notebook, write *your* podcast idea and all the possible audiences *you* can think of.

EXERCISE Target Audience

Now arrange these possible audiences into some kind of order to identify your "target market." Businesspeople talk about this a lot, so let's figure that out for your podcast with (why not?!) an actual target (opposite):

You want to define a primary audience—one you can name, aim for, and learn about—along with two more (secondary and tertiary) audiences so your podcast has room to grow in subject scope and market appeal.

1   Review that list of potential audiences you made in "Know Thy Listener."
2   Select the type of listener who's most likely to want to hear your podcast. This might be a combination of two or three very closely related audiences (for our hypothetical *Gettin' Crafty* podcast, it might be "craft beer drinkers/pub crawlers/ home brewers"). They are your core target audience. Write them down inside the bull's-eye.
3   Next, choose another audience that is likely to be interested in *most* of what your podcast will cover. Then choose another audience that might be interested in *some* of your podcast. Make them the next two rings of your target.
4   Now, assess: (a) Do you have information or ideas that will be of value to all these people, and (b) do you feel like you can't wait to communicate with them? Yes? Then you're on the right track for a potential match between your podcast idea and an audience.

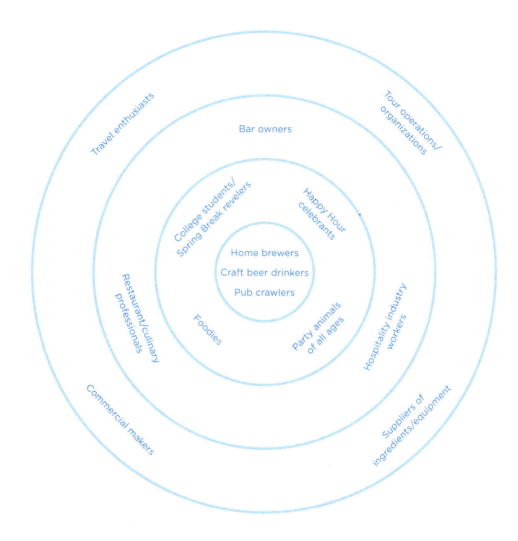

Travel enthusiasts

Tour operations/ organizations

Bar owners

College students/ Spring Break revelers

Happy Hour celebrants

Home brewers

Craft beer drinkers

Pub crawlers

Restaurant/culinary professionals

Foodies

Party animals of all ages

Hospitality industry workers

Commercial makers

Suppliers of ingredients/equipment

Boom. You've identified your primary, secondary, and tertiary audiences. You can add more circles/audiences, but like any relationship, you and your podcast can't be all things to all people. Without a clear target, you won't reach an audience.

Any trouble coming up with rings? That might mean your idea is too general, and it may end up appealing to no one in particular because it doesn't distinguish itself enough to stand out. Example: a podcast about history. Yawn. In this case, ask yourself:

—   What *specific* aspects of this topic will I cover?

— What will I say about this topic that hasn't already been said?

— How can I deliver the information in a unique or counterintuitive way, compared to what's out there?

On the other hand, too few rings can also signal an idea that's *so* niche-y that there isn't enough material or the potential audience isn't big enough to warrant the effort. Example: a podcast about eighteenth-century English tea sets. Ask yourself:

— What additional angles could I cover for wider appeal?

— Does this idea have enough scope to keep an audience interested over multiple episodes?

Maybe you expand to eighteenth-century English furniture, decorative arts, clothing, customs, and home life and call it *Jane Austen's Drawing Room.*

Keep your target handy when brainstorming episode ideas. Can you point to the rings each story will appeal to?

Question #2: Why Should People Care?

From the listener's point of view, this question is "What's in it for me?" A good podcast delivers the goods on something people care about. We could divide the options into two categories—pain and pleasure (bad and good; yuck and yum).

Here are some examples of **pain points**.

— **Problems:** From the baby who won't go to sleep to the stalled career to the latest head-clutching headlines—what keeps us up at night, stresses us out, limits our lives, keeps us from achieving our goals?

— **Needs:** Many needs, if unmet, can become very painful. Being healthy, managing money, succeeding at work, improving or fixing stuff (ourselves, our relationships, our kitchen sinks), to name a few.

Notes from the Pros: Do Your Homework

Liana Simstrom, podcast manager, *Invisibilia*

> This seems really obvious, but there are a *lot* of podcasts that already exist. Aspiring podcasters should probably take a look at the landscape of what's out there. Everybody is making a podcast right now. What are you adding to the space?

— **Flashpoints:** Clarifying controversial issues, teasing apart topical discussions, shedding calm light on a charged subject.

And the following are **pleasure points**.

— **Aspirations:** Helping us hope for, shape, and attain a dream, be it starting our own business, traveling to far-off lands, feeling good in our bodies, or looking good in our clothes.

— **Passions and diversions:** What do people love? Pop culture, stranger-than-fiction true stories, food (from grub to gourmet), elegance on a budget, vintage style, fly-fishing. True crime, one of the biggest podcast genres, slots in here, as does the arguably even bigger genre of Two or More Nerds Sitting Around Nerding Out Over a Nerd Thing.

— **Curiosity, inspiration, surprise, delight, awe:** This includes answers to burning questions. Questions we never thought to ask. Contrarian or counterintuitive ideas. Insights about something we thought we understood. Against-all-odds successes. Behind-the-scenes stories. Towering achievements, amazing discoveries, vivid world-building (real or imagined).

EXERCISE "What's In It for Me?"

Write your responses to these questions:

— Which of the pain and pleasure points in the list above does your podcast idea satisfy? (Could be more than one.) How will it do that?

— Imagine you're yakking about your podcast idea with a good friend at a bar, and your bold-and-honest friend shoots back point-blank: "So, what's in it for me?" What's your answer?

— How do you want your listeners to feel while listening to your podcast?

— When fans recommend or review your podcast, what would you imagine them saying? What do they love most about it?

Question #3: How Will I Find Them?

Now that you've named your target market and considered how your podcast will benefit your audience, let's learn about their interests and priorities by looking at where they spend their time. Focus on your primary audience in the center of the bull's-eye.

EXERCISE Where Does Your Audience Hang Out?

Jot down your answers to these questions:

— Where do they live (suburbs, cities, farms, states, countries)?

— What conventions or events do they attend?

— What magazines, newspapers, and books do they read?

— What websites do they read/visit?

— Which social media do they use the most?

— What platforms do they use to stream or download content?

Spend some time looking at those publications and lurking on those websites, feeds, and platforms. Then answer these questions:

- What tone does this audience find appealing (smart, with a snarky edge; measured and deliberate; sort of heady)?

- What length does this audience find appealing (short and sweet; long and detailed; something in between)?

- What engages them most, based on most-read or "liked" posts, greatest number of downloads, longest comments threads, most popular events, favorite blog topics, types of articles?

Psssst. This exercise just did something sneaky. It got you to do market research. Marketing intimidates some people ("I'm terrible at selling myself") and turns off others ("I just wanna do my thing").

But good marketing is really just alerting people to something you think they might be interested in—based on those pain and pleasure points.

Park this important info here for now. We'll come back to it in part 4. Meantime, answering these questions might help you build out your podcast's ideal tone, length, and content.

Question #4: Stripes, Spots, or Feathers?

We've been zooming in on your audience. Now let's zoom out to see which type of podcast might fit your needs.

Podcasts can be segmented by format (solo, roundtable), subject area (magazine show, advice show, news), or a combination of the two. The four "Podcast Profiles" below focus mainly on formats, describing those most likely to be accessible and scalable for start-up podcasters, though the narrative format is the most challenging. We'll come back to this, but for now just know that the kind of podcast you'll realistically be able to pull off depends on your supply of three crucial resources:

- The *time* you have available

- The *money* you have at your disposal

- The *passion* that will keep you going when *time* and/or *money* run low

PODCAST PROFILE: INTERVIEW SHOW

What it is: Host. Guest. Scintillating conversation.

Examples: These are as varied as the topics and personalities of the interviewers, from Terry Gross's subtle one-on-ones with celebrities and journalists on *Fresh Air* to Guy Raz's masterful conversations with crazy-busy business innovators on *How I Built This with Guy Raz*.

Host(s): One, maybe two.

Guest(s): One or two. If a group (such as a band), appoint a designated interviewee.

What makes a good one: Interview shows are like conversational tofu; they take on the character of their hosts and their guests/topics, from serious to funny to geeky. They're only as good as the conversation delivered to the audience—meaning they're only as good as the interviewer. As podcasting commentator Nicholas Quah wrote: "Terry Gross's interviews are probing and revealing, collaborative and investigative, comprehensive and singular. It's not too hyperbolic to say that the entire endeavor of podcasting would likely look different if it weren't for *Fresh Air*."

Don't let that intimidate you, because we can learn a lot from the masters. Primarily: An interview's got to be more than kibitzing between friends, a schmoozy puree of questions catering to the guest's PR talking points, or a delivery system for product plugs. Sure, all interviewers mention the guest's latest book, album, or achievement—but they have to know the difference between informing and shilling.

Jesse Thorn, who interviews culture creators on *Bullseye with Jesse Thorn*, says, "I'm looking to move past what other people have asked." Your listeners must learn something interesting, unusual, insightful, helpful, inspiring, or surprising—that improves their understanding. The best interview shows feel like a real conversation of rare depth. (For preinterviewing and interviewing techniques, including Jesse Thorn's key strategies, see chapter 10.)

Must-haves: Preparation is key, including researching your guest and pulling clips to read or play. Jesse Thorn says: "I try to take a full day to prepare. I try to give it at least six straight hours. I'm very fast at it, but in the early years it was maybe eight or twelve." Plus: Read the book or see the movie or show.

Pros: Interview shows are budget friendly; no location travel or studio rental is required. You can do the interview by phone. The limited number of sound tracks (just you, your guest, and maybe a few audio clips of their work) makes for easier weaving together when editing.

Also, while you need to note the important threads you want to follow in the interview, and you'll develop a list of questions and topics you want to hit, you're not writing a complete script for every episode. You just need to write an intro and an outro (more on those later).

Without fieldwork and scriptwriting, and needing less editing, interview shows are a good fit for time-crunched podcasters. You focus on developing and researching show/guest ideas, booking the guests, prepping for interviews, and recording the session.

Scalability: Interviews are friendly to schedules, budgets, and storytelling newbies—but require careful prep and a focus on interviewing techniques. Maybe start by keeping things short—say, a ten- or fifteen-minute interview—and grow from there.

PODCAST PROFILE: ROUNDTABLE/PANEL

What it is: Several panelists discuss one or several topics, depending on show length. The goal is to provide info you can use, seen from multiple points of view.

Examples: The tone can vary, from irreverent opinionated besties talking films and whatnot (*Pop Culture Happy Hour*) to journalistic team reporting on topical issues (*The NPR Politics Podcast*).

Host(s): One, maybe two. Maaaaybe.

Guest(s): Reasonable people differ on this, but remember that your listeners are hearing several voices, and they've got to be able to follow who's saying what. *PCHH* sticks to one host and three guests, max.

What makes a good one: A clear target audience, leading to a clear agenda of topics. Otherwise this loose format gets too grab-baggy to have a clear identity.

An engaging host who keeps the ball rolling, reining in humor or a panelist galloping off-point, and herding the gang to the next topic.

Ideally, having everyone in one room, so hosts can direct traffic with their eyes, seeing who's itching to pipe up, nodding to cue others in (if panelists dial or Skype in, be prepared to later edit out a lot of cross-talk).

Must-haves: Like roommates, panelists have to be compatible. They should share interests, as well as attitudes about respect, division of labor, and work ethic. But complementarity is important, too. The best roundtables draw on the power of diversity to deliver well-rounded content from multiple knowledge bases, points of view, and backgrounds.

Pros: Creators can share the research and episode development. Writing's minimal (intro, outro, and outline, not script)—allowing for some spontaneity. Roundtables can have audible fun, including (*if* subject-suitable/not overused) bursts of laughter, affectionate ribbing, and ongoing gags that the audience, as part of the family, comes to anticipate and enjoy as inside jokes.

Scalability: You can start with a defined topic and expand (for instance, home cooking expanding to entertaining; feature film reviews expanding to TV); introduce features (weekly roundups, industry awards/events/history); build engagement by incorporating audience ideas and feedback; go on vacation (not everyone at once!) and still tape the pod or bring in a guest panelist.

PODCAST PROFILE: PERFORMANCE PROGRAMS

What it is: A podcast that shares info and educates audiences about a particular performance medium.

Examples: *All Songs Considered,* a weekly podcast about "new music discoveries" by "hosts/nerds" Bob Boilen and Robin Hilton; and *World Cafe.* Both mix performance and interviews, but always with music as the subject.

Host(s): One or two.

Guest(s): Not required, but see Examples above.

What makes a good one: A clear show identity and a reason for everything you say and include. Your audience expects to learn from you. As host (curator, really), you must explain each episode's theme, and why you've picked this featured content. What's important, unusual, groundbreaking, historic, or innovative about it?

Must-haves: You need to be a passionate nerd, steeped and endlessly interested in your subject. Otherwise you won't have enough cred to build an audience, nor the drive to stay current and create innovative ways to explore the content.

Pros: Great for less chatty hosts. Editing's pretty straightforward: talk, clip, talk, clip. But podcaster beware: While some labels are happy to grant permission to use clips, others staunchly refuse. And unless you get permission or buy the rights, you'll need to keep clips short. (Basically, if you comment on, criticize, or analyze the clip, it will very likely fall under fair use[4]—but don't push it.)

Scalability: Similar to roundtables, these can start small and grow in subject breadth and length based on time, budget, and audience feedback.

4 Hopefully you're asking, "What the heck is fair use?" Even if you *think* you know what is and is not fair use (which defines how much copyrighted material it is "fair to use" without payment), look it up, and not just anywhere. Because what some people say is "fair use" might more accurately be called "fair abuse." Since it's in your interest as a creative yourself to see copyright law properly observed, start by reading chapter 8, check out the good ol' US Copyright Office (see Resources), and consult an attorney for specific questions.

PODCAST PROFILE: NARRATIVE

What it is: This ginormous umbrella covers fiction and nonfiction. In nonfiction, there are subcategories such as "knowledge shows" that demystify a topic (like *Planet Money*, *Radiolab*), investigative reportage shows (*Embedded*), and hybrids that combine information with reporting by interviewing one or more people dealing with that issue in their lives (*Invisibilia*).

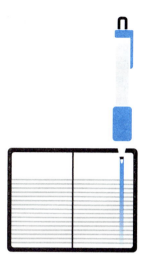

Examples: See above.

Host(s): One or two who guide the audience through the story, building vocal "bridges" between elements, adding detail, teasing out themes, anticipating questions the audience may be thinking, introducing twists and foreshadowings.

Guest(s): The topic may involve interviewing people on location, by phone, or in-studio, from experts to anyone pertinent to the story; gathering sound; and writing a script that assembles the pieces into a coherent, absorbing story.

What makes a good one: These are deep dives, even if short. The audience has to feel as if another world, fictional or factual, was opened up to them.

For fiction: Compelling stories, read by actors experienced in voice work (see "A Word about Fiction Podcasts," page 34).

For knowledge shows, investigative shows, and hybrids: Compelling stories that change how we see the world. Yup, that takes doing. Gene Demby, cohost/correspondent for *Code Switch*—which covers complex stories on race, ethnicity, and culture—recalls cobbling together the first "dummy" episode with cohost/senior producer Shereen Marisol Meraji: "It took about a week of Shereen wading through tape and me scripting to get fifteen minutes of a solid, reported podcast. Reporting takes a lot of time; producing takes even more. We are sometimes fixing the show right up until our episode publishes on Wednesdays at midnight. Sounding good, or even just fine, takes a *lot* of editing and a *lot* of production."

Must-haves: Time to research the story, gather the components, write the script, and edit the final product. Money for travel, field equipment, possibly professional editing, and permissions for music or other audio clips. Journalism skills—and a firm grasp of ethics—to report and tell the story (for more on interviewing, reporting standards, and legalities, read chapters 8 and 10). Audio production skills to record the tracks and assemble the podcast if it's DIY. And the project management skills to work far enough ahead to stick to your publication schedule (think *months*) and to get paperwork done, such as releases from interviewees (or actors for fiction) and permissions for music or other sound clips.

Pros: The satisfaction of discovering and crafting subtle, insightful stories and sharing them with others.

Scalability: This format is challenging for new or indie podcasters. If you're considering it but your real aim is to spout opinions thinly disguised as facts, save it for the family Thanksgiving dinner. Your cousins may never speak to you again, but they probably won't sue you.

If you do seek a scalable starting point, we suggest choosing a subject area you know very well, create superfocused episodes that limit the number of interviews and the scope of reporting, give yourself plenty of time, and keep your podcast short.

Question #5: What Is the Heart, Soul, and Spirit of Your Podcast?

Now let's look at matching up your possible podcast topic with the best format.

EXERCISE Test the Concept

Write down your answers to the following concept questions.

— **Why a podcast?** And not, say, a book, video, or website? What can you do in a podcast that you can't do as effectively in other formats?

— **Has anyone already staked a claim on your concept?** If so, why would someone seek out *your* podcast, and not someone else's on the same or a similar subject? In other words, assess your competition and define what you bring to the party that they don't. This will do yourself and your audience a huge favor!

— **What is the unmet need your podcast meets?** This is the question that launched NPR's *Code Switch.* Here is how Gene Demby answered it: "There was one story in particular that made us want to do the podcast thing. Back in 2013, Shereen and I went down to West Virginia to cover the oddest college homecoming ever: a historically Black college where the student body was 90 percent white. We came back with *so much tape*—too many great stories and threads to fit into a five-minute story on *Morning Edition* or *All Things Considered.* So we started to push for a *Code Switch* podcast—we even cobbled together a rough pilot—but in those primordial, pre-*Serial* days, there wasn't a lot of enthusiasm for it. (And frankly, we were so excited to tell that one particular story that we didn't think too much about, you know, what the *next* episode would be.) But we really believed that what we were doing—tackling tricky stories of race and identity in America—might work."

— **How long should it be?** Podcasts can last a few minutes or a few hours. You should be guided by format and subject. That said, data suggests that somewhere between eighteen and thirty minutes might be the sweet spot for holding listeners' attention—roughly the length of the average American's commute (probably no coincidence). But if that's the data-driven rule, don't be afraid to be the exception, if you're confident you've got something special. Your available time, budget, and story complexity are factors, too. It's better to launch shorter, higher-quality podcasts than longer, shoddier ones. Consistency in quality and length are key.

— **How often?** Again, aim for what you can consistently serve to your audience. You can always ramp up later. Listeners tell NPR they care more about podcast consistency than frequency. Remember, podcasts are about relationships: Your audience commits their time to you. They trust that your podcast will arrive when promised. Do everything you can to avoid breaking that trust, even once.

— **Who's your host?** Touchy question. Not every podcast creator makes a great host. You don't have to be the life of the party. But you should project an open, amiable persona, have passion for the subject, tenacity to keep up with the process, and the ardent desire to share what you know and love with listeners, with your words, your voice, and your presence behind the mic. If that's not you, find someone who shares your passion and put *them* behind the mic, while you partner closely in the background as creator.

— **Who is this podcast *not* for?** Look at that target you made. And your blue-sky list of every possible potential market. Get tough. Who's in and who's out? Need to revise your target? Go ahead. I'll wait.

A Word about Fiction Podcasts

Do you write fiction? You may want to try a narrative fiction podcast. But a great big honkin' warning up front: Fiction podcasts aren't just audiobooks split up into little bites. The best ones are written expressly for the medium. So before you start writing, think about how well the story you want to tell would work in an audio format consisting of small, discrete, serialized chunks. Most of the world-building you'll need to do will be aural in nature—whether short stories or long narrative; genre fiction or "literary" fiction.[5]

You may be attracted to fiction podcasting because it's cheaper than making films and easier than trying to get published. True. But when writing for a podcast, you need succinct, speakable sentences and dialogue that sounds like, well, what people actually say. And as mentioned, a world you can make audible. Is it set on a spaceship, like *Mission to Zyxx*? Inserting low, ambient engine noise will help place your listeners in space. Does it take place on a gloomy, windswept island in the English Channel, like *Wooden Overcoats*? Without the cries of seagulls and the sound of waves crashing on rocky shores, you might as well set the damn thing in Toledo.

As for how to write fiction for podcasts, listen to others, like the podcasts above as well as *This Sounds Serious*, to see how current practitioners are pushing the boundaries.[6]

With a fiction podcast, you'll be wading into project-management areas specific to that form, such as auditioning, hiring, and directing actors. But the general issues of audio production and editing discussed in this book, and the ground rules of scheduling and budgeting, will apply, as will figuring out and finding your audience.

5 Which is, of course, its own genre. DON'T GET ME STARTED.

6 Does it sound like I'm foisting you off on other people? That's because I am. NPR has more experience than anyone you can name in the art and craft of audio storytelling— but we don't do fiction. Contrary to what some politicians, and your Uncle Geoff's Facebook page, might say.

EXERCISE **What's Your One-Liner?**

Well, here we are. That place other podcasting how-to books, and indeed NPR's own training materials, arrive at eventually. The infamous assignment to come up with a tight one-sentence description of your podcast that captures its unique spirit.

Don't get sweaty. Your one-liner is key, but it could (will) change a bit (a lot) as you develop your idea. It's a touchstone for your podcast's core identity. It makes it real and easy to pitch to anyone whose help you may need along the way.

To get you started, here's a selection of one-line NPR podcast descriptions from our website.

Take a look and consider: How do they distill the show's essence—not just content, but *tone*? How do they answer the "who's it for" and "why should people care" questions? What pain or pleasure points do they address? How do they surprise us or make us curious? What's their promise to the audience?

"NPR's *From the Top* showcases the music, stories, and unique humor of America's best young classical musicians."

"*Pop Culture Happy Hour* is a fun and freewheeling chat about the latest movies, television, books, and music."

"*Louder Than a Riot* reveals the interconnected rise of hip-hop and mass incarceration."

"*Invisibilia*—Latin for invisible things—fuses narrative story-telling with science that will make you see your own life differently."

Your turn. Scribble a bunch of one-liners. Keep going. Stop. Circle words and phrases you like (because they answer the questions you've been asking in this chapter). Rinse and repeat. Don't discard anything. You might use outtakes in your official podcast description (see chapter 14). You might not nail your one-liner in one sitting. Keep at it. It's *that* important.

Question #6: What's Its Name?

Maybe you wanted to dive right into this question first. But sometimes the best way to find a name for a podcast is to back into it. After answering questions one through five, you will know *tons* more about your podcast than when you started. Once you've boiled your podcast down to a pithy sentence or two, the name should further distill its heart, soul, and spirit.

Go back to the list of NPR one-liners above. Look at the podcast names. What do they hint at or promise? What emotional experience do they suggest? Can you see how each name "hooks" together with its one-liner, each elaborating on and pointing toward the other? For example, the allusion to "happy hour" in *Pop Culture Happy Hour* evokes the "freewheeling chat" you'd likely have over drinks with a pal about what you're watching, reading, or listening to. *Louder Than a Riot*'s description makes a single, clear assertion—and suggests that there's a lot to unpack inside it. This is your goal.

A good podcast name often alludes enticingly (not cryptically) to its true identity. The description then fleshes out that identity for potential listeners, making its implicit meanings more explicit.

EXERCISE What Is Its Name?

You know what's coming. Set aside some pages in your notebook or create a separate file on your computer just for name brainstorming. Start banging out podcast name ideas now. No judgment. Just scribble!

As ideas occur to you, stash them away in your notebook or file. When an idea bursts forth in the steamy greenhouse of the shower, *do not assume you'll remember it*. Stash it!

When you find some ideas you like, search online to make sure they're not already taken or won't be confused with another podcast. You can also search the US Patent and Trademark Office directory (www.uspto.gov) to see whether the name has been trademarked, which might cause a problem for you. If it's not, you could trademark the name for yourself while you're there (though you might want to consult with a lawyer to help do this). Choosing a unique name is also important for marketing, in getting directories like Apple to list your podcast, and in enabling your audience to find your podcast in the first place.

Try your favorite titles out on people. Ask them to describe your podcast based on the title. Does it make them want to know more? It has to be intriguing enough to make someone scrolling through podcasts click on it to find out what it's all about. You want a sense of essential mystery, but not *in*essential mystery. You don't want to just confuse people. Your podcast name should entice people to *find things out*; don't expect them to *figure things out*.

Sometimes the best podcast name is purely descriptive, like NPR's *Life Kit*. Just two words that say "tools for life." Straightforward podcast names tell your target audience exactly what they're getting.

Make sure that the name works without its artwork (see chapter 14). Your podcast name needs to do the job on its own.

Also, look at the name requirements of Apple Podcasts (previously known as iTunes) to ensure your name and description meet them. As of this writing, Apple dominates the downloads scene, so you need to be included there.

A word about keywords. Keywords are those terms people might use to search for podcasts on your topic. While you want to be aware of them and use them intelligently in your marketing materials, you also want to use them honestly. Search algorithms are always shifting, so your strategies for using keywords and tags will need to be agile to keep up. There was a time when loading up your podcast description with a keyword salad ("tv media television hbo cable streaming watchmen comic graphic novel Rorschach lindelof") would cast a wide net certain to snag you some downloads. Today, that strategy gets you rejected by Apple Podcast's server. Again, there's no hard-and-fast rule, except to stay alert and constantly tweak your strategy. More on this in part 4.

Is all this advice about names making your hair hurt? Then just do this: Keep it clean, simple, and pithy.

Question #7: Why Are *You* Doing This Podcast?

Almost done. But first, you're going to make a pie. Not the eating kind. The chart kind.

EXERCISE Know Thyself

Draw a circle in your notebook. Now ponder these questions:

— How much *time* do you have to devote to your podcast?

— How much *money* do you have to devote to your podcast?

— How much *passion* do you have to do this podcast?

Section your pie chart with each. Don't think too much. We'll delve into these in later chapters. For now, go with your gut.

These three segments comprise the Time + Money + Passion Equation. Knowing this equation can help you decide what kind of podcast you'll do and how often (and maybe whether) you'll do it.

Perfect world: Your pie chart has equal portions—enough time to execute your dream podcast, enough money to buy the services you don't want to learn/do yourself, and the passion to keep it going. Most people have more of some, less of others. Let's break it down, with some work-arounds.

Time: If your "slice" of time is small, you may need a bigger budget to engage help to get the job done. Money tight, too? Then try publishing shorter podcasts, less often. And/or partner with a cohost or panel.

Money: If money's your small slice, you'll need more time on a limited number of things you can't figure out yourself and then doing research to find good freelancers with rates you can afford. Here again, having a cohost or panel show could distribute the workload (and maybe costs, too). You may also choose to look into crowdfunding. Again, shorter length/longer pub schedule could help.

Passion: Earlier, you were asked why other people should care about your podcast. Now, consider why *you* do. Do you love your subject? "Doing something that you're not passionate about will not be sustainable," says Shereen Marisol Meraji, cohost and senior producer of *Code Switch*. "Know what your passions are, the things that drive *you*."

People have lots of reasons for podcasting, and lots of different goals they hope to achieve. Think about what spells "podcast success" to you. Is it sharing something you deeply care about? Raising your professional profile and reputation? Showcasing your knowledge and presentation skills in hopes of booking speaking gigs or other appearances? Connecting with your customers? Driving traffic to your website to check out products and services? Getting downloads and developing a community and committed conversation? Receiving reviews or awards? Building enough audience to get subscriptions, sponsors, or ads, so eventually the podcast can (maybe!) pay for itself? What might this podcast achieve for you that couldn't be achieved through other means (blog, social media, webinars, and the like)?

You don't need hard-and-fast answers to all these questions. But if you're not passionate about your reason, STOP now, do not pass GO. Why? Because your audience will sense it and tap out— fast. Or *you* will because you just won't have the juice to put in the sustained time and effort. Find another approach, another angle, a purpose for your podcast that you *do* feel passionate about, and start again.

Congratulations! You've done a ton of heavy lifting. You now know much more about the podcast you yearn to create: You've identified the audience you're trying to reach, the kind of podcast that suits your strengths, and what you hope to achieve. The chapters coming up will help you get an even clearer handle on the process. Onward!

CHAPTER 3

Who's on My Team?

So! You've got your podcast idea, and—bonus!—it's a solid one. Take a moment. Bask in it. That's no small feat.

Okay, enough lollygagging. It's time to build your team—maybe.

Traditionally, a new podcast involves a cast of characters, each with a different specialty, who join forces to do what must be done.[1]

But it's likely you're going to have to wear multiple hats—maybe all of them. Even if you don't have a hat face. That comes with potential benefits (*you* control everything!) and potential pitfalls (you control *everything*!).

Before we commit to a new show, we ask many people to put in extra work and time[2] to develop, test, and revise the concept, with no guarantees that it'll get green-lit. So we *do* know what it's like to be shorthanded, short on time, and short-circuiting over all there is to do to pull a podcast together—which maybe describes your state of mind right about now?

> *My advice for people who want to make a podcast is the same as my advice for anyone who wants to get a big, weird, cumbersome project off the ground: Collaborate with people you like and trust and mutually support; produce new work on time every time, over and over again, so your audience can build rituals around you; get yourself the best editors and producers you can find; and don't dither too long in the crushing drudgery of meetings. (That last one is probably vastly truer for podcasting than it is for, say, launching an airline.)*
>
> —Stephen Thompson, writer/editor, NPR Music, cohost, *Pop Culture Happy Hour*

1 Adopting a team battle cry in the "Avengers, assemble!" mold is strictly optional, but advisable.

2 Read: Meetings. Just...so *many* meetings, you guys.

This chapter profiles the team members commonly involved in making podcasts (there's plenty of overlap, caveats, and exceptions, as you'll see). This will help you get your head around the various tasks involved. You probably already have a sense of what you're good at, what you're willing to work on to get better at, and what you have no freaking idea how to do. By the end of this chapter, you'll have a solid grasp on what lies ahead, so you can determine the following: if you can make your podcast with your current team; whether you want to outsource some responsibilities; and whether you need to revise your podcast idea so that it fits your resources better.

The Usual Suspects: Podcast Team Members

Editor (The Taskmaster)

Beats the podcast's structure and story into shape.

Mixer (Prime Minister of Microscopic Detail)

Fine-tunes audio quality.

Producer (The Workhorse)

Handles/oversees audio production, technical editing, sound design, mixing. May also edit, plus possibly many other tasks.

Engineer (Minister of Almost Inaudible Audio Anomalies)

Does the final polish.

Host (Brains 'n' Brawn)

Creates (often) and delivers (always) the story.

Composer (Cleftomaniac)

Writes original music or licenses existing music for podcast theme, and/or for individual episodes.

Sound Designer (Soundscape Architect)

Develops, obtains, and/or creates the sounds needed to make the story effective.

Art/Logo Designer (Visuals R Us)

Creates the podcast artwork.

Chances are, your team will consist of one, two, or a brave few. All good. However, one way or another, someone has to take care of each of these eight roles. Your goal: Figure out which tasks you can do, which you can learn, and which you can hire out, as resources allow. Let's take a closer look at each role.

Think Like an Editor (Your Story Will Thank You)

Editors are to stories as yellow Lab puppies are to chew toys. They obsess over them, jealously guard them, tirelessly gnaw on them, and sometimes tear them apart—*that's* how much they love them.

Editors track every aspect of a podcast—structure, language, music, sound—and how they unite to bring value to the audience. They ask endless questions: Where's this headed? Is it accomplishing what we hoped? What's needed to get the full dimensions of this story? Is it taking a new direction?

At NPR, we involve editors early, when the story's barely a concept. For radio pieces, which are often pegged to news, the reporter and the editor meet briefly to discuss how to approach and shape the piece before the reporter tackles it. But for narrative (particularly investigative) podcasts, editors are leaned on hard, and often, throughout the process, helping transform a broad concept into a rich, detailed episode.

Editors ask (and keep asking!) questions like, "Why should listeners care about this story?" "Who will we interview?" "Is there a better/faster/cleaner way in?" "What's an angle that hasn't been done to death?"

Then, once the pieces of the podcast are actually in hand—we call the clips of people talking "actualities," actually—we read the script aloud to our editor (over the phone if necessary), playing the sound clips where they're supposed to go. The editor listens with two sets of ears—the I'm-interested-but-if-I-get-bored-or-confused-I'm-outta-here ears of your audience, and the I've-been-doing-this-audio-editing-thing-for-dog-years ears of a veteran editor—and gives feedback: "The scientist used a technical term there. You need to define it." "One bad pun is okay. Two is too many." "This part drags."[3] "That clip wasn't so clear. Got a better one?"

Editors sometimes tell you things you don't want to hear. But man, your story will benefit. The earlier you put your discerning, ruthless, eagle editor ears on (more on that in later chapters), the better your podcast will be.

3 This is a good editor's go-to comment, deployed with annoying gusto.

Producers: Turning Knobs, Twirling Dials, and So Much More

The producer manipulates the digital files and pulls together the pieces of the podcast, with minute focus on the sound itself.

The difference between editor and producer? Generally speaking, the producer's hands are on the knobs and dials (or the computer mouse), literally assembling the sound tracks and improving their quality: pulling out those sixty seconds you actually use from a sixty-minute interview . . . fiddling with the tracks to make any "p-pops" less annoyingly plosive . . . sensing when a spontaneous burst of laughter during a roundtable discussion crosses the event horizon from "fun" to "self-indulgent" (and blading it out like a skilled surgeon) . . . fading the sounds of organized madness in the kitchen of the hot new restaurant in town—and the voice of the chef, your interview guest, giving orders to the crew—up and down to make things intelligible.

But producers can wear many other hats, basically becoming project managers, doing everything from corralling interview guests to handling the recording session to keeping the books and even getting involved with marketing. The mix of skills you may look for in a producer depends on your podcast's needs.

Later chapters will dive into best practices for audio production. There's a steep learning curve. But you *will* get better with practice. You'll also get a sense of what a producer could do for you, if you decide to work with one. I, for example, know that I'd make a lousy producer. Scheduling and chatting up guests would flummox me, inasmuch as they involve (1) organizational skills, (2) coordinating disparate schedules, and (3) talking on the phone. I don't record my own vocal tracks often enough to remember how to set or adjust the levels, so I always have to ask someone to remind me (read: corral a long-suffering producer foolish enough to look up when I loom over their desk).

The Host(s): The Face—Er, the Voice (and the Spirit!) of the Show

The host is the public face and voice of a podcast and, as such, embodies its identity—especially if the host is also the show's creator, which may be the case for you.

Often, hosts bounce around episode ideas with their editor and/or producer and/or own damn self, drive story development, conduct interviews, and (if you're going the DIY route) assemble them into final form.

You may see yourself as the host, considering your knowledge of and passion for your subject and your gift of gab (and your love of the spotlight). But be prepared: Hosting is a lot of work. Which is why you might decide to consider cohosting.

Your first impulse might be to turn to a friend and fellow podcast nerd and say, "Hey, friend and fellow podcast nerd, wanna do a podcast together?" It may be the beginning of a beautiful partnership.

Or the end of a beautiful friendship. Tuh-*rust* me.

Yes, cohosts need to share interests and like each other, the way friends do. But that's where your quest for a cohost should *start*, not end. Check out the exercise below before bringing aboard a podcast partner in crime.

EXERCISE Cohost Considerations

Think about or write your answers to the questions below. First, ponder the podcast process:

— What aspects of podcasting do you think you're likely to be good at (or know from experience you *are* good at)?

— What aspects do you need to improve or learn more about?

— Of the latter, which are you most interested to learn?

Next, think about your podcast subject:

— What areas are you most knowledgeable about? What, specifically, nay—*uniquely*—are *you* bringing to the table?

— What areas do you know less about?

Now, consider your work habits and personality:

— Do you like slow and steady progress? Or do you tend to procrastinate, but then work well under deadline pressure?

— Do you like pitching ideas, asking for help, and getting others on board with plans? Or are you more into working behind the scenes?

— Are you happier doing big-picture thinking? Or do you like keeping track of things and methodically ironing out details to get something just right?

Maybe you've noticed that the title of this exercise is about cohosts, but the questions are all about you. That's because good cohosts *complement* each other's strengths while sharing a passion for the subject. Having different areas of knowledge, opinions, and experience makes for more interesting, varied episodes. And it can be a smart move to divide and conquer podcasting by pooling multiple talents. If you don't love keeping things organized, you might seek a cohost who'd take pride in making sure every dang episode publishes on time and on budget. Or maybe you need a cohost who's good at working the phone to bag interviews while you dive into learning audio production. For some, the "opposites attract" model creates a great balance; for others, it causes unproductive tension, especially when work styles (or work ethics) clash—it's an individual thing. What's key is awareness and being clear and honest with yourself and each other. Questions like the above help you hammer out a division of labor and turn up areas where, as a solo or even a duo, you may decide to recruit help.

Sound Designers, Mixers, and Engineers: Valuable Ears

Sound designers may wear creative and technical hats, developing sound that fits the spirit of the podcast and doing the technical work of audio production. Mixers do what the name implies: Blend the audio into a buttery whole. Depending on the operation, a producer may do both.

Finally, at places like NPR, engineers bring up the rear with a fresh set of ears and access to technologies even producers don't have, to make a given audio piece ready for radio or (in some cases, but not all) podcast. They sweat the picky details—lots of 'em. Details you might not notice consciously but that infuse the final product with a richness, roundness, and consistency we take pride in. If there's a hiss or a delay on the line when we're recording a remote guest, engineers can minimize it. If an interview done in the field comes back with wind noise, they can twiddle it into nonexistence. They're the watchers on the wall.

That said, not every episode of every NPR podcast goes through this final stage. An unscripted podcast like *PCHH* only does so if

Notes from the Pros: A Producer at Heart

Jessica Reedy, producer, *Pop Culture Happy Hour*

When I was an intern at *All Things Considered*, the first producer I ever shadowed was a guy named Brendan Banaszak. And when he sat down with me, he said, "You will hate being a producer if you hate sitting here and cutting out people's ums. This is what the job is, at the heart of it. If you're bored by this, you are not meant to do this because you will spend hours of your life doing this and either you like it or you don't." That really stuck with me because I liked it. I found it kind of, like, meditative.

something specific and technical calls for it: An old movie clip we pulled to illustrate a point needs cleaning up, say.

While it takes years of experience to do what these audio production pros do, this book will clue you in to ways you can start to "edit with your ears," as they say in the biz.

Composer: Advancing Story Through Music

Music can set the mood of your story, shift the mood dramatically, or signal transitions between sections of a story—in just a few notes.

Basically, as you'll learn in later chapters, music packs a wallop. So, no surprise, there's a lot of interest in using music—and a lot of misinformation out there about "free music" and what's considered "fair use." Bottom line: While the cost can vary, permission is always required to use another person's creative content (for more, see chapter 8).

Art/Logo Designer: Making the Verbal Visual

It seems like an afterthought, right?

It shouldn't be. It *really* shouldn't.

Art is hugely important to your podcast. It snags restless eyeballs and attention spans as they race around an increasingly crowded internet. You need a strong logo that conveys what your podcast is called, and what it's about, simply and cleanly.[4]

The same issues of permission and payment apply to art as to music. For legal tips, see chapter 8; for design tips, see chapter 14, whether you're commissioning art or (gulp) trying it yourself.

What About Podcasting Communities, Podcast Production Services, and Classes?

Let's deal with these one at a time. Podcasting communities are groups you can join to connect with others who are also making podcasts. You can google to find online and local podcast groups. They can be places to network, ask how-to questions, give and receive suggestions and even hands-on help, and learn about the art, craft, and business of podcasting while helping others do the same.

Look for groups that provide just what you want and need, with supportive, positive members who give the group as much as they get from it. Shop around, follow the rules of engagement, do your part to contribute, and bow out if the fit isn't right. "Surround yourself with other passionate people who challenge you to be better," says Shereen Marisol Meraji. "Nothing great comes from a crew of yes-people."

Can't find the right group? Start one! Yowei Shaw, cohost and editorial lead at *Invisibilia*, helped organize a listening group when she was starting out. Check out her advice in "On Community," page 50.

As for classes, there are lots of online tutorials for audio production software, such as Audacity, GarageBand, and Final Cut Pro. You can also enroll in formal classes to build your audio production skills and connect with fellow podcasters (including the pros teaching the class) to build your podcasting network.

Speaking of services, podcast production services abound. Just type the phrase into your browser and see. They can produce your podcast on just about every level you can imagine—for a price, of course. Most aspiring podcasters aren't intending to outsource the process, but still, life is busy, and you may decide to go that route. Businesses may choose outsourcing if in-house staff is too busy with content creation atop their usual workload to take on production—though check first before you farm stuff out: Staffers might jump at the chance to learn podcasting and carve out a specialty niche in the company.

4 Maybe not *too* simply, though. I know, everyone thinks they can gin up a crackin' logo on a cocktail napkin. And maybe you can! I don't know! But, real talk: Graphic designers are your friend—they can help 'zazz that too-many-cocktails napkin-scribble into something that'll look great sitting atop the podcast charts. Look, just *think* about it, okay?

Solo podcasters might outsource time-intensive production because they're busy building their community or broadening the scope, length, or frequency of their podcasts.

As with any service, the watchwords are "buyer beware." The higher the stakes with your podcast (and if it's part of a business strategy, they can be pretty high), the more critical it is to be able to count on the service to meet your quality and scheduling needs.

Being a smart consumer of such services starts with educating yourself and knowing what best practices are. Keep reading.

EXERCISE So, Who's on Your Team?
Now that you know the people and processes involved in creating a podcast, it's time to assess your podcast's production needs. Let's return to the trusty Time + Money + Passion Equation from chapter 2. Here are some ways that might play out:

1 **Are you short on money, so it's gonna be a DIY operation?** Then nurture your premium assets of time and passion by thinking of ways to (a) build in time for your learning curve and (b) keep your energy/passion strong. Here are suggestions:

— *Hit pause.* Spend a couple months just playing with audio editing software, taking tutorials, and learning how things work (consider reading this book as part of your crash course). Then be honest with yourself. If you're passionate about doing this but a little overwhelmed, could a cohost share the job?

— *Pad the schedule.* Give yourself the time you realistically need. The rule of thumb is to take every timeline you set and increase it. Every one. Got that? *Every. One.*

— *Before you publish anything, finish several episodes.* Podcasts in the can are like money in the bank. They help you meet your publishing schedule the way money helps you meet your financial goals. The more episodes you bank today, the less you'll sweat—and the more you'll sleep—tomorrow.

— *Publish less often.* You can always pick up the pace later. The most important thing is keeping your commitment to your audience to publish on time.

On Community

Yowei Shaw, cohost/editorial lead, *Invisibilia*

People in audio are extremely nice and generous. If you're part of a community—and there are lots of these communities all over the world—then you can say, "Hey, I'm having problems with recording at home," or, "I'm having problems with this particular editing software." And the wild thing is, you can ask for help and oftentimes, other makers will help you!

For example, tracking is the hardest part for me. There's the performance aspect of it—it's really hard for me to sound natural. I need help. I still need help. But in the beginning, I struggled with the actual technical setup, like making sure I got it to sound good. You need to understand how a microphone works, you need to understand where to put your mouth; it doesn't come naturally to me.

I was part of this local listening group in Philadelphia that I helped organize when I was starting out. We'd rotate which house the potluck was at. And we had a wide range of experience levels. Some people were just starting out like me, and then we also had veteran editors and veteran engineers. And we happened to have Jeff Towne as one of our members—who is a technical audio legend and also unbelievably kind. So I brought up my problems with recording at one of these groups, and he was like, oh, I've been wanting to work on a piece for Transom [a radio production training workshop]. Why don't we get together and work it out?

So we worked together to try out some different techniques. That's just one example of bringing a problem to a community and someone jumping in. If you make a practice of offering to help others, people will often reciprocate by volunteering to help edit your stories, or you can go to them with specific questions.

Having a community of producers around you is really key when you're doing things on your own because you don't have the apparatus of a whole institution or big-time studio behind you.

— *Shorten your podcast.* It takes hours to create mere minutes of content. Is it really necessary for people to listen to your dulcet tones for half an hour, when fifteen supersuccinct minutes might get the job done as well or better, plus cut your work process by half?

— *Change the format.* An interview format is far less demanding technically than a story-driven narrative. A roundtable might need more editing (all those voices!), but it spreads around the heavy lifting of episode development.

— *Narrow the scope.* For example, limit travel expenses of a food/review show by focusing on local farmers, stores, and restaurants. Or keep the national focus but turn it into a phone interview format with farmers, artisanal makers, chefs, health/diet experts—no location work—for no travel and easier, faster editing.

2   **Are you short on time, but you've got the fire in your belly to make this pod?** Okay, so you've got passion. You might also need some money and/or some podcasting peeps to help you out:

— *Consider a cohost or roundtable format.* Share the load, Mr. Frodo.

— *Turn to your community.* Maybe you can trade services with a podcaster in your group. Or get referrals for reasonably-priced-but-well-trained audio pros—maybe students or new grads starting out.

— *Outsource the most time-intensive processes or the things you know least about.* Generally, this is audio production, but it could be, say, marketing. Whatever's not your thang.

See where this is headed? It's about lowering the stakes in some way—not to compromise, but to claim your power to kick that arch-villain of quality named "Overwhelm" out of town once and for all. Only then can you put the power to accomplish *your* goal of podcasting, at the best level of quality *you* can provide, realistically within *your* reach.

CHAPTER 4

How Long Will It Take and What'll It Cost?

In chapter 2, you started working out your personal Time + Money + Passion Equation for your podcast. This chapter takes the first two components deeper. Because while your passion and aspirations for your podcast count for a lot, the anchors of time and money bring your aspirations within reach.

Here you'll find scheduling fundamentals, time-saving tips, and key budget points to keep in mind. The goal: to give you a clearer view of how you'll accomplish the podcast you want to do.

Starting to Schedule

Abe Lincoln said, regarding a person's optimal leg length: "I should judge they ought to be long enough to reach from his body to the ground."

He might have been talking about podcasts. A podcast should be as long as it needs to be to get the job done. That depends on the kind of podcast you're doing, how much you're doing yourself, and your experience level. And all of *that* affects your schedule.

Story-driven and investigative podcasts take longest: developing and researching the story; finding, booking, and doing the interviews; gathering sound; reviewing it all to pull out the *real* story; revising and editing till your hair hurts; then polishing.

At the other end are roundtables: two or three people sitting around chatting about something of terrific interest. And review shows: one or more voices interspersed with clips. Once you get good at these, you might be able to finish an episode in a few days, even hours.

In the middle are interview shows: You've got to book and prep for the interview, then record and edit—but with fewer audio tracks to tangle with.

The more topical the topic (pop culture, current events), the faster you'll need to publish, or you'll be yesterday's news talking about yesterday's news. No one wants to hear my *Pop Culture Happy Hour* colleagues and me wax eloquent about a film three months (heck, three weeks) after its release.

Compare that to *Invisibilia*, which requires months to develop the long-form, complex narratives it's famous for. It publishes less often—"seasons" of six or so episodes, twice a year—but those are heavily reported and painstakingly constructed, and they sound fantastic, rich and layered and satisfying.[1]

There's a marketing factor, too. An irregular publishing schedule invites your audience to forget you exist (or might cause their podcast app to just up and quit downloading episodes to them).

Not to scare you. This is nothing you can't handle without a schedule and an honest look at your abilities.

The Two Things You've Gotta Track

Whatever type of podcast you're doing, you're basically tracking two processes.

1 **Production:** the steps for assembling each episode
2 **Publication:** a record of the release of each/all of your podcasts

To help you out, on page 55 is a list of the processes and checkpoints often involved in producing and publishing various types of podcasts, which you can customize to your needs.

Wondering *where* to track this stuff? A computer spreadsheet and your calendar might work fine if it's just you. Or search online (try typing "podcast schedule template" into your browser) for more robust scheduling, project-management, or collaboration tools, especially if you're coordinating with others or if your podcast has a lot of moving parts.

EPISODE PRODUCTION SCHEDULE

Your production schedule is your nose-to-the-grindstone view of the podcast process. It tracks the stuff you've got to do to get the dang thing *done*.

PODCAST PUBLICATION SCHEDULE

Imagine you've been podcasting for a year or so. Suppose you want to update a story (*Uh, when was that episode published?*); set up an

1 Have you considered breaking your output into discrete "seasons" of, say, ten episodes each? If your podcast isn't keying off current events, that might be a good way to build some breathing room into your schedule—but make sure your listeners know that's what you're doing.

Production Checklist

Preproduction

- ☐ Start conceiving episode
- ☐ Make interviewee/guest list
- ☐ Assign research and other tasks with due dates (if working with cohosts/team)
- ☐ Research topic and/or guest(s), which includes reading/viewing/listening to the guest's books/films/music as needed
- ☐ Draft script or outline
- ☐ Edit script or outline
- ☐ Book interview/guests
- ☐ Pull clips to play during interview, if any
- ☐ Send interview releases and permission requests for music and/or other clips as needed
- ☐ Prepare interview questions

Production

- ☐ Record interview(s)
- ☐ Collect sound (see chapter 9)
- ☐ Fact-check
- ☐ Revise and finalize script or outline
- ☐ Record your script or outline
- ☐ Audio editing
- ☐ Mixing

Postproduction

- ☐ Insert ads, if any
- ☐ Transcription (more on this, and why it matters, in chapter 14)
- ☐ Write show notes
- ☐ Prepublication promotion

Publication

- ☐ Publish episode
- ☐ On-publication and postpublication promotion
- ☐ Thank-yous to interviewees/guests (with a link so they can listen and share!)
- ☐ Podcast production postmortems and metrics checks (chapter 16)

One Example of a Long-Form Podcast Schedule

Liana Simstrom, podcast manager of *Invisibilia*, shared the basic production framework she applies to the enormously complex process of assembling this story-driven/investigative show renowned for its depth and discernment. You don't have to follow this schedule, and don't get fazed by the lingo, which is defined briefly here (and will be explained fully in later chapters). But hopefully this will give you an idea of how NPR approaches this type of show and how intense the process can be, even when performed full-time by a team of seasoned pros.

This is the basic outline of how Liana tries to schedule their longer spring episodes:

— **Pitching and framing: 2 to 3 weeks.** (Pitching means selling your editor on your idea, and framing is figuring out with your editor how to approach and accomplish it.)

— **Reporting: 3 to 4 weeks,** which includes research, contacting sources/guests, and recording interviews.

— **Log and pull sound clips: 1 to 2 weeks.**

— **Outline script: 1 week.**

— **First draft of episode: 2 to 3 weeks,** which includes rough, placeholder "dummy" vocals.

— **Host edit and revise: 2 weeks.**

— **Group edit and revise: 1.5 weeks.**

— **Review with brain trust/outsiders and revise: 1 week.** (This means asking a handful of trusted folks outside the process—like a focus group—if they get lost or lose interest.)

— **Fact-checking and production: 2 to 3 weeks.**

— **Send link of draft episode to team and revise: 1.5 weeks.** (This gives team members a chance to review the rough draft.)

— **Send link of revised draft episode to team and revise (optional): 1 week.**

— **Final track and production: 1 week.** (This is when hosts record final vocals.)

— **Final pass: 2 days.**

— **Mastering: 1 week.**

interview with a previous guest who has a new book, film, album, or restaurant (*Uh, what's the contact info?*); pitch a new guest by sending episode links to other interviews you've done (*Uh, what the heck were the titles?*); or rank your sponsors— maybe you've got those!—by how much they've paid you (*Uh, where are those invoices?*).

Your podcast publication schedule puts this info at your fingertips. Consider it your thirty-thousand-foot view of your podcast enterprise. It's your master record of your podcast's history—and a resource for charting its future. This is business, baby.

A podcast publication schedule might contain info like:

— Episode title and number, description, and publication date

— Interviewees/guests, with name/title/company, contact info, and social media handle(s)

— Transcription, with transcriber and post dates

— Prepublication, on-publication, and postpublication promotion, listing what you did and when

— Postpublication metrics checkpoints

— Sponsors and ads, listing name, contact info, ad description (length, placement), cost, and date paid

Consistency Is Key

Your podcast schedules should help you stick to a reliable publishing program. Will you do a series that releases on a set schedule (weekly, every couple of weeks, monthly, or on some other time frame)? A seasonal podcast (and if so, how long is a "season")? A limited series with a finite number of episodes? It's up to you, but I can tell you this: As with work, romance, and life in general, 'tis better to underpromise and overdeliver than the opposite.

Remember, podcasting's different from broadcasting. You aren't just putting your show out there and hoping someone tunes in when you do. You want your audience to make your podcast part of their life. In turn, they want to be able to count on you to be there for them with a new episode (a) when they expect it and (b) at the length they've come to look forward to, since it fits perfectly in the time they spend cooking dinner, running errands, or working out.

When you succeed, you hold up your end of the relationship, which builds trust and loyalty.

Consistency is also a great discipline for when you're getting paid to put ads in your podcast (still dreaming big, right?). Businesses will expect ads to run when promised, and you may need to prove it with an episode link plus time stamp.

Eleven Time-Smart Podcasting Tips and Tricks

Check out these ways to save time, make time, and understand the time you need for your podcast.

1 **Fools rush in, but you are no fool.** So don't rush. Start out by giving yourself ample time, knowing you face a steep learning curve. You can always accelerate once you're more familiar with the production process.

2 **Baby steps.** That is, start with a smaller plan so you can learn from any mistakes and glitches before going all-in with big plans. For example, if you're a de-cluttering expert, create a three-part series on office organizing; this will give you a sense of how long things take and how many shows can realistically be in your "season." That way, too, if a listener stumbles across part 3, "Filing for the Flummoxed," and enjoys it, they might seek out parts 1 and 2: "Dominate Your Desk" and "Abolish Your Inbox." Now you're building an audience—an incentive to keep podcasting if there ever was one. Just make sure your audience knows that they're listening to a limited series, so *they* know that there are other episodes to explore, and give them a way to let *you* know if they want more. Also, know this: Your first effort at podcasting might be a steaming pile of unpublishability. Hey, it happens. But take heart. The teachable moments will not be forgotten. You'll do better the next time, and the next.

3 **Expose your dream schedule to the harsh light of cold, merciless reality.** Track when you plan for a task to be done and also when a task is actually done. That way, during your production postmortems (see #4), you can pinpoint problems when something goes off-course. Here are some possible remedies:

— "Steal" time from other processes.

— Lengthen your publication schedule.

- Take tutorials or seek out other instruction to improve your skills.

- Pay or swap services with a fellow podcaster or engage an audio pro to perform that component for you.

- Rethink your podcast format.

4 **No laurel resting! Do postmortems.** Review your podcast schedule after an episode publishes. Where'd things go off-track? What could you do more efficiently? Evaluate your podcast's quality and, of course, be sure to note what went *right* and pat yourself on the back!

5 **Include your squad.** (Do the kids still say that? *Squad?* Yikes.) If you're working with a cohost or a panel, include them in the planning, scheduling, and postmortem processes to get and keep everyone on the same page. It helps when everyone participates to hammer out schedules, assign tasks, and address stumbling blocks.

6 **Move forward by planning drawkcab.** In "Project Blueprint," our NPR Training team suggests working backward from a designated launch date to develop your schedule, with weekly goals broken down.

7 **Stockpile episodes so you can swim in them later like a trademarked cartoon Scottish billionaire waterfowl.** Once you get rolling with podcasting, you'll be working on multiple episodes at once, in different stages of completion, to maintain

---

Week: May 14–18

GOAL	TO-DO	OBSTACLES
(What do you want to accomplish this week?)	*(List the action items necessary to meet your goal.)*	*(What stands in the way of meeting your goal?)*
• Complete script for first episode	• Finish pulling tape • First edit • Rewrite • Second edit	• Getting time with editor • Troubleshooting music licensing issue

your publication schedule. (Side benefit: You can promote future episodes because you'll know what they are!)

That's why you should have several finished episodes banked and ready to publish before you launch your podcast. While those episodes are publishing, you'll be working on the next several, which you'll then bank and launch, and so on, in staggered fashion ("stagger"—*such* an apt word for this).

8   **Do long-range planning. No, longer. Looonger.** At *PCHH*, for example, we look ahead and add major movie releases/series premieres to our calendar (not too far ahead, though, as these dates often change—maybe a month or two ahead). We have at least two weeks of shows planned at any given time.

9   **Start an Idea Bank and rob it regularly.** Your podcast pipeline starts with ideas. You must incubate them. Keep a file where you stash any and all podcast ideas as you think of them. Don't judge. Just deposit. Encourage your team to do the same. Have regular idea meetings when you look at what's in your Idea Bank, kick those concepts around, add new ones, and pull some out to develop. It might be a weekly check-in with just you, your coffee, and your notebook. Or a half-hour call with your team. (Details on developing ideas and telling stories in part 2.)

10   **Throw some softballs.** Keep a stash of some easier-to-do episodes in development. So if an episode—or life—throws you a curveball (a guest cancels, you have a tech-tastrophe, or your kid gets his eighty-fourth ear infection of the school year), you can accelerate one of the easier ones in the queue to keep your publishing schedule. If you generally do interviews in the field, do some shows with in-studio guests. If your discussion subjects are topical or time-sensitive (such as current events), reach into history with roundups by decade or on themes. If your show comments on current events or fast-changing pop culture, bank some "evergreen" episodes—those that can stand alone, without a specific news peg, so you run them, or even rerun them, should the need arise.[2]

2 The need? Will arise.

11   **Make time for mixing thoroughly.** All production takes time. But mixing—editing and sequencing audio tracks so they sound like they magically happened all smooth and natural-like—takes hours to finish a few minutes' worth. So, especially at first, pad your schedule with extra time to get mixing right.

What'll It Cost? Beginning to Budget

Someone's gotta pay for all this. How much you spend may depend on your podcasting goals. Doing this for love? Then spend what you can afford, be it shoestring level or hand-tooled leather with brass buckles, fringe, and custom orthotics.

Are you hoping your podcast might eventually bring in income to cover your costs, and maybe a little more? Or maybe you aim to seriously monetize this thing? In any case, even if you start off lean and/or mean, eventually you'll need to make enough of an investment to produce a reasonably polished product, and then gradually increase your investment based on (a) your growing production skills, (b) the reach of your podcast, and (c) whether you're still loving this crazy podcasting thang.

You'll read more about monetizing strategies in chapter 16. The focus here is on costs.

Some costs are one-time only (such as a mic) and some are recurring, like fees for the hosting platform where you'll upload your podcast for distribution to directories.

Equipment is covered in chapter 6, but if you go no-frills, it's pretty much the cost of your computer, smartphone, and editing software (unless you're using a free version). If you invest in a couple of mics for you and your cohost or interview guest, plus headphones, that can run a few hundred dollars. Headed into the field? Field recording equipment (that is, portable audio recorder and other stuff) can add hundreds of dollars more. Staying inside? If you don't have a sound-dampened space to record in (tips on this later), but want the high-sheen sound of a production studio, you'll have to rent one, and that might run you as much as a couple hundred dollars or more per hour. Oh, and are you planning to put sweat equity into learning how to do every step by yourself or to hire outside help?

Whatever you decide, you need to track how much you spend and how much (hopefully, eventually) you make on your podcast. Some reasons why: If you're hoping to write off podcast expenses on your taxes as business deductions (check with your accountant first)—you need to track expenditures, plus make sure you have supporting documents like receipts to back up your claims. If you're reimbursing others on your team, you need to track what they spent—and if you decide to seek funding, you'll need to know what your podcast costs to make your pitch.

The following is a list of commonly incurred expenses for a basic podcast. You might not incur them all, nor is this a comprehensive list. But it's a realistic overview of what most podcasts spend money on. The goal? To operate your podcast in a lean, efficient manner without ever sounding cheap.

Another way to cut costs? Learn good sound collection habits (keep reading). Just knowing how and where to place or hold the mic can prevent audio problems that'll cost significant time or money to fix.

Do your homework. Go online for price ranges and reviews of services and products.

Possible Podcast Budget Items

Equipment/Software

☐ Computer

☐ Recorder

☐ Mic(s)

☐ Mic stand(s)

☐ Shock mount(s)

☐ Headphone(s)

☐ Pop filter(s)

☐ Windscreen(s)

☐ Editing software (unless using free software)

☐ Call recording software (unless using free software)

Production

☐ Editing

☐ Producing

☐ Mixing

☐ Transcription

Marketing

☐ Podcast art

☐ Podcast hosting service

☐ Streaming service

☐ Website domain name

☐ Website hosting service

☐ Website design

Additional/Other

☐ Outside professionals and team members

☐ Studio rental

☐ Sound treatment equipment/materials (portable recording booth, acoustic foam, etc.)

☐ Travel

☐ Fees (to license or commission music, sound effects, etc.)

☐ File storage/backup

Tap into your community. Talk to other podcasters doing your kind of podcast about what they use, how they budget, where to cut corners, and when it's worth paying for quality. For example, if you want to put your energy into developing ideas and marketing, maybe invest in engaging a producer to oversee recording and the time-intensive process of editing. You'll learn a ton, boost your podcast's quality, and stay on schedule. Trade services with other podcasters ("I'll create some music bits for your next season if you'll help me with editing" or "I'll teach you bookkeeping if you'll teach me Audacity"). Start a communal list of affordable indie professionals you've used and liked.

EXERCISE **What's the Bottom Line?**

Now that you've got a general idea of costs, answer these two questions:

— **Do you need to tweak the concept?** You've got format, length, and schedule to play with. Examples: Turn a travel-heavy show into an interview-based one with occasional road trips; bring in a cohost to share work and expenses; shorten your show to a punchy ten minutes instead of a rambling half hour (trust me: short-but-good is *good*); turn a weekly crafts show into a holiday crafts show and publish around selected holidays.

— **Where could you get affordable help?** Examples: Join or form a podcasting group and trade services, ideas, and info; take audio classes or free tutorials online; engage students in design, composition, and audio production to help.

Are you wondering how you're gonna pull off the podcast you're interested in doing? That's good! This part of the process is all about honing your idea and getting it in line with reality. Getting real about this stuff is the best way to end up with a podcast . . . for real.

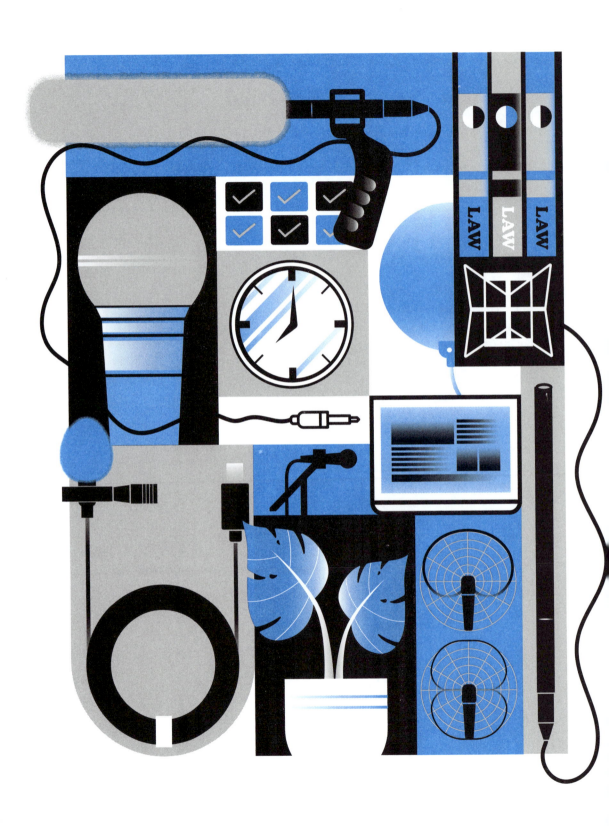

PART 2

PLAN

Prepare to Podcast

Once you've determined the core idea of your podcast, it's time to get behind a mic, right? Not quite. A surprising amount of podcasting happens before you record one second of sound. There's a lot you can do to set yourself up for success before you record. Your editor¹ will thank you for this prep work!

First and foremost, you need to be heard clearly, so we'll delve into voice—one of the most distinctive features of a podcast. I'll explain ways to evaluate your voice, decide what you love about it and what, if anything, you might want to change—plus provide exercises for getting comfortable with your voice, avoiding common vocal mistakes, and infusing your podcasts with expression.

Before you can press Record, you need to have the best mic for your purpose, as well as the equipment necessary to ensure that your podcast sounds good to your listeners. I'll provide essential info on how to get started and level up without breaking your budget.

Oh, and how to create content that people will actually want to listen to? And tell a compelling story? Here, too. Storyboard versus script. Intro and outro. And the questions and storytelling strategies the pros use to grab and keep audience attention.

And because none of this matters remotely if you end up getting sued pantsless, chapter 8 provides the absolute, bare-minimum basics of media law—to help keep you out of jail and fully pants-clad.

1 Um, you?

CHAPTER 5

Finding Your Voice: Three Steps to Your Best Vocal You

We've all heard it. That unmistakable, warm-yet-authoritative Radio Voice.™ Relaxed. Polished.

No one is born with it. Many of your favorite NPR radio personalities developed their voices over years of training and experience. Think *All Things Considered*'s Audie Cornish and *Morning Edition*'s Rachel Martin. Their voices are practiced, engaging, and—crucially, for a newsmagazine host—totally adaptable as they guide listeners through the day's news stories, from tragic to technical, heartwarming to hilarious.

But you don't need a traditional, voice-for-all-occasions Radio Voice™ for podcasting. Open secret: *Everyone* is born with a voice for podcasting because podcasting's about the individual voice—as real, unusual, and untraditional as yours may be. Your listeners want to hear *your* passion, *your* knowledge. You.

Read on for three steps to finding and making friends with your unique voice, discovering common vocal errors, and learning simple techniques to help you sound like your best vocal you.

Step 1. Accept How You Sound

Your voice makes you sound like *you*. It's your special sauce: a natural mix of flavors distinctive to you—wtone, pitch, cadence, volume, inflection—shaped by the emotions of the moment (curiosity, delight, doubt, certainty) as well as your life experiences, where you and your parents grew up, or any other languages you speak.

Ask some trusted folks this question:

— "Will my audience find me hard to understand in any way?"

Then ask yourself:

— Am I okay with how I sound?

Being understandable is crucial for audio. If you get consistent feedback that your audience might find you hard to understand, you may decide on some vocal coaching. This is *not* to eliminate your unique vocal qualities—the ones that set you apart—but to enunciate more clearly and learn other techniques (like slowing down) to help your audience understand and stay with you.

Friendly feedback might also uncover some vocal habits you'd like to say goodbye to, while taking loving ownership of what could become your vocal signature: the smile that seems to lurk just behind your words, the way your voice goes flat and deep with ironic humor, that laconic Southern drawl, that New York edge, your British gift for the clipped whopping understatement, or the wonderful way you say "Dakar."[1]

Don't accentuate your sound to cultivate a brand or podcast persona. You're a person, not a persona. If you normally throw in a Yiddish expression because nothing else says it better, or you quote wise words in your German granny's fractured English, do it because that's you. Own it, don't exaggerate it. Be understandable. Sound real. Sound like you.

Step 2. Avoid the Three Vocal Tics That Turn Listeners Off

At NPR, listeners tell us what they like about our podcasts, and we're grateful for that. They also tell us what they don't. We appreciate that, too. Three complaints turn up over and over: low energy, vocal fry, and sounding scripted.

LOW ENERGY

You know it when you hear it: a flat, monotone speech pattern. No lilt. No variations in pitch, pace, or volume.

If this is your natural speaking style, great, but know that you're leaving on the table one of the most essential tools to hold listeners' attention.

Easy work-around: If you're working from a script, mark the words and ideas you feel are most important for listeners to understand. Highlight, underline, or circle 'em—make them pop—so you'll see them coming up, slow down, and *punch* them:

1 (NPR International Correspondent Ofeibea Quist-Arcton only.)

Yesterday was the first Monday of **May**, which means some of New York's fashion elites put on their most outrageous outfits for the **Met Gala**. Actor **Billy Porter** looked like a **winged, golden Egyptian god,** carried in on a platform by shirtless men. Singer **Janelle Monáe** went **surrealist** with a giant **eye** for a bra and a stack of **hats** tumbling off her head. This year's theme was **"Camp: Notes On Fashion."** And we are **not** talking about **summer** camp.

Hit those key words or phrases hard. Increase your volume, raise or lower your pitch, draw out the syllables slightly, pause a fraction after. Those changes perk up listeners' ears. It's the best way (besides music and sound cues), to signal something's happening in the story they won't want to miss.

Lack of vocal energy is often a symptom of poor breath control, nerves, or both. When you run out of air before you run out of sentence, you can't modulate your tone. Your vocal cords may rasp against each other—a phenomenon known as *vocal fry* (a loaded subject; see page 70). Ever hear a radio or podcast guest sounding tight and croaky when they start talking? That's nerves. Adrenaline has caused their lungs and throat to constrict, so not enough air passes over their vocal cords when they talk.

Again, easy fix: Take a big, deep breath before you start talking. That full breath supports your voice, lending it resonance, agility, and range, so you can supply the variety that keeps listeners hanging on your every word.

This isn't hard. It just takes some practice. In time, it'll be as natural as, well, breathing. In your script, look for breath breaks (usually at punctuation, but elsewhere, too). Mark them in the script in a way that'll cue you. Add breath breaks to the script above and try it again. Breathing helps, right?

EXERCISES **The Three-Dog Pant and Candle in the Wind**
At NPR, we've learned a lot about breath control from Jessica Hansen, an actress, voice-over artist, vocal coach, and NPR announcer. You've likely heard her telling you that support for the show you're listening to comes from listeners like you. Jessica swears by her simple, daily warm-up routine to help her sound more natural and take good care of her voice—and once you try it, you will, too.

The Three-Dog Pant

"A lot of low vocal energy comes from poor breath support," Jessica says. To help strengthen that support, "the first exercise opens up the rib cage and gets the breath flowing freely in the body. It involves pretending you're different kinds of dogs."

First, a Chihuahua. "Focus all the breath at the very top of your ribcage" and take "short, shallow little breaths." For ten seconds, just pant as fast as you can.

Next, Jessica instructs, a Labrador. Feel the ribs right below your armpits? Now, as you pant like a bigger dog—a little deeper, a little slower—you want to make sure those ribs are moving in and out. Do this for another ten seconds. "Once those ribs are open and swinging, the breath can move more freely."

Finally, a St. Bernard. This is focused at the bottom of your ribcage and your belly. Breathe deeper, in and out, for ten seconds, feeling your belly and lungs swell and contract like an accordion as you pant.

Once you've limbered up your lungs and the bones and muscles around them, it's easier to take the supported breaths you need to read your script, work from an outline, or talk off the cuff. It just takes half a minute, but it energizes your vocal delivery, every time.

Candle in the Wind

Here's another simple exercise Jessica suggests for breath control.

Hold one finger in front of you and pretend it's a birthday candle. Now take a deep breath, and try to blow that candle out by exhaling in five discrete puffs of equal length and power. Repeat another four times.

You'll feel silly (like *that's* never happened before)—but this exercise teaches firm control of how you exhale. Seeing that "candle" helps you focus and train your body to keep your breaths regular and even, sustaining vocal energy through sentences short and long.

VOCAL FRY

Hoo boy. A fraught subject.

Vocal fry is the tendency to draw out the last word or phrase in a sentence in a creaky, low-register voice. It occurs when the voice emanates from the back of the throat. Vocal folds in your voice box, which usually vibrate quickly with the air passing through during speech, get shorter, grow more slack, come together—and

Notes from the Pros: On Finding Your Voice

Sam Sanders, host, *It's Been a Minute with Sam Sanders*

Should I make an effort to sound Black on the radio, whatever that means? To prove that I have a unique perspective and yadda yadda yadda? Should I purposefully sound Texan? Or like someone who was raised Pentecostal? I could go on.

I've had to let that go.

Some of my friends think I always sound "Black" on the radio. Other colleagues say they never would have known. Sometimes my Texas comes out. Sometimes I actually sound like a Californian.

But what is most rewarding for me now is that people know it's Sam Sanders when they hear me on the air. I sound like myself, and that is a mashup of all the things I am, and it is a tone that I can subtly shift based on the needs of a story. I can be somber for a story about death, or play up the charm in a fun feature. But it's all a point on this spectrum of this voice called Sam Sanders.

Manoush Zomorodi, host, *TED Radio Hour*

Everyone cringes when they hear their own voice. Get over yourself. If you're convinced you have something to say, don't worry about what you sound like when you say it.

Cardiff de Alejo Garcia, cohost, *The Indicator from Planet Money*

Don't be afraid to listen to your own recordings, again and again, to understand why you (likely) sound so different from how you first imagined you would sound. Maybe that clever intellectual joke about the Bulgarian central bank is funny, or maybe you sound like an irredeemably highfalutin jerk. The only way to know is to hear yourself tell it. And then tell it again a different way. Just as it's hard to know how you look in a fresh new outfit without checking yourself out in the mirror, you won't really know how you're capable of sounding until you've listened to yourself enough.

then spring open when the air passes through, producing the creaky "fry" sound.

In addition to being something people variously abhor, barely notice, debate from socioeconomic-cultural-feminist vantage points, or do themselves—unconsciously or not—vocal fry is associated with some voice box conditions, is a trick singers can use to hit low notes outside their range, and is part of certain languages, such as Zapotec Mayan.

It's something NPR listeners complain about a lot, along with its cousin, upspeak (the tendency for vocal pitch to rise at the end of a sentence).

But the thing we at NPR have noticed? Most of the complaints come from older men, mostly about younger women. Which is funny because speech pathologists tell us that vocal fry is much more common among men. In fact, it's considered a sign of hypermasculinity. But some men of an older generation tell us it makes younger women sound like "valley girls" or "faux socialites," and thus, by their rubric, nonauthoritative.

There's real evidence that this antifry bias is generational (and sexist)—so ask yourself: Do you care?

Your podcast will go out into the world as a reflection of your sensibility, passions, and personality. How you sound is a huge part of that. Maybe you don't like how you sound and want to make some changes. If you happen to be one of the millions with this increasingly common vocal tic, you could choose to correct it.

If you've already envisioned your target audience, and if that audience includes a lot of older men (will you be podcasting about golf, say? Or military history?), maybe you'll want to take those steps, if only to spare yourself the complaints that—trust me—will come your way.

If you decide to keep your fry, you won't be alone. But I'd be remiss if I didn't mention something that gets less attention: Vocal fry can damage the voice. "From a vocal technique standpoint vocal fry is not a really healthy way to make sound," Jessica Hansen says. "The little vocal folds [in your throat are] banging up against each other in a way they're not designed to do. [This] can hurt your vocal folds, eventually creating calluses called nodes, then leading to surgery."

Jessica trains her students to keep the voice "forward in the front of mouth," where it resonates against the front teeth, the hard palate (the bony area on the roof of the mouth, behind the front teeth), and the sinus cavities. This makes the voice more resonant and also amplifies it.

EXERCISE The Lip Trill

To train your voice to be naturally placed forward, away from the back of the throat, practice the lip trill. Jessica Hansen instructs to first take a deep, supportive breath, and then blow it through your closed mouth, so that your lips "trill," or flap together, as you exhale. As you do so, adjust the pitch of your voice, sliding from the bottom of your register to the very top, and back down again.

SOUNDING SCRIPTED

People say that one of the things they love most about Sam Sanders, of *It's Been a Minute with Sam Sanders*, is that he sounds "real"— loose, relaxed, relatable—not stuffy or artificially precise. "It sounds like he's winging it," an NPR listener once wrote. "It's like we're sitting at a bar and just chatting."

Sam's intros are famously winning. From his signature greeting ("Hey, y'all") to his garrulous, open speaking style, he guides us through the show on a wave of warmth and good feeling that seems completely spontaneous.

It's not, of course. Sam and his producers script those introductions carefully for clarity and accuracy. When they record in-studio, it's timed out precisely. For many of us, writing a script is part of what makes us sound stuffy. But Sam's great at, first, writing copy that sounds like his voice, and second, reading it in a breezy, natural way. It's a skill he's developed—one that few have naturally.

People read aloud from prepared texts all the time. At weddings, book readings, in church, at conferences. How many sound natural? Precious few—few enough that when someone does it well, you remember.

If you're doing a scripted podcast, you need to make sure you don't sound like Uncle Doug doing his reading from Ecclesiastes at your cousin's wedding.

Stiffness is understandable. For most of us, public speaking is our number-one fear. We're anxious, sweaty, and desperately trying not to screw up. Everything that makes us interesting to listen to—demeanor, pacing, vocal range—flies out the window.

The goal: to relax enough so that it sounds, not like you're reading copy, but telling a story.

First step: Make your copy clear and simple. Chapter 7 is devoted to storytelling—how to write the way you naturally talk. For now, remember that your listeners have nothing but the sound of your voice to go by. That means short, simple sentences. The first rule I learned at NPR when I started converting my website text into radio and podcast pieces was: "Say goodbye to your clauses."

When I write, my prose naturally fills up with parenthetical statements and dependent clauses that nest in my sentences, one inside the other, like Russian dolls. I'm not alone. It's a stylistic tic that can work great with readers, who can easily reread if a sentence becomes a bit too Faulknerian to follow. But *listeners* have a hard time picking out the most important parts of a story from prose filled with filigreed bits and asides. They need clean, clear copy—which is also *much* easier for you to read into the mic. [2]

Once you've cleaned up your copy and you're ready to record, the goal is to sound like you're talking to the listener, using all the

[2] When I recorded the audiobook for my second book, Reader Me kept cursing Writer Me for all those clever, circuitous sentences that defied being read aloud.

vocal tools you naturally use when telling a story to a friend at a bar: inflection, pitch, pacing, and volume.

At first, you might sound and feel like Uncle Doug. But there's a way to relax into the compelling cadences of natural speech.

EXERCISE **Reading in Character**

The idea is to knock your voice out of the one narrow channel it can too easily lock into when you get too much in your own head. Instead, you allow your voice to do what it naturally does when you're telling someone a story in the moment—to rise and fall, to hurry up and slow down. To let what you're saying guide how you're saying it.

If you read your copy in a series of distinctly different character voices—voices you know well, so you don't have to think about them—you'll open up your voice and allow it to move through various pitches and tones naturally. It doesn't matter *what* characters, really—just make them different from one another.

Jessica Hansen, for example, first has her students read their copy "straight" as they plan to record it. Then she has them read it again in several wildly different styles or voices—could be as a cowboy, an opera singer, and Bugs Bunny. Do this, playing with voices. Now reread your copy in your own voice. Invariably, this exercise helps people sound more open, engaged—and natural.

Try it! Take the sample passage from our discussion of vocal tics (see page 69) and read it aloud in the voice of a character—any one that strikes your fancy: movie gangster, televangelist, Captain Kirk, Greta Garbo, Yoda.... Notice a difference when you return to your voice?

Step 3: Know How the Pros Do It

Here are some other vocal tips to keep in mind before (and when) you hit Record:

— **Script aloud.** At your keyboard banging out your script, try saying it aloud while you're writing, so it'll sound more like you.

— **Play with formatting and markup.** Try boldface, as in the sample on page 70, to remind yourself to stress certain words, or ALL CAPS, as NPR correspondent Carrie Johnson

Mind Your Ps and Ss

Plosives (aka p-pops) and sibilance are normal speaking sounds that get magnified by the mic. They can be distracting and downright annoying to your audience (plus, they scream "amateur"). Here's how to diagnose and prevent them. (Trust us, you don't want to spend time editing this stuff out.)

Symptoms: Plosives generate a gust of air that hits the mic like a fist to the face: *Pow!!* This often happens with words containing Ps and Bs; sometimes Ts and Ks.

Sibilance is a hissing sound from air rushing across the mic surface. Common culprits: S, SH, TH, and F.

Diagnosis: Hold your hand a couple of inches in front of your mouth and say these phrases:

"Bobbing for popovers."

"Speak the speech, I pray you, as I pronounced it to you, trippingly on the tongue."

"S**t, stop sitting on my throbbing f***ing thumb!"

Feel those gusts?

Treatment: P-pops and sibilance can be tough, time-consuming, and sometimes impossible to edit out; you may need a pro's hand. The best offense is a good defense:

— Practice pushing out less air when speaking. Practice the sentences above till you feel just a *tiny* puff on your palm.

— Nail down proper mic placement: several inches away from your mouth, angled right or left—out of range of those gusty pops and hisses (try it, pretending your palm is the mic, and see!).

— Equip the mic with a windscreen or pop filter (see chapter 6).

This isn't about changing your voice; just practicing vocal habits that'll improve audio quality, cut editing time, and produce a more pleasing podcast (say *that* three times without plosives).

does. Circle or highlight key points. Cue your breaths. Johnson also uses "a lot of ellipses to remind myself to stop and breathe." She also tries to distill ideas to a line, and "I leave a full line of space in between to make the script easier to read."

— **Hum and meow.** Jessica Hansen suggests both humming and meowing "for keeping the voice more forward and out of the throat" to avoid vocal fry and add energy. For humming, find the placement of your hum where the lips are the buzziest and most tingly. If it tickles, don't back off, you're doing it right! And yep, that's right, meowing. Pretending to be an annoying, loud, meowing cat will place the voice right up front. Test it by speaking a sentence, meowing your alley-cat best, then rereading the sentence. Feel a difference?

— **Go slow.** Since your audience can't see your lips moving, it's easier for them to miss something. Speak a little more slowly than usual. It'll help you speak more clearly, too.

— **Stand and deliver.** NPR's Scott Simon records *Weekend Edition* standing up in Studio 45. It adds energy and authority—it's one reason he's got such a dynamic delivery.

— **Get the mic right (or left).** Holding the mic too close to your mouth will pick up plosives and sibilance (see "Mind Your Ps and Ss" opposite and more on mics in later chapters). Super-important: Keep the mic a little to the right or the left of, and several inches away from, your mouth.

Now, play with this! Start recording vocal notes to yourself on your smartphone. For proper mic placement, hold the phone near your cheek, angled as if you're chatting with someone, or about four inches in front of you. Capture stuff you observe, musings, podcast ideas. Listen and correct for p-pops and sibilance (adjust mic distance and "push" the consonants less). Try for that slower-but-conversational, key-words-and-phrases-emphasized voice. You'll get used to how you sound, find the vocal delivery and mic placement that make you sound like your best you, and get into the creative habit of scanning your world for interesting stuff and stopping time to capture it. All good!

CHAPTER 6

The Well-Equipped Podcast

Before you step behind the mic, you need to know the best mic for your purpose. And whether to plug it into your computer or a portable audio recorder. And what software you will use to edit. And which headphones[1] to get (like in those studio pix of audio people looking all cool and pro-like). And...

Don't panic. And don't overspend. This chapter introduces you to the fundamentals of podcast gear, from low-frills to midlevel frilly, and it will help you find the right equipment for the podcast you want to make.

I'm about to wade into some technical weeds here—but you won't get lost in the woods. This chapter will help you sort through the options for important initial tech decisions. From there, just do what everyone does: Keep learning (technology having that annoying habit of always changing), read product reviews, and yak with other podcasters. Audio geeks love to talk tech and trade tips. Tap the hive mind for opinions and help.

The Basic Basics

You might already have the equipment for a low-frills podcast:

— Your smartphone

— Your computer

— Sound editing software

You can use your smartphone's recording function or download a sound recording app to record yourself and sounds. Then email the

[1] "Cans" in radio lingo. Though no one really calls them that, in my experience. We're NPR, not *Drive Time with Burly Bob and the Stinkmeister*, you know?

Notes from the Pros: Get Enough Gear to Get You Started

Yowei Shaw, cohost/editorial lead, *Invisibilia*

One of the lazier reasons why I got into podcasting rather than film is because there's simply a lower barrier to entry, and there are so many resources online. Like, it just felt more possible. Basically what I did was read everything I could get my hands on, and then get the bare minimum setup that I could.

audio files to yourself or connect your phone with your computer to upload the file. Audio files can get big quickly, so be sure you've got enough storage space on your phone.

Then use free sound editing software (such as Audacity) and online tutorials to learn how to cut and combine ("mix") files to tell your story and improve the sound.

EXERCISE Making Tracks

An audio file is called a track.[2] Each component of a podcast is (should be, better be, really has to be—you'll learn why in a sec) recorded on a separate track.

Practice recording your first vocal tracks (as I suggest at the end of chapter 5!), and use them to play around with this basic recording/emailing/uploading approach. Take breaks so you can keep saving your files as you go.[3] Get used to how it works. Listen back and think about where you'd trim a track. You may not have the skills to actually do this yet, but you will. And you'll develop the beginnings of an editor's ear.

You'll probably discover that while phone audio might work fine for a one-person voice-over, it's not great for interviews. Trying to record two people on one device makes for uneven sound collection. Obviously, it doesn't work long-distance.

2 Old-school radio types reserve the term "track" for the reporter's vocal files versus files of other people talking ("actualities" or "clips"), music, or ambient/background noise ("ambi"). To this day at NPR, when we record ourselves reading our scripts, we still call it "tracking." But you're not an old-school radio type, are you? An audio file's an audio file.

3 "Pfft," you're thinking. "That's too much of a hassle. I can just keep recording, I'll be fine." Um. Have you...*met* technology? (Save your files. Do it. Trust me.)

Basic Options for Interviews and Cohosts

For interviews—or if you've got a remote cohost—try the recording features of platforms you've probably used for online calls or web conferencing (such as Skype and Zoom).

First, though, look into how to record your voices on separate tracks. That way, you can edit each track separately, and problems in one track won't bleed through to the other(s).

For example, maybe *you* sound fine, but your interviewee keeps clearing her throat while you're talking (she didn't do the chapter 5 vocal warm-ups). If you're both on one track, how will you edit that out without chopping your words?

Or suppose you're interviewing two people, you're all dialed in, and one person's Schnauzer goes berserk when their doorbell rings, trampling all over everyone's lines. Good luck editing that mess.[4]

Another issue: internet connectivity. We've all had it happen on online calls: Someone's connection craps out and they're dropped. What if that happens during a roundtable?[5]

Finally, the audio might sound tinny ("bright") or muffled ("muddy" or "bass-y"). This happens when there's imbalance between high-frequency and low-frequency sounds—known in the biz as tone or equalization (EQ) issues.

Still, these more home-brewed options may work fine

— during your learning curve,

— for a solo podcast,

— if your pod's short (less risk of losing internet connection), or

— if you've already got a devoted community who'll overlook quality glitches to hear your dulcet tones.

But if you want to be competitive in the larger marketplace—or if you're a stickler of an audiophile determined to produce the cleanest, crispest sound you can[6]— you'll need to level up a notch or two.

Try software such as Ringr, Zoom, ClearCast, or Zencastr that records each voice on each computer. You might have to pay, but the sound quality may be worth it to you.

[4] You may think all that yipping adds a roundedness, a lived-in charm and character. Maybe. Up to you. All I know is that, during the COVID-19 pandemic, when everyone at NPR was recording from makeshift home studios (read: closets, pillow forts), listeners were tolerant of things like our dogs yipping, our kids screaming, our spouses blowing leaves *right outside the damn window when they knew we were taping but do they listen NO THEY NEVER LISTEN*—at first. But it got old quick. Both for our listeners...and for us.

[5] During the pandemic, it happened often while taping *Pop Culture Happy Hour.* Like, *often.*

[6] This...is NPR.

Some questions to ask when evaluating options:

— Is it compatible with Mac, PC, or both? (Look for both, for maximum versatility with interviewees.)

— Is a particular browser required? (If so, make sure your interviewees use it.)

— How many participants are allowed on a call?

— Any limits on duration of the call?

— Do the other participants have to install or set up anything (such as Zoom, Skype, or Google Voice)?[7]

— Is it possible to record on independent channels, and if so, for how many participants?

— What type of file is produced? (MP3, WAV, AAC, or FLAC? NPR podcasts tend to work with WAV files because they're uncompressed and most audio folks think they sound better— but that means they tend to take up lots of space. MP3s are the most popular way to store music and are more efficient in terms of size. It's possible to convert file formats using online tools, or save yourself that extra step.)

— Where is the file stored?

— Can recording be done on a smartphone as well as on a computer?

— What's the price? If it uses tiered pricing, what's offered in each tier? If there's a free version, what does it offer?

Talk to your community about what works for them and what snags they've hit, and shop around.

Next-Level Setup

Willing to invest several hundred bucks to level up? Read on.

If you're not going out in the field, your upgrade might be

— Stationary mic(s) or handheld mic(s) with stand

[7] When an NPR guest can't get to a studio, and if they have both a smartphone and a landline, we tell them to download an app that turns their phone into a recording device. The thing is, we *then* have to send them a series of detailed instructions on how to record themselves (a complicated affair that requires them to hold two phones to their faces at the same time), how to monitor their levels, how to name the file they create, and how to send it to NPR. Walking less-than-tech-savvy guests through this process is something NPR producers spend…just a surprisingly large chunk of time doing. It gets great sound, but during COVID-19, a lot of shows and podcasts settled for voice memos. Much simpler. Bottom line: Don't assume your interviewee is as fully equipped as you, and build in time for troubleshooting before you can start.

Notes from the Pros: On Tooling Up (or Not)

Yowei Shaw, cohost/editorial lead, *Invisibilia*

> I wouldn't go fancy right away 'cause you don't know exactly what
> you need. So I would get a serviceable microphone, recorder, audio
> editing software, and then that's all you need in the beginning. And
> then just start making things.

J. C. Howard, producer, *TED Radio Hour* and *How I Built This with Guy Raz*

> I wish someone had told me to invest in an editing software
> (Adobe Audition, Pro Tools, Hindenburg, etc.). It doesn't have
> to be expensive or super high-tech; just something to make cuts
> where needed. Having a podcast is good. Having a well-edited
> podcast is better.

— Headphone(s)

— Recording/editing software (aka a digital audio workstation,
aka DAW)

If you're going out in the field, for reasons of portability, you
might choose handheld mic(s) instead of stationary versions, and
possibly a portable audio recorder.

Let's break this stuff down.

Making Friends with Mics

Nothing in audio happens without a mic. An external mic steps you
up from the mic in your phone or computer.

First level: Get a mic you can connect to your computer or
smartphone. A mic with both a USB connection and an XLR connection (a cylindrical thingy with prongs/pins inside) will let you

level up from computer to higher-level recorder when you're ready. Next level: Connect the mic to a portable digital recorder (see page 87) so you can collect sound in the field.

Whatever you decide, everyone—including you, your cohost, and any guests—should each have their own mic.

Some mics, called condenser mics, need what's called phantom power in order to work. This puts extra demand on your recorder's batteries, so it's something to be aware of and ask about when buying a mic.

There are lots of different kinds of mics, but for podcast purposes, focus on mics suited to the kind of voice recording you'll be doing (see below).

PICKUP PATTERNS
Different mics pick up sound differently. The key pickup patterns are cardioid, omnidirectional, bidirectional, and shotgun.

Cardioid
Cardioid mics are good for voice recording because their most sound-sensitive part is a little place in front shaped like an upside-down heart, making them more sensitive to the voice they're pointed toward. They are less sensitive to sounds from behind or on the sides—also a plus if the room isn't treated to dampen sound. These mics are sensitive to wind, though—whether from Mother Nature (known as wind buffeting) or plosives as you speak—so they need protection (see "Accessories for Mics," page 86).

Omnidirectional
This mic picks up sound from all around, equally. It could work if you've got, say, several folks around a table and one mic between you. Given the intimacy of many podcasts, this may not be the best choice. When there are other sounds in the environment, you've got to hold it close to what you want to record. If you can do that, the sound will be strong, and this mic is also more resistant to wind and p-pops than cardioid and shotgun mics. If you can't get up close, and/or if there's a lot of echo or other noise in the room, it's not your go-to.

Bidirectional
This mic is great for one-on-one interviews using one mic, as it picks up sound from front and back, but not the sides.

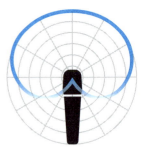

Cardioid

Omnidirectional

Bidirectional

Shotgun

This long mic gives you that boardinghouse reach to get close to your recording subject when you're not that close. But their sensitivity means that they can pick up p-pops and wind buffeting. They also pick up sounds in loud settings, so not ideal in noisy environments.

These mics register handling noise (the sound of your hand on the mic) like you wouldn't believe. Don't hold the mic itself—you'll see people do this; they shouldn't. Invest in a pistol grip (see page 86). This is one of those condenser mics that requires phantom power.

Shotgun

MIC DESIGNS

Then there's mic design. Let's break it down for podcasting needs:

Stand

These stalwart, stationary babies can be found for a reasonable price, with a USB connection to plug into your computer.

Handheld

Handhelds are affordable and versatile on location and in-studio—though you'll need a stand for studio work to eliminate handling noise. Options include USB and XLR connections.

Lavalier

You can attach this mic to your or a guest's clothes. Seems efficient, but in podcasting, sound is everything, and the sound's not great. The mic's not close to the mouth, clothing can muffle it, and it can pick up other sounds. Plus you're giving up control of mic placement. No no no, and heck no.

Stand

Handheld

Lavalier

ACCESSORIES FOR MICS

In addition to picking the right mic, there are extra accessories you can get to boost the sound quality and recording experience of your podcast.

Mic Stand

A mic can pick up handling noise just by fingers sliding along the surface. A stand holds a handheld mic so you or your guest don't have to.

Mic Stand

Shock Mount

A shock mount helps stabilize a mic from picking up vibrations due to being moved and handled.

Shock Mount

Pistol Grip

Described by Rob Byers, who was a production specialist with the NPR Training team, as "basically a shock mount with a handle," a pistol grip gets your hand off the mic, reducing the vibrations that create handling noise. It's especially needed for the shotgun mic, but can be used with other mics.

Pistol Grip

Pop Filter/Pop Shield

This is plosive (see chapter 5) protection for a stationary mic. It also helps keep saliva off the mic—peace of mind for the next person using it (for more on hygiene, see also "Keep It Clean: Protecting, Cleaning, and Sanitizing Your Equipment," page 90). A filter also protects the mic surface from corrosion. The mesh can be metal or nylon (dual-layer fabric is really good). What it does is diffuse gusts of air. Make sure it's 1 to 2 inches away from the mic. Inexpensive and effective. But no pop filter screens out every pop—so watch your breath control, mic placement, and handling, and keep your ears peeled during editing!

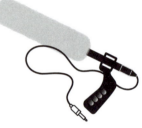

Pop Filter/Pop Shield

Windscreen

A pop filter is a type of windscreen, but there are other types, too—from simple foam covers to furry caps. They disperse the wind and create a capsule of still air around the mic. They're especially important when working outdoors, where you'll need more than a foam cover.

Then there's the ginormous windscreen that'll make you feel like you're reporting from the nor'easter blowing in over Lake Erie. Sometimes called the "dead cat," it's best for high-wind

Windscreen

environments. Indoors, it might serve as an intimidation device for interviewees (kidding!) or a chew toy for your pooch (not so kidding and not recommended).

Digital Recorder

If you don't want to be chained to your desk recording your podcast on your computer, investing in a portable digital recorder lets you take your podcast on the road, cover events, interview on location, collect sound, and step your podcast's complexity and quality up a notch. Many can more or less fit in the palm of your hand or in a pocket; others not so much. You transfer the tracks to your computer from a memory card. Higher-end recorders let you monitor and adjust your levels on the fly, saving you editing time later. Here are some factors to consider:

— What's the quality of the built-in mic(s)?

— If you're planning to record music, is it up for the job?

— Can you plug in one or more external mics?

— Does it have an XLR connection only?

— What type of external mic can be used?

— Is the speaker good enough that you can listen back without needing earphones or a computer?

- What's the trade-off between size/portability and capability?

- What batteries are needed, and what's the battery life?

- Is the battery rechargeable?

- Does it need phantom power?

- How much built-in memory does it have?

- What type of memory card?

Headphones

Becoming a podcaster means educating your ears about audio quality and all the stuff you need to prevent or fix, such as sibilance, p-pops, handling noise, and wind buffeting. Headphones reveal subtle sounds your ears may overlook without help: the hum of the air conditioner ... your breathing ... that moment when you leaned back and your voice retreated from the mic. You'll need headphones while recording (inside and out) and while editing.[8]

Don't get the noise-canceling or wireless kinds (both require power—why add to your to-do list?—and they work in a way that doesn't provide the sound quality you need for taping/editing), nor the ones people use to listen to music. Just get a closed-back pair, snug-but-comfy on or around your ears, high-quality enough to hear the usual problems and editing challenges that happen in audio. Ideally, ones that are easy to carry, maybe folding or with a bag for stowing, and with a cord that easily reaches the recorder, not too short or too long. Better yet? Ones with replaceable ear pads (which wear out) and cables (which break).

Mixers (Not the Dating or Drinking Kind)

A mixer lets you record from multiple mics simultaneously *and* tweak the sound while actually recording. If you know what you're doing, it can save time during editing and give you a lot of recording horsepower, but they aren't recommended for those just starting out. It's one of those things you kind of graduate to (cost-wise, too) when you're looking to reduce time in the editing booth and you have some extra money to spend.

8 Should your guests wear headphones, too? Up to you. In our experience, NPR guests who aren't used to hearing themselves talk tend to become self-conscious when they wear headphones.

As for Software...

I could fill a book yammering about recording and editing software, but this would be more overwhelming than helpful. At NPR, we use a proprietary software to mix our shows and podcasts. It's versatile and powerful, but it's also idiosyncratic as hell. Even audio producers who come to NPR with years of experience take weeks to get fully up to speed on it.

Let me summarize:

— Popular versions like GarageBand (Mac-compatible only) and Audacity (Mac or PC) can be good (and free) places to start your learning curve.

— Shop around, get what's compatible with your existing systems, find out what types of audio files the DAW works with, notice what's free (or offers a free trial period), what's paid, and what's subscription. Look into student discounts (if that applies).

— Read reviews and how-to articles, check out online tutorials, and talk to other podcasters about what they started with, what they use now, pros and cons, and features they'd recommend for you based on the type of podcast you're doing and your experience level.

— If you're collaborating with other folks, make sure you've all got the same audio editor and plug-ins (see chapter 11). It's hard to shift a story across different audio editors, and important stuff can be lost in the process.

— If possible, find something that has a loudness meter to help you even out volume based on how the human ear hears loudness. If you can't, you may decide down the line to get a plug-in, but make sure what you choose is compatible with your editing software.

— Start with what doesn't kill your budget or make you hyperventilate.

That is all.

Decisions, Decisions

How to choose among all this stuff? Consider your needs and the type of podcast you're doing. Is it a solo show: just you, in a quiet, sound-dampened space? A decent stationary mic and headphones, with recording and editing software to match, may do you fine.

Will you be doing a lot of long-distance interviews? Maybe start with recording functions built into internet calling services, and graduate to recording software for a more polished result.

Will you be on location, in noisy or windy places, doing a lot of in-person interviews? You might need mics for yourself and your interviewee; headphones; mic protections against the elements, p-pops, and handling; and a portable recorder.

Ask podcasters with podcast formats similar to yours what they started with. Anything they'd do differently? Ask if you can sit in sometime to watch them work the technology while recording and then editing (bring treats). Volunteer to help with location work—you'll get a chance to learn setup, see how the equipment works, and maybe try it out, too.

As always, read product reviews and watch tutorials. Check out the Resources section on page 266 for tech help. And make friends with the audio geeks in-store, explaining your needs and budget. If they're smart, they'll realize it's worth helping you without a hard sell because, if you're a happy camper, you'll come back to them for all your podcasting equipment needs.

EXERCISE Geared Up? Start Having Fun!

Test it out! Play with the switches and dials, in an *ooh-what-happens-if-I-try-THIS?!* spirit.

Start inside. Talk into your mic and make mistakes—pumping out preposterous p-pops, holding the mic too close to your mouth, creating handling noise, p-p-pounding the table as you p-p-pontificate. Listen to how that sounds.

Got a high-pass filter on your mic? Record with the filter off, then on—listen to the difference. Or play it back on your audio editor, using the filter there.

If appropriate, take your show on the road, recording yourself outdoors, on a windy day, or with street noise. Make "mistakes." Play with the filters, knobs, and dials. Compare results.

Recruit a friend for a mock interview. Try it remotely by phone (how's the sound with internet recording?), then in person both indoors and outdoors: maybe in a diner (don't drop the dang mic in your eggs), on a park bench (tweet, tweet—yup, audiobombing by *boyds*), in a building lobby (do I hear an echoooo?), or next to a busy street. If sharing a mic, note the challenges for mic placement and handling. Working with two mics means setting up both and using them correctly, including accommodating someone else's plosives, sibilance, and table-thumping.

Then listen to your recordings the way your audience might—earbuds in or headphones on, on the bus and subway, in the car, at the gym, doing housework. Are the words clear? If not, what's getting in the way? Audio collection and editing is addressed later. For now, notice what your ears are hearing.

Playing with your gear lets you practice making audio—setting up, putting away, holding the mic, working the controls, and making it all second nature—plus it starts educating your ear for audio editing by assessing recording environments and peoples' speech habits the way audio makers do. When the time comes to record your podcast for real, you'll be so much more relaxed (and your guests will be, too). That's how you wanna roll.

CHAPTER 7

Audio Storytelling 101

Here it is. Storytelling, the big, beating heart of podcasting. Data's dull; stories are startling. You know this, you feel this, you've experienced it all your life. But how do you tell said story—whether talking about financial planning, charting the immigrant experience, or conducting a boisterous roundtable on exactly what makes Batman, Batman?[1]

1   Nerd.

There's the rub. There are tons of stories and tons of ways to tell them. No single Golden Path to follow, despite what your workshop teacher told you. But NPR is all about storytelling, so here are some tried-and-true directions, based on our experience.[2]

2   We've tried 'em; they're true.

This interactive chapter is peppered with exercises and podcasters' common questions. I'll share key differences between writing for audio versus print and help you find the essence of your subject and start developing it. Do you need a script? Or would a storyboard or outline work better? How do you write for *your* voice and not, say, Audie Cornish's? What storytelling strategies can help you put your own story out there in a way that'll make listeners put down their dang laundry?

I use the term *story* broadly here. Could be a long-form investigation à la *Invisibilia*. Or a roundtable, or an interview show, or you crooning into your mic. Whatever it is, you've got something you want to say. That's your story. How you tell it depends on your podcast format, your personal style, and storytelling best practices. Choose what works for you from this chapter, get storytelling tips from fellow podcasters, and learn with your own ears from good podcasts.

It's all about holding your listener's interest. There's a trick to it. Actually, several.

Notes from the Pros: Key Questions to Ask About Your Story

J. C. Howard, producer, *TED Radio Hour* and *How I Built This with Guy Raz*

I think the most challenging thing is trying to take the mounds of audio that we have and cutting it together in a way that tells a good and interesting story. You'll have to make some judicious choices to best use the time you're given to tell the story. You might start by asking these questions: Does my work...

1 **Do justice to the story?** This is usually my primary thought. You've been entrusted to tell a story, and I think when the subject of that story listens back to it (even with massive cuts), they should say, "Yeah, that's about right."

2 **Make that story clear to the audience?** Starting with an outline is really helpful; sometimes I just do this on a couple of Post-Its. Life is messy. The stories we tell are complex, sometimes even convoluted and winding. Maybe *you* know the story really well, but for many your work might be their first and only encounter. So as you tell the story, it helps to start with an outline and follow a simple timeline.

3 **Include the fun bits?** There may be parts that you just love; those are the things that make the story worth telling. Sometimes you've got to dig a little for those nuggets, but if they pull you into the story, they'll probably pull others in, too.

4 **Leave some nuggets behind?** The other side of that coin is that sometimes, even though you just love this bit or that bit, you have to leave it out. Maybe it doesn't serve the larger story or would take too long to explain. Some really good parts get left out, and you have to be okay with that.

The Three Tools of Audio Storytelling

Everything in audio stories happens with three tools:

1 **Voice.** Yup, people talking and actively moving the story forward. At NPR, we call other people's voices—your interviewees or guests—"actualities" or "acts." Your guiding voice as narrator/reporter? That's a "track."[3]

2 **Sound.** Sound helps your audience orient in space and time with their ears. There's *active sound*: nonverbal audio that propels the story—the thunk-thunk of the chef chopping chives—and *ambient sound*: birds chirping, sneakers squeaking on a gym floor, or the unique hum in a room (impress your friends: call it "room tone").

3 **Music.** Music is a power move that can set a mood, establish a scene, or change the subject. Use it wisely. Which is to say: deftly, and with restraint. Music should only be used to communicate what your best efforts with words and sound can't express. More on music later.

These get recorded on their own tracks, which you'll assemble and edit into the shining expression of you-ness that is your podcast.

Your skill with these three tools determines how rich, how believable your audio world is. That world gets built differently in audio than in movies or print.

Movies feed you images, words, sounds, music. They sort of push their world on you. Print doesn't push. It arranges the world in orderly symbols on page or screen. You allow those symbols to enter your eyes and activate your brain, where you build the world being described. Audio doesn't push or arrange so much as it winds a tantalizing trail into your mind via your ears, enticing you to follow that trail through a world built entirely of sound.

In that world, if we can't hear it, we can't "see" it. Your storytelling task: Figure out how every scene, event, and idea can be evoked with sound, be it the artist's studio, the arena, the factory floor, the town square, the painting, the layer cake. All sound, all the time.

Story Elements Your Audience Needs

Since humans can only hear one thing at a time,[4] audio stories can't lay out an array of elements like in, say, a newspaper, where readers can scan to pick up multiple streams of info—photo, caption, headline, subheads, chart, graph—at a glance, and can

3 You'll see this term again—and again, as it's loosely used to refer to any audio file that goes into the mix. But in NPR-speak, the "track" is the reporter's voice, and "tracking" is the act of recording the reporter reading their script.

4 Prove me wrong, kids! Prove me wrong!

easily page back to refresh their memory or revisit something that confused them.

If listeners miss something in audio, it breaks their immersion in the story, which streams on as they're thinking, "Wait, what?" Odds are, they'll be confused, annoyed, and less likely to stick with the episode.

Which means: In audio, information has to be dropped in slower, smaller bites, with signals (aka signposts) to keep listeners oriented, and recaps in case their attention drifted to the whistling teakettle, their itchy toddler, or the cutie on the next treadmill over.

That's why sentences in audio tend to be shorter. Too much distance between subject and verb, and listeners get lost in thickets of phrases, clauses, and indirect objects. Plus, normal speech doesn't sound like that.

Be careful, too, about stacks of facts and rattling off names. Data, stats, and numbers need explanation, not recitation. Names and titles need periodic repeating.[5] Besides, stacks of facts aren't really a story. What makes a story is *how* all of that happened.

Like the yarns of childhood or yesteryear, audio stories have to grab attention from the start (surprise, horror, a chuckle, curiosity), and then drop information in pieces that assemble the puzzle, bit by bit. These "little reveals"—called *story beats*—give listeners time to build the world you want them to envision, keeping them tantalized to hear more.

> *We talk about beats, like, how many beats does the story have? How many interesting, surprising beats does this person's story have? If you're gonna sustain somebody's interest for twenty, thirty minutes, you gotta have some beats. How many beats can one character sustain for one scene? In long-form podcasts, it's figuring out: What is going to keep people listening?*
>
> —Kelly McEvers, host, *Embedded*

Stick with one purpose per episode. Develop one idea at a time. Wanna dive deeper? Do a follow-up episode. (A two-part series—smart marketing!)

The story has to travel somewhere—usually from knowing less to knowing more—with unexpected twists and turns along the way, clearly signposted: "But here's what surprised us." "You'd think that with all of these heads in the room, a vote would've happened. But

[5] Think you that even I, veteran listener of thousands of pods, will remember who "George" is twenty minutes into the episode? Reader, you flatter me.

no." "This was just the beginning of the journey for these migrant families." As you draft your script or outline, ask yourself what "little reveal" will grab your audience's attention every several minutes. You want to make listeners curious, not confused. That's the fast track to Skip.

That said: Don't feel you have to change someone's life with every episode (though maybe you will!). That can lead to toxic levels of bloviation (second-fastest track to Skip). Instead, according to Alison MacAdam, who was a senior editorial specialist with the NPR Training team, try asking: "What will the audience remember when it's over?" An insight, a strategy, a vivid detail, a hilarious punchline, a glimpse into a different world, a different perspective?

> *We use the term* delight *a lot at* Planet Money. *We don't go about picking stories that'll, like, "educate" people and be pedantic. We'd much rather pick stories that will surprise people. There's some meat and potatoes hidden in there, but we'd much rather delight people.*
>
> —Nick Fountain, producer, *Planet Money*

Script or Outline?

Audio scripts are a written road map of every audible element: what people are saying, the "voices" of active and ambient sound, and music (such as when to "fade" or enter/exit under a spoken track, and when to play them solo "in the clear").

Some NPR podcasts are tightly scripted, even if they don't sound it. They have to be because their intricate stories coalesce over months of research and reporting and interweave actualities, collected sound, music, and narration. Sometimes the topics are sensitive or topical, requiring precise language. While *The NPR Politics Podcast* might sound like a relaxed back-and-forth, it's been carefully written beforehand because the hosts must accurately convey what polls and pundits are indicating. *Code Switch* has an informal vibe, but the subjects it covers (race and culture) are complex and sensitive and require careful planning. The hosts sound casual because they've learned how to write to their natural voices.

Long-form narrative especially needs this level of detail to build a vivid world, a scaffold of credible information, a platform for insight. "We're very, very, very scripted," Kelly McEvers says.

"Every word is written, overwritten, rewritten, drafted, workshopped, group edited, approved pretty much before it goes out." Longer stories might break into scenes or chapters (signposted by the host, by a short silence, or by a shift in who's talking, sounds, or music).

Other podcasts follow a looser framework—a storyboard or an outline. These tend to work when the podcast format or topic has to be more elastic because listeners enjoy and expect a certain amount of real-time, authentic spontaneity. Even so, there's prep and revision.

While you can't really write a final script until you've done your research, collected sound (chapter 9), and gotten your interviews (chapter 10), you can start to develop it beforehand with notes that evolve as you learn more. Revision is writing's middle name.[6] Your script will take shape as you assemble this audio puzzle and find the story (more on that in chapter 12).

If your podcast doesn't require a script, this isn't a license to not prepare. Yeah, I know. You've got the gift of gab. You're eloquent, witty, thoughtful. You don't want to sound slick or rehearsed. You think you can you wing it.

You can't.

I've unfollowed countless podcasts because hosts or panelists convinced themselves that a sardonic "What's *that* about?" amounts to a point of view. Attitude isn't enough. Listeners need more. Think about what you're going to say: Bring notes, plan phrasing.

But ... leave room for discovery. Some podcasts—roundtables, interview shows, recap shows—need to invite listeners in. We want to feel like we're in the room with you. So prepare, but plan ways to say things that will *open* the discussion, not shut it down. Invite your fellow panelists or guests into your thinking, and follow theirs. Reach for insights ... together. Which is to say: Listen.

A basic outline might look like the following:

— Your standard template for starting: maybe music, you saying your name and the podcast name

— Enticing one- or two-liner about what this show's about

— Ad (if you're doing those)

— Interview with guest

6 Alternately: Writing is rewriting. Pick your hoary axiom!

Notes from the Pros: Pulling the Story Together

Jesse Thorn, host, *Bullseye with Jesse Thorn*

While I'm prepping, I keep a document open on my computer in a writing app called Q10 that saves a text file automatically to a folder that's synced across my devices. If a thought I want to make sure to ask about occurs to me, I drop it in there. Not usually in question form; mostly just a phrase, like "loves to play mandolin but isn't good at it" or something.

I'm often thinking in a way improvisers call A-to-C. There is a piece of information, and I think: *What does this make me think of?* Then I think: *What does* that *make me think of?* It helps avoid obviousness. Because generally you don't want someone's patter. You want a fresh, in-the-moment thought or reaction.

In the end, I have maybe a list of six or eight things I want to try and remember to ask about, a list of six or eight clips, and a lot of information in my head about who the person is. Once in a while, I'll have a question written down, but generally only because it's something sensitive and I want to say it exactly correctly. Like a question about a crime someone was accused of or a time someone's colleague was harassed or a time someone said something particularly shitty. Generally, though, it's just a few phrases so I don't forget to ask. I just interviewed the soprano Renée Fleming, and my list had "singer breaking wine glass: is that real" on it.

> To sound casual, you really have to put the work in. And it's hard. Basically, we read through a script, and then sometimes we just turn over our scripts and try to tell it back to each other so that we can have this casual vibe.

— Promos (guest's new album, for example)

— Thanks to guest, podcast credits, and thanks to audience

— Where to find your pod

— Special requests: call for audience participation (experiences, ideas, opinions, reviews)

— Standard template for ending: music, name, podcast name, etc.

Whether outline or script, it's practical to set up a template that includes the episode title and number, guests' names, recording and publication dates, and time segments if you're tracking those to keep your pod to a certain length (for example, start at 0:00 and then mark when you want to change the subject at the five-minute mark, introduce the guest at ten minutes, and so on). You can keep a timer during recording and have a sense of where you should be at any given point.

Story Questions Good Editors Looove to Ask

Editors have fifty thousand different ways of asking the "why should anyone care?" question. They're tactful about it (usually). A pitch session might go like this:

PITCH: "There's this art festival coming up."

EDITOR: [Silence. Thought bubble: **An episode about an event? Because it's there???**]

PITCH: "I am **obsessed** with the organizers of this incredible art festival."

EDITOR: [Swigs coffee. Thought bubble: **Great. Ask them out.**]

PITCH: "There's this art festival coming up. It used to attract boho types and that's it. But the new organizers have revamped it to keep the boho vibe but make it interactive, so it's like an art happening in itself. They're filming it and will release highlight videos online to promote it and build word of mouth. If it works, it could change how these events happen and really grow the audience."

EDITOR: [Puts down doughnut and starts asking questions.]

Our point: It's not the "what" but the "why" and "how" that give a story the arc that story geeks wax grandiloquent about. They're what take us on a journey from point A to point B and discover new stuff on the way, whether you're telling a fairy tale, covering the Oscars, or investigating a phenomenon of the mind, culture, or current events.

One of the first lessons I learned at Planet Money *was: If you want to understand a thing, do the thing. To get a handle on the oil industry,* Planet Money *bought 100 barrels of crude. To explain the commercialization of space, we launched a satellite. These are expensive examples, sure. But you can find your own version of this. Jumping into a complex world with a mission and some skin in the game gives you—and your listeners—a concrete way to learn about an unwieldy subject. Also, it's incredibly fun!*

—Kenny Malone, cohost, *Planet Money*

Below is a list of story-shaping questions to help you zoom in on the how/why of stories:

— What's your story's likely focus?

— What's new or surprising about it?

— Is there *one question* you're trying to answer? (Sometimes called the "driving question.")

— Who—or what—is the main character?

— Where's the tension? (Or ask, "What's at stake?")

— Is this the right time for this story?

— How will you make this relevant/interesting to people who don't already care about it?

— How might the story begin?

— What are your dream ingredients? Examples: What voices would be ideal? What quotes would address your driving question? What moment or scene would make the story unforgettable?

Now, imagine the desired effect on your audience:

— After listening, what will they talk about?

— What might they need from your story and why?

— Will they think that this is the best way to get this information?

— Will they find your approach different and/or better than what's already out there?

— How might your audience benefit from this story? Will it inform them? Empower them? Connect them to other people? Inspire them to take action? Improve their lives?

Story Questions Good Producers Looove to Ask

Time to slap your producer hat atop your creative hat and your editor hat. An injection of "How will this thing get done?" in the story development phase can help you focus your ideas.

Preparation Meets Creative Conversation

Sami Yenigun, supervising editor for *All Things Considered*, describes the story development process at the late, lamented *What's Good with Stretch & Bobbito*, an interview podcast that tackled music, politics, and more. You can see how much legwork and editorial back-and-forth went into finding the episode's arc:

We would have weekly check-ins. Before I started scripting or anything, I would prepare a press packet. It would be all of the interviews the guest has done recently, new projects they're working on, stuff they said in the press. We'd have a preliminary conversation with the hosts to sort of say, "Which parts of this are interesting to you? Which angles would you like to bite on? Okay, you wanna talk about this album in particular? Great."

I'd script according to the hosts' interests. Then I'd send a draft script to the editors and to the hosts. Then we'd have another phone call a day or two later. That's where we really whittled down, okay, what is the arc of this conversation gonna look like? We're gonna start with some small talk, hey, how are you doing? What's your latest project? And then maybe we'll go back in time to say, okay, this is the evolution of your career. And then we're gonna end the conversation looking forward—who do you hope to collaborate with next year; that kind of thing. That's where we really get into the nitty-gritty of what the editorial arc is gonna be. And that guides what's gonna happen in-studio.

In chapters 9 and 10, I discuss creating detailed lists for sound collection and interviewing. Here are some questions to help you get started:

— Who do you want to interview? Your reading will probably turn up some names—preliminary, but you never know where these leads might take you.

— Will you be able to get all necessary points of view?

— Are you going to the right places and sources to report the story?

— What scenes and sounds would bring this story alive—and why? How will you collect them?

— Are there special considerations (interviewing minors, or not using a person's full name, for example), that need preapproval from the interviewee?

— Are there possible legal considerations (see chapter 8)?

— Do you have the time to assemble this story? If not, can you move it later in your publishing schedule? Narrow the scope?

— What challenges are there? Examples: location/travel expenses, difficulty finding interviewees, and permissions for clips or other materials. How might these affect story scope, budget, or schedule?

— What would help you tell this story across multiple platforms? When you publish the episode, you'll be promoting it. It's great to have some extra stuff to post. Audio or video clips, photos, maps, charts, stats . . . ? Start a wish list with thoughts about how you might obtain each item (time-consuming permissions/releases might be needed, so it's good to work well ahead; see chapter 8 for more).

— What's *not* going to be in this story? Trying to do too much in one story is how good podcasting intentions (scripts, budgets, schedules, relationships) go horribly awry. Get strict. What helps answer the driving question?

EXERCISE What Do You Need to Tell Your Story?
First, do your preliminary research:

— What articles, audio/video clips, or other resources are you finding?

— What are you learning that's surprising?

— What's making you curious?

— How would this appeal to your target audience (see chapter 2)?

Now, start your Preliminary Sound Collection List and your Preliminary Interview/Guest List. Create charts that contain the information in the following columns; customize as necessary.

Preliminary Sound Collection List

SOUNDS	AUDIO/VIDEO CLIP

Preliminary Interview/Guest List

NAME	PROF'L TITLE/DESCRIPTION
SOURCE/REFERRAL	CONTACT INFO
NOTES	

Mapping Your Story

As you dig up facts, curiosities, contradictions, details, and interview leads, start sketching the big-picture story. Storyboard, flowchart, outline—whatever helps you see it. The concept will sharpen as you dig more.

As your story map develops, consider the following:

— What's directly related to the story arc: developing or explaining key ideas, action, or characters' motivations and decisions?

— What's a digression—nice to have, but not necessary to have?

— What new angles are there? How do they change the story?

— What's beyond the scope of what you can cover, given budget, time, episode length?

— How can you use sound to make the important points?

— Is there info that contradicts what you thought you "knew"? How might this change the story arc?

Bang Out a Title (and a Little More)

What?! Before your story's even half-baked? Yeah. Because you need one eventually. Because you need to get over Fear of Titling.[7] And because it's a great exercise for finding the story's essence, knowing it might change (a little or a lot). Try making it funny if it's appropriate, and if you're good at funny.[8]

Also, try banging out a one-liner (or a few-liner—two to three max) episode description. This, too, helps you hold onto the core idea. It'll come in handy for interview pitches and emailing sources and might evolve into your episode description.[9] (And if you're having trouble with this, it might mean your idea needs focusing.)

EXERCISE **Your Episode Working Title and Description**
Okay, you ready? On a fresh page in your notebook or computer where you can easily come back and revise (because where's the fun in getting it on the first try???), write down your working title and working description.

[7] Won't happen. But you *will* get into the Habit of Titling. Next best thing.

[8] "How do I know if I'm good at funny?" is a question people who aren't funny ask themselves. So, congratulations, now you know. It will save you a lot of time and effort.

[9] Chapter 14. Don't say I didn't warn you.

What's the Structure?

I could spend hours describing story structures: the Hero's Journey, David vs. Goliath, blah blah. No disrespect. NPR has used them all. They're great (anything good enough for Homer, the Bible, and a few others over the millennia is good enough for us). You should study them. We do! In books, movies, and in our own storytelling medium of audio.

But this isn't lit class. You're an audio maker with a busy life. Let's approach your story the way veteran audio reporters do.

EXERCISE The Big Picture

The best reporters have a story structure in mind before they start gathering audio. They've thought about what needs to be laid out at the beginning (and what tape or scenes might achieve that), what the order of the narrative might be (such as telling the story chronologically), who they're following (what character and idea) and maybe even where they need to end. Of course, these elements can change during the reporting process. But it's good to start out with a "hypothesis." Some guiding questions:

— What intro do you hear in your head?

— What would be the best first bite of tape (or scene)?

— How could this story unfold—what's the narrative arc?

— Who/what is the main character?

— What about the last bite?

— What final thought do you expect to share with listeners in the last track?

Now, you don't just want a lineup of audio clips glued together by narration. That's the tail wagging the dog—or the actualities wagging the audio maker. So here are some basic story structures you could test:

— **Chronological.** This happened, then this, then this. Gets the job done. May be appropriate for news or a topic needing a neutral approach. A little vanilla. Could spice it up if delivered with attitude. (Corollary: reverse chronology; start with the end of the story, then back into how it all went down.)

— **Three-act.** A workhorse for short pieces. Each act builds on the one before. Example: Act 1: Scene-setting/driving question/ stakes. Act 2: How it all went down. Act 3: How things are different after it all went down. Sometimes the emphasis shifts between acts to a different scene or character. You signpost these shifts to the audience so there's a sense of momentum and increasing complexity.[10]

— **News feature.** Former NPR editor Sara Sarasohn had this model: Problem » Solution » Complication » Future. It can be useful for a story with more complexity—that "complication" phase can open up all kinds of actions, reactions, re-reactions, and what-happened-nexts before we get to a resolution (and even the resolution can be: "Here's where things stand for now.").[11]

— **Detective story.** Here you're Sherlock Holmes, stroking your chin, puzzling over the evidence, and wondering, "Why?" You go into the mystery maze, taking your audience with you as you uncover the "clews." What you discover, they discover. Case closed.

EXERCISE Anatomy of an Audio Story, Part 1

Look up a story-driven podcast that you love and choose an episode. Listen to it with an ear for the stuff we've been talking about:

— What are the stakes or the driving question?

— How does the host set that up?

— Who are the characters? What are their dilemmas, choices, challenges, questions, changes?

— What story arc(s) do you hear for the host, character, or you as the audience (discovery, insight, learning, catharsis, decision, resolution, wonder, more questions, etc.)?

— How are the arcs developed (narration, expert interviews, interviews with main character(s), visits to locations)?

— How are changes, twists, shifts, or important points signposted (narrator, other voices, sounds, music)?

Try this exercise once you've got a rough one-liner/description of your story, with some research to flesh it out a bit.

1   Write the story "flat": There's this point, this point, and this point. This happens, then this, then this.

2   Where might the arcs be? Are there dilemmas, decisions, processes, learning curves? What's at stake? This is what gets people engaged in the journey.

3   What would you need to build those arcs or stakes? Let's say you're writing about a medical issue. Sami Yenigun says, "I think one of the best ways to tell that story is to talk to somebody who has personal stakes involved, who is actually having their life affected by something. If somebody pitches me a piece that's just statistics and numbers, I immediately go to: Okay, who is a character who can explain this to me and help me understand why this is important?"

4   Based on your answers to these questions, add your ideas to your sound collection and guest lists (people to interview, locations to visit, clips to gather).

How to Start? The All-Important Intro

No matter what kind of podcast you're doing, you have to grab attention in the first *minute*! Our NPR One platform lets us see listeners tuning in, staying tuned, and (gulp) dropping out. We've learned that the highest-performing intros are twenty-two seconds or less.

Get those ears to commit! Grab one of those pleasure or pain points you mapped out about your target audience (chapter 2)—what's got 'em worried, makes 'em curious, tickles 'em pink. Consider this menu of tried-and-true ways of opening an audio story:

—   **Ask a question or introduce a mystery.** What will you explore in this story? What's your mission? What should the audience listen for? Better yet, explicitly present a mystery: "What if . . ." "Have you ever wondered . . ." "How'd they do it?" "Imagine . . ." Bottom line: What makes listeners stick around is the promise that they will learn something by the end of the story that they didn't know at the beginning.

— **Dive immediately into the narrative (aka the "cold open").**
It might be someone saying something truly startling: "I didn't
set out to kill her. It just kind of happened." Or sounds that grab
the ear: a very odd gurgle . . . a swish and a thud. Cold opens
can work—if quickly followed by an explanation: "That was
the sound of a human swallowing . . . of an arrow as it leaves
the bow and hits the target."). *But* is the overall message too
complicated or unfamiliar and in need of explanation *before*
listeners can keep up with a narrative? (See Gene Demby in
"Notes from the Pros: On Intros," page 113.)

— **Establish the concept.** Remember how Sarah Koenig began
the first-ever episode of *Serial* by asking readers to think—
really think—about how difficult it can be to account for your
time? She asked a few random people to tell her where they'd
been, say, a week or two ago. No one could provide a confident
answer. With this introduction, *Serial* quickly gets its listeners
thinking about time and memory, which aligns them with both
Koenig and, to some extent, the podcast's central character,
Adnan Syed. Focusing first on a large concept rather than the
story itself can elevate the story beyond its basic facts, injecting
it with depth and gravity.

— **Get personal.** If the story isn't about you, is it still okay to begin
with "I"? Sometimes! Maybe you have a unique perspective
on the topic. Maybe the topic is nearly universal, and you're as
good a subject as any. Maybe the story stems from your own
curiosity, or you need to illustrate an experience and it's easiest
if you make yourself the guinea pig.[12]

EXERCISE **Try Some Intros on for Size**

First, listen to the intros of several podcasts in your category. Do they
use any of the conventions above? Or something else that grabs your
attention? What exactly pulls you in? How do they achieve that?

Once you've spent some time listening to intros with the ears
of an audio maker, think about your episode idea (or maybe it's a
rough concept you've been mulling over and testing to decide if it
has the legs to be an episode). Looking at the intro ideas above and
thinking about what you've heard, what kind of intro gambits might
work to grab your audience's attention for your story?

12 But don't be a pig about it.
Putting yourself in the story
can work, but only if you're
doing it to provide your listeners a way in—a means to help
them relate. Sometimes going
small and personal helps you
speak to what's large and
universal.

Notes from the Pros: What Makes a Good Story

Nick Fountain, producer, *Planet Money*

Finding stories is the hardest part of the job, I think. But there are a few things we look for.

We look for a strong character we can identify with, or the audience might be able to identify with. That sometimes could be us going on a journey. The reporter's quest.

It's good if the character either has a goal or changes their mind about something. We don't want anybody who's static; we want somebody who has an arc.

We want some action, something happening, and we want that action to be motivated by something our character wants, generally.

We want something with stakes. It could be stakes for the character: It's really personal, they're putting their reputation on the line, they're in physical danger. Or the stakes are just *big*, a big idea. The future of America is at stake; something like that.

We're looking for surprise. Part of that is good storytelling, but you can only structure a story to be surprising so much. The story has to actually be surprising. There have to be twists you really cannot expect. People have to change their mind about things. Another way is to have delightful moments on tape. For example, something crazy happens on tape. That takes us off into a little tangent.

And we look for a big idea that makes it seem like we're not just trying to entertain you; we're also trying to educate you about the world a little bit.

You'll write your intro for reals and revisit it (um, often) once you've worked more on the story and have the details and arc more firmly in hand (see chapter 12). What you're shooting for here is to play with sketching out the beginnings of the beginning, as a jumping-off point. Just always make sure, for ethical and marketing reasons, that your intro doesn't overpromise on what your story actually delivers.

What About Music?

Music expresses emotion without saying a word. In the first couple of minutes of *Code Switch*'s "Is This What It Means to Be White?," a single repeated note plays under the voices like a hurried heart-beat, heightening the intro's ominous setup about the 1965 killing in Selma, Alabama, of white minister and civil rights organizer James Reeb. In *Short Wave*'s "Seeing Monsters? It Could Be the Nightmare of Sleep Paralysis," a scientist talking about brain wave activity during sleep and dreaming is underscored by soft—yup, dreamy—arpeggios.

"Imagine your audio story is like a song," suggests Ramtin Arablouei, cohost/producer of *Throughline*. "[A song] has different elements like bass, guitar, drums, and so on. All of the elements of your story—like the narration, ambient sound, guest interviews, and music—fit together just as a song would. Think of each element as an equal part. This is the best way to make sure the music, that oh-so-important spice, doesn't sound canned or devoid of any care-ful consideration."

Music is a powerful tool that needs a delicate touch. For one thing, it can be kind of a luxury. For another, it can become a crutch. Let me explain.

The luxury part? You can't use music without permission of the copyright holder. That entails at least some paperwork, and (depending on various factors) a fee of some kind. Head over to chapter 8 for details. And talk to your podcasting peeps. Some may be musicians and willing to license their work for a modest fee or for free in exchange for a credit line and the exposure—and maybe you can return the favor by helping them out with *their* podcast.

Making, or scoring, your own simple sound streams to run under words (a "music bed") might be an option for, um, some. Type "free music-making software" into your browser for informa-tion, ideas, reviews, and options. "Music isn't a magical power. It is an acquired skill," Ramtin says. "You don't need to play guitar like

Notes from the Pros: On Intros

Sami Yenigun, supervising editor, *All Things Considered*

The smallest tweak in that first sentence can change whether or not a listener feels this is something that's important to them. Saying, "Beauty pageants are on the rise," versus saying, "Two weeks ago, there was another beauty pageant," can completely change whether or not a listener is gonna be engaged. Even the smallest details matter when it comes to buy-in from your audience.

Jessica Reedy, producer, *Pop Culture Happy Hour*

For a conversational show to work well, you have to really think about how you're gonna start the conversation, who you'll go to first in that conversation, and what you're expecting them to do—because they set the tone. We call it table-setting. Then people will build on that.

Gene Demby, cohost/correspondent, *Code Switch*

One of the things that we learned—with a lot of help from some of the old pros at NPR—is to be judicious about cold opens. I know, I know: They're sexy! All that *sound*. All that *ambience*. The slow reveal. This sounds, uh, tawdrier than I mean it to. But we realized that we couldn't wait until five minutes into an episode to explain to the listener what the episode was about—the central stakes in the story—except for those rare instances when we had a really, *really* compelling speaker or short anecdote. That's the key for us.

Prince or write chords like Hans Zimmer to be able to compose music for your story. Pick up a twenty-dollar keyboard from the music shop, dust off the old guitar, or grab a shaker, and start experimenting."

The crutch part? Nick Fountain nailed it: "You shouldn't use scoring to get yourself out of a writing problem." Meaning: There are thin spots in the story, your research, your narration, the interview tape, or other elements, so you use music to push our emotional buttons: *Feel THIS now!*

If used at all, music should add emotional dimension, not flatten a story into cliché. These days, a more stripped-down approach is preferable. It can be helpful to listen to how music is used in podcasts in your category. "For instance, what types of music work best for podcasts about mysteries or true crime?" says NPR Training's Argin Hutchins. Cardinal rule, though: "Never be obvious," Ramtin cautions. "If you are telling a story, for example, about a particular time in history—let's say the 1950s—do not use Bebop jazz. Surprise the listener. The goal should always be to use music to transport the listener into a different space emotionally or intellectually. The first step toward an emotional experience for listeners is novelty. Respect your listener enough to give them something they aren't expecting."

Play with it. "Sound design and music have infinite possibilities," says Rund Abdelfatah, cohost/producer, *Throughline*. "Sometimes the more abstract they are, the better."

Try something contrarian, unobvious. "It's often good to go against type," Nick says. "If it's a cowboy story, don't use Western music. If it's a noncowboy story, go ahead, try using cowboy music."

Unless music is the focus of your podcast, it shouldn't be distractingly complex, or like music you'd listen to for pleasure. Think: "The score should underscore." Once you know what your story is, then drop in music.

Bottom line, says Ramtin: "Have fun. Regardless of the kind of story you are telling, scoring it should feel like a joyous experience. If you aren't having fun and feeling something, then neither will the listener."

While you probably won't finalize music until you've collected other sound and have a better idea of your story, it's smart to think about it early, so you can research your options.

What About Other Sound?

From the sound of your own breathing to autumn leaves skating across cement; from the THWOMP of the basketball dunk to the guttural purr of a lioness nursing her cubs; from the wind in the trees to the unique tone that trained ears can hear in every room: Our world is awash in sound. Learning to hear it, capture it, and use it to tell a story is a passion quest for audio makers. It's so important that chapter 9 is devoted to collecting sound—vocal tracks, active sound that propels your story, and ambient sound that evokes a believable environment for your audience. For now, just know that there's a world of nonverbal sound out there that speaks as loudly as words do. Particularly if you're doing a lushly produced, many-layered podcast, you are going to have a grand time with that.

EXERCISE Anatomy of an Audio Story, Part 2

Pick a podcast, any podcast. Or use the one you listened to in part 1 of this exercise. As you listen, jot down each sound element you hear, as you hear it. The show intro. The host doing the episode intro. The first interview. Host recapping key points, asking more questions to transition the story to the next level. Music fading in as the story moves to the first location. The sounds you hear at the location. Host introducing the second interview. Host recaps, transitions, and so on.

Other stuff to note:

— Sound or music fading in or out under vocal tracks, or played solo ("in the clear").

— Clips played from lectures, albums, movies.

— The "little reveals" where we learn something new. Mark them with an asterisk (*). These are spikes or "beats" along the story arc.

— Surprises, twists, the unexpected. More story beats. Mark them with an exclamation point (!). These, too, spike the story arc and keep it interesting.

— The wrap-up: what we've learned and intriguing questions raised.

— Outro: the episode sign-off.

— With multiple hosts: Does one do more leading and the other(s) more following? Does the "lead" change? How do humor, disagreement, and diverse interests/ideas create the arc to hold interest and inform?

— If it's a solo, interview, or review show, how does the host create an arc of deepening information/insight to keep you listening?

— How does the story end? What are the takeaways? What will you remember? At *Planet Money*, Nick Fountain says, "We try to write an ending that's sort of like, 'What does this tell us about the world?'"

Congratulations. You just roughed out the rudiments of an audio script.

Scripts, in Short

If you weren't great at writing in school, worry not. This isn't writing to be read. It's writing to be *heard*. Big difference. Scripts and outlines are covered in chapter 12, but as you learned in the "Anatomy of an Audio Story, Part 2" exercise above, they're basically a road map or blueprint of the episode—who's talking, what other sounds we're hearing, in what order.

If you're doing a story-driven podcast, you won't finalize your script until after you've collected your sound (see chapter 9) and done your interviews (see chapter 10). If you're doing a roundtable, interview, or solo podcast, you'll pull together an outline (or maybe something more script-y, depending on your experience level and preferences) before you record.

Scripts vary across podcast formats. An interview script will look different from a long-form, location-driven story script, which will look different from a roundtable. Yours might be unique to you, if you're the only one who needs to understand it. But there are norms worth noting. Here's a superbasic, totally hypothetical version with explanations in brackets of the various script elements:

PODCAST OPENER [This is consistent every episode—so your audience knows they're in your world: title, your name as host, maybe opening music that fades as the host starts talking.]

HOST: Hey, Glen Weldon here, with *Everything Batman*: All you want to know about the Caped Crusader, plus some stuff you don't.[13]

13 I am what I am.

EPISODE INTRO [Incredibly compelling teaser about what this specific episode is about.]

HOST: Every year at Halloween, according to [some source], more than [some amount of] Batman costumes are sold in the US. But did you ever wonder what happened to the *original* Batman costume? [Evokes curiosity.] We did, too. We figured it was [name some reason]. But the truth turned out to be surprising, even for geeks like us. [Signposting and surprise.]

Intro to Interview #1

HOST: I spoke with Batman über-geek [name person and give short bio].

Interview #1 [Scintillating interview with Batman über-geek.]

HOST: Of course, *that* led us to wonder—to BOY wonder[14]—who has the world's largest collection of Batman memorabilia. [Transition/leveling up.] We tracked him down.

Intro to Interview #2

HOST: He didn't want us to know where he lived. And he only agreed to let us use his first name: Bobby. Bobby met us at an amusement park—which somehow seemed in keeping with the theme of our show. Plus, maybe I could score myself an off-brand plush Pikachu. So we went for it.

[Fade up/fade down location sounds.]

Interview #2 [Back-and-forth between host and reclusive-eccentric-mega-collector, who reveals something truly shocking/amazing/never-heard-before.]

Episode Wrap-Up

HOST: Well, I struck out on the Pikachu. But I learned a lot about what makes mega-collectors tick. [Summarize what we've learned/discovered: humorous, pithy, profound, quizzical—whatever the content calls for.]

14 I'd put this joke into the script; a good editor would strike it. Repeatedly with a blunt object. Not just because theline works better on the page than it does in the ear, but because it comes too early, while we're still setting expectations, and would just distract the listener.

Outro

HOST: That's it for this episode of *Everything Batman*. And hey—we need your help. We're doing a roundup of best lines from the TV series for a future episode. What's your favorite line from the TV show? Go to our website [name URL] and shoot us an email. *Your* favorite line might be featured in our roundup! Thanks! And if you like what we're doing, please share *Everything Batman* with your friends. Look for us on [name podcast service] or wherever you find your podcasts. Till next time!

Below are some more general pointers on script development. (And if you're the type who skips ahead in novels, fast-forwards videos, and likes to know what's happening next, you can get an advance look at how to finalize your script once you've got your sound collected and your interviews done by just heading over to "Script Tips," page 188).

— **Keep time in mind.** Limit yourself to roughly five to six hundred words for a four-minute story. "Longer is not better," Nick Fountain says. "Every time you waste a minute on your show, you're wasting that minute times however many listeners you have. If you have ten thousand listeners and you waste one minute, you're wasting ten thousand minutes in the world."

— **Create a format you can see at a glance.** The sample script format above is basic. You can customize it to make your speaking lines stand out.

— **Set up templates.** If you always open the show the same way, set that up ahead of time. Same for any outros (see below).

— **Write out words or names phonetically if you need pronunciation reminders.** Mark accented syllables, too.

— **Mark emphasis and breathing.** See chapter 5.

— **In roundtable and cohost discussions, (respectful) disagreement is good.** It's more interesting for listeners if everybody is not in lockstep, agreeing with everyone else. People can hear the regard you have for one another even while you say, "Nope. I think what you're missing is X, Y, and Z."

— **Don't leave the best for last.** Grab your audience's attention in the first minute. Keep new things coming every couple of minutes: a new sound, a new voice, a story twist, a new beat.

— **Put your outro to work.** Thank your guests and any others involved in making the episode. Also, now's your chance to connect with your audience. Thank them for being there. Remind them where to find your podcast. Keep them engaged with your content. And sometimes, ask for something (the old "call to action"). Options abound. Listen to other podcast outros for ideas, and use or customize some of these:

  — Direct them to your website for more about the episode they just heard (such as the full interview or additional excerpts, photos or video, a blog post drilling deeper into the subject).

  — Tell them where to find your guest's latest album or book.

  — Ask them to join you on social media, share your podcast with their friends, or review it if they enjoyed it.

  — Ask for input on an upcoming show, vote on something, take a survey (aka an "audio callout")

  — And of course, sign off with your show name, your name, and where they can find your show.

— **Be careful with numbers.** Hearing numbers is far harder than seeing them. Keep data, stats, and metrics selective. State them simply. Don't ask the audience to retain them for long. Always explain what they mean.

— **Write the way you talk.** Think living room, not classroom. "If you are aiming for a conversational tone, write how *you* actually talk," says Science Desk's Madeline K. Sofia, host of *Short Wave*. "That might seem simple, but we're programmed to write in a very different way than humans actually communicate. Finding your voice is all about being honest about who you are and putting it on paper." One great tip to get your scripts to sound like you: Speak your story aloud, then script what you say. Of course, as Madeline notes, this "means you have to come to terms with how you actually speak. Which can be horrifying. But you're in podcasting now! Pride is a thing of the past."

Take a moment now to breathe and think about your podcast concept. Let's revisit the Time + Money + Passion Equation we looked at in earlier chapters. With what you know about the process so far, do you have what you need in terms of these three key resources to fulfill your goals?

If not, good on you for honesty. But that doesn't mean you have to give up.

A story-driven podcast could rescale to an interview-driven one. An "on the road" podcast could pivot to an "on the phone" one. A solo podcaster might share duties with a cohost or become a spicy roundtable. Stretch out the schedule; shorten the length.

Remember, it's better to be consistent than overambitious.

Sami Yenigun says about pursuing stories: "Definitely go after things that you're passionate and interested in. Look at those things with a critical eye. I think a lot of times people are fans of movies, say, and they want to do a podcast about movies, and they don't often think critically about it. There's plenty of place for fandom. But I would say to challenge your assumptions constantly when you're going into pieces."

Bring that clear-eyed honesty to your process and growth as a podcaster. You've got a sense of the variables now. Figure out what "your best" can be, for now, for you. Be that podcaster who questions and wonders how your work could be better. Your audience wants your best work. So do you.

Notes from the Pros: Write in Your Voice. You. Yes, You.

Kelly McEvers, host, *Embedded*

My practical advice on writing—which I will scream from the rooftops and everyone who's ever worked with me will roll their eyes and be like, "Oh my God. I can't believe she's saying this again"—is just write the way you talk to your friends. Turns out that's not easy. I am such an annoying stickler that I won't say, "Spoke to" because I don't say that to my friends. I say, "talked to." Or, "For more tips on how to . . ." I don't say "tips." It's just not a word I say. Would you say to your friends, "Do you want some tips on how to fry this egg?" No. I say "advice" because that's just what I say. If you say "fire" in the first sentence, in the second sentence, you think you have to change the word and say something else. You have to say "the blaze" because that's like the most newspapery thing ever. Who would talk that way? Like, "Oh, by the way, there was a fire in my house last night. That blaze was . . ." No. I would just say "fire" twice. *Write how you talk*. It's actually hard. You get in front of that page, and you're like, "I'm making this thing that's gonna be recorded and I think I'm supposed to sound like all these other people sound or just like this person in my head who I think I'm supposed to be." Nah, just be you. This is my biggest piece of advice.

CHAPTER 8

Legal Issues for Podcasting

And now I'd like to introduce a guest speaker: Ashley Messenger, NPR's senior associate general counsel. When we threw ourselves upon the mercy of Ashley to educate us about media law for podcasting, she graciously volunteered to put her thoughts in writing. Turns out we had stumbled on just the right person, because she has literally written the book (*a* book, anyway—and its newly revised edition) on the very issues of media law for podcasting (as well as broadcasting) entitled *Media Law: A Practical Guide* (see Resources, page 266).

There's some serious stuff in this chapter. That's because NPR takes being honest and ethical seriously, and you should take your podcast seriously. And I thought that the best way to share these foundational professional principles in media law with you was to let Ashley do it in her voice, clearly and without distractions. So for this chapter at least you'll be free of my footnotes and their demi-jokes.[1]

1 Mostly.

Not all the legal topics covered apply to every type of podcast or to every subject matter, and some might not apply to you and your podcast, but I urge you to read the whole chapter. First, you never know when you might find yourself in a situation or pursuing a story you hadn't anticipated—podcasts have a way of going in unexpected directions. And second, anyone who publishes creative work needs to be familiar with these best practices and protections.

Understand: In a very real sense, worrying about legal protection isn't about your intentions, which may be good and virtuous and true. You may think that throwing a little shade at some public figure is harmless, or that speculating about a scandalous rumor with a few friends will be seen in the fun, freewheeling spirit you intend, or that playing an excerpt from a new song you love is fine as long as you comment on it (fair use, right?). Or maybe you assume that your podcast is too niche, too small, to ever come to the attention of a high-powered team of attorneys from some tetchily litigious hyper-mega-globocorporation.

Simply put? Wrong. Or at least, you very easily—too easily—could be noticed and find yourself in legal peril. What matters isn't how you think you'll be heard by your audience. What matters—and what can wind up costing you time, money, stress, and more—is what someone with an ax to grind, for whatever reason, can reasonably argue that they heard and which has, even if you didn't mean to, broken laws or caused the person harm.[2] You owe it to yourself to protect yourself.

And please keep in mind: While Ashley's gonna give you a broad overview of this extremely complicated area of law, this chapter isn't giving you legal advice with an eye to your specific (and doubtlessly fabulous) circumstances. You know the drill: Consult a lawyer to discuss any of these issues if you feel them relevant in your situation.

Take it away, Ashley.

Legal Basics You Should Know

There are several legal issues you might come across as a podcaster. This is not an exhaustive list, but here are the most common problems:

— If you say something that could harm someone's reputation, they might sue you for libel.

— If you disclose private facts about someone, they could sue you for invasion of privacy.

— If you use music or audio from other sources, like TV shows, film, news reports, or other podcasts without permission, you could be sued for copyright infringement.

— There are laws that govern when and how you can record audio. You can be sued or criminally prosecuted if you don't adhere to the rules.

2 At this writing, it's still not possible for someone to do a quick keyword search to find out if you've mentioned them, or their product, on your podcast. But this technology is coming. Probably faster than you think.

— When interviewing people, you should consider whether to get releases and whether to grant anonymity or use first names only in certain circumstances.

— If you gather material, like interviews or documents, that are relevant to a criminal prosecution, you could be subpoenaed for those materials or to testify.

— If you ever want to use the Freedom of Information Act (FOIA) or state information laws to gather material, or get court records or access to court proceedings or news scenes, there are rules about when and how you have a right of access.

— If your podcast is distributed internationally (and if it's online, it probably is), then you might be subject to liability in other countries—and their laws may be very different from the United States.

Each of these issues is extremely complicated and would warrant an entire chapter on its own, so this is only a short summary of the issues, and it concentrates on US law. If you think you have legal issues to consider, you should consult with a lawyer who specializes in media law.

Libel and Privacy Claims

People can file lawsuits if they don't like what you have said about them. It's important to be thoughtful about what you say as an ethical matter, but there can be legal consequences, too. In general, if what you've said about someone is false and defamatory (meaning that it hurts their reputation), they can sue for libel. If what you've said is true but private, they can sue for invasion of privacy.

The challenge with avoiding libel claims is that it can sometimes be difficult to know whether something is true or false. Suppose a woman accuses a man of sexual assault. Is the accusation true? You don't actually know. What you can do is try to corroborate the information and see whether it seems to be true. Questions you might ask include:

— Are there other witnesses who can verify the woman's version of events?

— Are there witnesses who contradict her?

— Is there physical evidence that should be considered?

— Was any kind of formal report filed?

— Are there other accusers?

In some instances, you might not have any information except the accusation itself. You might also have a denial from the man. Denials are not necessarily helpful. A person who is falsely accused will deny an accusation because they didn't do it. A person who is justly accused will typically deny an accusation because they don't want to be caught. Courts have therefore said that denials are not, on their own, indicative of truth or knowledge of truth. You are therefore left with the difficult task of weighing the likelihood that the accusation is true and the importance of reporting on it. Anyone who repeats an allegation can be liable for damages if the accusation turns out to be false, unless some kind of defense applies.

The law gives the media (and everyone, actually) certain protections for reporting potentially defamatory accusations. For example, most states have a defense, usually called "Fair Report Privilege," that allows the media to report on court proceedings. If a lawsuit is filed or if someone is criminally charged, you have a privilege to fairly and accurately report on the case. But there are usually conditions attached to that privilege: The report has to be (1) a fair description of the case, (2) an accurate description of what was alleged, and (3) all accusations have to be thoroughly attributed to the court proceeding or pleadings. Some states extend this privilege to other kinds of government records, like police reports or other statements by government officials.

The other primary defense to libel claims is that people who are public officials or public figures must prove "actual malice," which means that the speaker knew the statement was false or recklessly disregarded the truth when the statement was published. Most people don't intentionally publish false statements, so it's difficult for public officials and public figures to prevail in libel cases.

Taking the example above, if a man is accused of sexual assault on your podcast, can he successfully sue you for libel? If the assault is the subject of a lawsuit or criminal prosecution, and if you have fairly and accurately reported the accusations in the case and properly attributed them to the pleadings or proceedings, then it would be difficult for the man to win if the court applies Fair Report

Privilege. If the man is a politician or celebrity, and you have no reason to doubt the accuser, then it would be difficult for him to win because he would be unable to prove "actual malice." But if the accused is an ordinary person and no case against him has been filed, he might have a better argument. You might have to litigate the truth of the accusation, and then you may be at the mercy of the jury, who will decide who they believe is more credible.

Another consideration in libel cases is the concept of protected opinion. The law generally protects critiques or statements of opinion from liability. Courts have given First Amendment ("freedom of speech") protection to restaurant reviewers who have said that food at a restaurant is "too salty," for example. General insults, like calling someone a "loser," is usually protected, too.

Libel law is extremely complicated, though, and it will be interpreted through the law of the state where a person files a lawsuit, so it's not possible to discuss in this chapter all the issues that could arise. Here are the main points to take away: (1) You can potentially be liable for a defamatory statement that gets included in your podcast if it turns out to be false, (2) you should scrutinize accusations to the best of your ability to determine whether they seem true and are worthy of repeating, and (3) if you are going to include a potentially defamatory statement, you should consult with a lawyer to see if you have defenses available to you. Keep in mind that truth is always a defense against libel/defamation—but that means doing the shoe-leather reporting to ensure you get the facts right.

However, true statements can be just as problematic as false ones. While the law gives media great leeway to publish newsworthy information, it is possible to be liable for invasion of privacy if a podcast reveals private information about a person that is not considered newsworthy. This is particularly true if it reveals medical information, financial information, information about sexual activity, or other sensitive material.

Great storytelling often requires using a real-life anecdote to tell the story. However, courts have said that you don't have the right to force a person to be your anecdote if the information is not already publicly known. If you want to tell a story about, say, having cancer or being transgender, you need consent from a person to disclose that information about them in your podcast (again, assuming that it's not already public information). You can't just find a random person who has not been public about their status and use their story as your anecdote without their express consent. It may be permissible to publish otherwise "private" information about a person if the circumstances are truly newsworthy. For example, if the president of the United States were diagnosed with a fatal disease, that information would be truly important for the public to know regardless of whether the president consented to the disclosure of the information, so a court could easily find that such a disclosure was not an invasion of privacy.

In short, it is wise to get consent when featuring a person in a story. There isn't a requirement that consent be in writing, but it's still wise to have it recorded in some way in case you ever need to prove you had consent. You could have someone sign a release (discussed below) or get their consent on tape. Consent is not required if the person is legitimately newsworthy, but that determination requires careful analysis. Again, consult your lawyer if you have questions.

Copyright Claims

You can be liable if you use third-party material—that is, material created by someone other than you—in your podcast without consent. Examples that tend to come up in podcasting include music, sound effects, excerpts from print or digital media, sound tracks from film or TV, or visual art of the kind one might use for podcast art. The main exception to this principle is called "fair use." Fair use is the concept that it is "fair" to use copyrighted materials under certain circumstances.

The fair use test is described in the Copyright Act as having four factors:

1   **The nature of the use.** Is it for commentary or criticism? Does the material illustrate a point? Is the use "transformative," making a use that is different from the original? If the use is critiquing a work, making a point, or using material in a way that adds context and new meaning, then courts are more likely to find such uses to be fair.

2   **The nature of the original work.** Unpublished works are given more protection than published works (because the author has a presumptive right of first publication), and fictional works are given more protection than factual materials (because facts cannot be copyrighted and fiction requires more creativity).

3   **The amount used.** You may have heard or read that you can use twenty seconds of audio and it's automatically fair use. That is not necessarily true. The law does not set specific amounts

that are fair or not. The question is whether the amount used is proportional in light of the purpose of the use. Courts will consider both how much of the original you used and how much of it is necessary to make the point you are trying to make. For example, using a twenty-second clip from a two-hour film to illustrate a point about how an issue has been treated in pop culture will likely be fair use. It's a small percentage of the original, and it's only the amount necessary to illustrate your point. But even a larger amount can be fair use in certain circumstances. If a celebrity posts a twenty-second rant on TikTok that is offensive, and you want to discuss the clip and explain why you found that rant to be offensive, it might be fair use to use the entire twenty seconds if it is necessary to hear the whole thing to understand the context of what was said. Conversely, using twenty seconds of a song you like for no obvious reason might *not* be fair use because you're using a significant amount of the work without a purpose that justifies it. In short, there is no amount that is automatically fair or not fair. It's a question of whether the amount is appropriate in context. A lawyer with expertise in fair use can help you assess how much is too much.

4   **The effect on the market value of the original.** Does the use compete directly with the original? If you use someone else's material, and your use supplants theirs (in the sense that the listener would now have no need to go to the original source), that would weigh against the use being deemed fair. Also, you should consider whether there is an established licensing market for the material. For example, there is a well-established market for music used to score shows. Courts therefore usually expect those who use music to pay for it.

In sum, a use is usually considered fair when you use a short clip for the purpose of commentary or critique, or to illustrate a point. But there are no guarantees! It can be difficult to assess what is fair use, and it helps to have a lawyer guide you.

An issue that often comes up with podcasting is using music to score your podcast. You typically need a license to use music. The easiest and most cost-effective way to get music is to use a precleared music library. These libraries contain hundreds if not thousands of compositions that convey mood and tone and are perfect for scoring. They do not contain pop songs, so you won't have music from your favorite artist. If you want to use a specific song, you would need to reach out to the rights holders to obtain a license, and that process can be expensive and time-consuming. Using music can be fair use if you are commenting on it; a podcast focused on music criticism that uses fifteen-second clips of songs to critique the trombone piece, for example, would be fair use. But scoring your entire podcast with your favorite songs probably would not be considered fair use.

Audio Recording

There are federal and state laws that govern when it is a crime to record a conversation. The federal law and many of the states say that you may record a conversation if you are a party to it. That means it is illegal to record a conversation if you are merely listening in—eavesdropping—or otherwise accessing a conversation in which you are not participating. This holds true whether the conversation is in person, over the phone, or anything else.

Some states prohibit recording a conversation unless you have the consent of all parties to the conversation. Because these states are more restrictive, you have to know whether their law will apply to your recording. If you are recording a conversation in person in those states, you would have to comply. If you record a phone call that crosses state lines, you may need to comply with the most restrictive applicable law. The danger is that you might not know which state's law applies. If you call someone who has a Maryland phone number (an all-party consent state), but they live in New York (a one-party consent state), but they're visiting family in California (an all-party consent state) at the time of the call, which law applies? If you want to be cautious, it's a good practice to get consent before making a recording. If you're arranging a phone interview by email, for example, you can state in your email that you will be recording the call, which could serve as evidence of consent. And of course, you can always record consent on tape when you start your call.

However, most courts recognize that you have a constitutional right to make recordings in at least some circumstances. It is generally not a crime to make recordings in public places where there is no "expectation of privacy." Courts have also said that there is an affirmative constitutional right to record on-duty police officers in public places. (In many states, the police are recording you with body cameras, too.)

In addition to the criminal aspects of recording, most states also allow people to bring civil suits if you record them in a context where there is a "reasonable expectation of privacy." Usually, that means that you can make recordings in public places, but you could be sued for making recordings without consent in people's homes, offices, or other private places. As with all other issues, talk to a lawyer if you need guidance.

Recording in courtrooms has its own protocols (see "Access to Information," page 132).

Releases and Anonymity

One of the issues to consider when making a podcast is whether you want to get releases from people you interview or talk about. In most circumstances, releases aren't legally required, but there are circumstances where it's in your best interest to get them anyway.

Some content producers, often in the entertainment industry, will obtain releases from participants all the time, for everything, no matter what. They do it as a matter of course to make sure that they have consent whenever they need it. This is a perfectly legitimate choice! Other producers get releases only in certain situations, such as when there is a specific legal risk, such as disclosing private information or interviewing minors. This is also a perfectly legitimate choice. How you choose to handle this issue depends on your personal level of risk tolerance and organization.

In any event, you may want to get releases whenever you use private, sensitive, or controversial information, as described in "Libel and Privacy Claims" on page 125. Having a piece of paper (or audio recording) that shows that the person consented to your using the information can be helpful. You may also want to get releases whenever you interview minors. Those releases would ideally be signed by both parents or a legal guardian, although consent of one parent is better than none. Releases do not guarantee that you won't get sued, but they do show that you have consent, and consent can be a defense to most legal claims. You will probably want a lawyer to tailor a release for you to make sure you have the kind of consent you need for whatever kind of podcast you are creating and the kinds of claims you might be trying to prevent.

Another way to protect people's privacy is to use only a first name, a nickname, or some descriptor (such as "the big sister," "the little sister," or "the ex-husband") that protects their identity. Now that material lives online forever and can be easily searched, people are often more protective of information about themselves. They would prefer that the one embarrassing fact about their lives is not the first search result when others search their names. One simple way to prevent that problem is not to use their full name. Of course, not using a full name goes against the traditional journalistic principle that reporters do use real names. (NPR has a policy against using pseudonyms because they are false; however, it does permit only first or middle names, nicknames, or descriptors to be used, as long as the reasons for doing so are disclosed to the audience.) You may still want to obtain a release from a person, even if you are not using their full name.

Subpoenas

If you have obtained material that is somehow relevant to a lawsuit or criminal case, someone might subpoena you for it. Whether you have to turn over your materials will depend on many factors, such as whether it's a civil or criminal case, whether it's in state or federal court, and what they are seeking. While this may not be likely to happen, depending on the type of podcast you're doing, it's important to know that it is a possibility so you can get legal guidance if you need it.

It's important to think about these issues in the context of offering confidentiality to a source. If you promise to keep a source's identity a secret, but you are subpoenaed to disclose the source, you are faced with an impossible choice: Do you risk being held in contempt for not complying with the subpoena, or do you break your promise to your source? It is better to think through these issues before you promise confidentiality and discuss with the source what circumstances would allow you to disclose their identity or other information. Here again, even if you think this might not happen with regard to your podcast, it's helpful to know about it in case the matter of confidentiality comes up.

A somewhat more common scenario is when a podcast features an interview with someone who then gets sued by someone else. If one of the parties thinks your interview has information that could help them in the lawsuit, they might ask for the recording of the interview. This is particularly true when you used only a portion of the original interview in your podcast and have a lot of unused tape. As an ethical matter, most journalists don't want their materials—especially unused tape—used in lawsuits. If you get a subpoena, you may need a lawyer to help you figure out how to respond.

Access to Information

There are laws that govern when and how you have a right of access to information that you might want when preparing your podcast.

First, it's important to know that you cannot demand access to private places or private records. However, you may have a right of access to records held with the government or certain public places.

The federal Freedom of Information Act (FOIA) allows any person to request any record from any government agency. There are nine exemptions that allow the government to deny your request, and agencies are notoriously slow in responding to requests, but FOIA can be an effective way to get records if you plan in advance and make a proper request. An important thing to know about FOIA is that the government isn't required to do research for you. You have to know what you're asking for when you make the request. Simple requests that ask for specific documents tend to be most successful. For example, asking the FDA for a (hypothetical) report entitled "The Effects of Smoking on Minors" by Joe Smith dated January 12, 1993, is easy for the agency to identify and provide. A request that asks for all records related to smoking and children will be difficult for the agency because they have to do research and make judgment calls about what counts for inclusion. For more information, visit www.foia.gov.

States similarly have FOI laws that allow people to ask for records held by state agencies. The requirements of each state's laws vary, but there is an excellent online resource called the "Open Government Guide" at the website Reporters Committee for Freedom of the Press (RCFP, www.rcfp.org) that allows you to search the requirements for any state's access laws.

You also generally have a right to attend court proceedings and access court records. Note, though, that recording the proceedings in the courtroom might be prohibited. Different courts have different rules about when audio recording is permitted, and you must comply with the rules of the court you're in. If you think you're being denied the right to record a proceeding, you can ask a lawyer to help you intervene to be allowed to record, but recording a proceeding is generally something you should arrange in advance. Showing up with a recording device unannounced is usually not a good idea.

If there are press conferences or news scenes and you want to record there, you may have the right to do so unless you're creating a security risk or interfering with the safety perimeter set up by law enforcement. You might need a "press credential" to attend certain events, and government entities are allowed to restrict entry only to those who have a credential, as long as they set up reasonable and nondiscriminatory rules for issuing them. Some states have laws that specifically say that you have an affirmative right to record state or local government proceedings. Those rules can be found in the RCFP's "Open Government Guide," noted above.

In short, if you have questions about where you're allowed to record or what records you can get, it's wise to check with a lawyer.

International Issues

Podcasts are typically distributed online and might be available in any country. That means that you could also face legal issues in any country. And most countries have laws that are more restrictive than in the United States. This chapter couldn't possibly mention all the laws in the world, but here are a few important differences to know.

— **Hate speech laws:** Most countries prohibit any statements that could be viewed as "hate speech" or denigrating a race, religion, ethnicity, or other group. Including any such statements in a podcast could subject you to liability for them.

— **Libel and insult laws:** Some countries have laws that prohibit insulting the monarch (or other leaders) of that country. There are no defenses. If you insult the monarch, you can be thrown in jail. Other countries also have stricter libel laws that do not give protections to speech that is about government officials or that would count as protected "opinion" in the United States. In fact, in some countries, libel claims are as routine as parking tickets. If you criticize a government official, you might get a notice that you have been charged with libel. (And they're often criminal charges, not civil lawsuits.)

— **Prohibitions on reporting on court proceedings:** In the United Kingdom, Australia, and some other countries that have adopted similar legal systems, you can be held in contempt for reporting on a court proceeding before it has been completed. That's not the rule in the United States, where you're allowed to report on a case as it's unfolding. These laws aren't intuitive to Americans who are accustomed to reports on court proceedings, but such reporting is indeed a serious offense overseas.

— **Privacy laws:** Privacy laws are much stricter in other countries. In general, you should assume you need someone's consent to use information about them. While there are exceptions for "journalism," those exceptions are interpreted narrowly to be things that are of utmost importance to the public as a whole. The conduct of government officials while on duty may not be "private," but their personal affairs probably would be considered so.

In general, a foreign court cannot impose a penalty on you unless you have assets in that country or you're physically present there, and the US government generally doesn't extradite citizens who are convicted of violating speech laws in other countries. So if you don't travel or have assets overseas, you might be safe even if your podcast runs afoul of foreign laws. But you should be aware that if you go overseas, you can be detained. It has happened! For example, an American citizen who traveled to Thailand to visit family was detained and jailed there for statements he made—while in the United States—about the king of Thailand.

Foreign libel judgments might also be less of a concern in terms of having them enforced in the United States. If you're found liable overseas and a party wants to collect damages in the United States, they have to have the judgment recognized by a US court. Courts usually respect foreign judgments. However, in 2010, Congress passed the SPEECH Act, which prohibits US courts from enforcing foreign libel judgments if that country fails to provide as much protection for the speech as the US law would. That means that if they couldn't sue you in the United States and prevail, they cannot have the foreign judgment enforced here (although it can still be enforced on any overseas assets you may have).

However, other kinds of foreign judgments can be enforced in the United States, so it's important to deal with lawsuits and get good legal advice if you are sued in another country.

Hand in hand with legal awareness should go ethical awareness. As people and as professionals, we at NPR aim to do not only what is legal but what is right. Often, doing what is right will also help prevent any legal liability. *NPR's Ethics Handbook* (www.npr.org/ethics) is a document we've developed over the years and continue to amend and refine to ensure that it remains relevant and useful. Visit, read, and make use of its help and guidance![3]

3 Ashley hands the writing of the book back over to me; we now return you to your regularly scheduled litany of sweaty footnotes and labored near-puns.

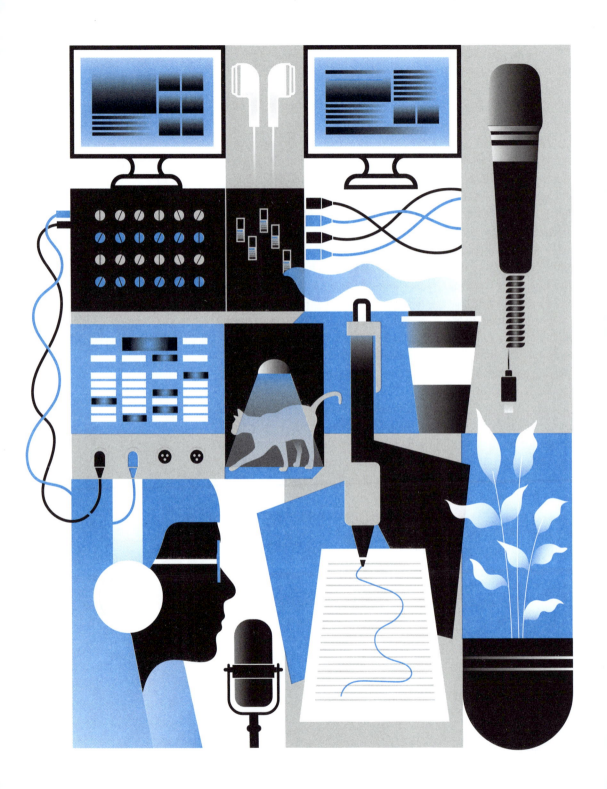

CREATE

Putting It Together

You've imagined. You've prepared. You've got a team, a mission, and a plan. (And some snazzy gear.)

Now comes the fun part! Part 3 walks you through what dedicated audio collectors do before, during, and after pressing Record. How insightful interviewers prep for and conduct memorable interviews. How producers get the sound to, well, sound good (including a typical podcast production workflow). And how expert editors shape a motley assortment of vocal and sound tracks into an absorbing story. Because of course you want to be in that (still-all-too-) rare top group of start-up podcasts that do this important stuff well.

Not talking about "polish" here. Following the steps outlined in this section will not make you sound "slick," "overrehearsed," or "inauthentic." But they will help you find and develop the excellent essence of *your* podcast in ways that will help ensure that your listeners love it as much as you do.

CHAPTER 9

Collecting Audio Like a Pro

As humans we use the sounds around us to assess our safety: What am I hearing, and what does it mean? If sound is painfully loud, too soft to understand, jarring, or garbled, we get uncomfortable, confused, annoyed, and want to get the hell out of there.

That's why we care about which mic to use and how to hold it; how to sound-dampen a room; how to deal with wind, p-pops, and background noise; and getting just the right sounds to evoke an environment.

Plus, the soundscape you create is competing with the real-world soundscape your audience is in at any given moment: rattling through the subway tunnel, zipping along the highway, pounding the treadmill, or chopping carrots. Your podcast has to sound clear, draw people in, and *keep them there.*

Or . . . just know this: Good sound collection gives you the best shot at making a successful podcast and will save you untold editing time and agita.[1]

This chapter covers sound collection fundamentals—whether you're doing a phoner interview from a nook at home or going on location—that'll help you tell the story you want to tell. How do you prepare the room to get the best sound? What common sound glitches should you listen for, and what do you do about them? What nonvocal sounds will help tell your story?

Your attention to detail here is crucial—because your podcast's credibility starts with your sound collection. Do it poorly, and your listeners will stop dead on the dang treadmill to hit Skip. Do it well, and they won't know you've been there. They will think *they've* been there.

1 Plus, some audio problems aren't fixable in postproduction, so there's that.

Make Your List(s), Check It ('Em) Twice

Chapter 7 touched on this. Now, get granular: What sounds could help tell your story?

For a roundtable, interview, or review show, who will you interview? What will you review? What sound clips should you get hold of?

Going on location? What's your wish list for direct sound (people talking) and ambient sounds (everything else)? What sounds would help your audience feel like they're there? Maybe cattle lowing in a story about yogurt-making at a local farm. Sewing machines and cutting shears in a piece on custom suits. Start a list.

Your Sound Collection Worksheet/Checklist

For sound collection planning, set up a chart like the sample opposite, where you can build a list of all interviews, active sounds, ambient sounds, and music, plus notes. Ideally, it'll eventually include every sound you'll need to record for a given episode. Then you can convert this into a checklist to make sure you actually collect all those sounds. The sample chart has entries based on chapter 7's hypothetical podcast *Everything Batman*. (For now, don't worry about the lingo—active and ambient sounds are discussed later in this chapter, and interviews are in chapter 10.)

Choose Your Weapon, er, Mic

Time to assemble the gear you collected in chapter 6!

For sound collection, a basic approach might be recording (then editing) using a downloadable audio program/digital audio workstation (DAW) like GarageBand or Audacity. For solo or remote interviews, an internet-based recording service can be fast and easy, but you're at the mercy of connectivity hiccups—risky for longer shows.

Ideally, there's a mic for each person. If you're seated, it should be on a stand, for best stability and placement, minimal handling noise, and so each voice gets recorded on its own track for easier editing.

If you're holding the mic and moving it between you and your subject, all beat-reporter-like, a pistol grip will help reduce handling noise.

On location, mic yourself and your interviewee. You never know; some of your questions or reactions (see Nick Fountain's bite on this: "Notes from the Pros: Be You," page 164) might end up in a story-driven podcast.

Sound Collection Worksheet/Checklist

PODCAST	Everything Batman
EPISODE #/TITLE	Ep. 03: Whatever Became of the Original Batsuit?
INTERVIEWS *(name/title, contact info)*	"Bobby" (use first name only); Bobby Donwell [contact info]
ACTIVE SOUND *(List the action items necessary to meet your goal.)*	Unfurling of cape, fabric sounds, zippers, opening box/bag containing costume
AMBIENT SOUND *(What stands in the way of meeting your goal?)*	Amusement park sounds (barkers, games, sounds of rides, bells, kids yelling). If need quieter interview location, then bench outside park entrance OR use car?
MUSIC *(title, composer, contact info for licensing)*	Snippet of Batman theme [who owns the rights? Contact them.]
NOTES *(status, to-dos, etc.)*	Can he bring the suit? If not, can he do second meeting where he keeps it? Visit park in advance to scope out recording area.

Field Equipment

Equipment

- ☐ Fresh batteries
- ☐ Spare batteries (charged)
- ☐ Mic + battery
- ☐ Mic cable
- ☐ Wind protection
- ☐ Pistol grip
- ☐ Headphones + adapter
- ☐ Recorder
- ☐ Formatted memory card + spare (both formatted on recorder)
- ☐ Mic clamp

Misc

- ☐ List of anticipated sounds (your Sound Collection Checklist)
- ☐ Phone (charged)
- ☐ Phone charger
- ☐ Phone battery pack (charged)
- ☐ Business cards
- ☐ Pen/pencil/notepad
- ☐ Rain gear/hat/gloves/ sunscreen
- ☐ Snack
- ☐ Money for parking/ transportation
- ☐ Tote bag[2]

2 This…is NPR.

Location, Location, Location

Suppose in a public space you come upon a large pile of fabric on the floor. Upon inspection, you see it's a coat. There's movement under it. And mumbling. What do you conclude?

Why, naturally, you would conclude this is someone recording audio in a noisy space. No, seriously. Audio makers have done this[3] to create an ad hoc sound-dampened recording space.

Dead isn't usually a term we consider positive. But you want a "dead" recording space. That's hard to find in a world that's vibrantly alive: air conditioners and fridges humming, radiators clanking, people coming and going, garbage trucks garbaging, toddlers and dogs being very happy or very sad, or someone's phone ringing (including yours).

Now you're hearing the world like an audio maker.

Take a listen where you want to record. Are people constantly walking by? Is there conversation? Traffic noise? Loud equipment? Vibrating sounds like appliances may be tough to screen out. Background music? *Huge* no-no: How will you edit vocal tracks without the music sounding all chopped up?

Outside, listen for wind noise—nature's giant p-pop. Sometimes it's unavoidable, but it can make audio annoyingly hard to understand, it's tough to edit out, and strong buffeting can pretty much tank your tape. A foam mic cover isn't enough. If taping outside, get one meant to handle wind noise. Try an omnidirectional mic. If your mic has a high-pass filter, turn it on. Try standing between the wind and your interviewee, or record behind a large structure, truck, or car (or get *in* a car—see the following).

Indoors, there's "roominess." Great in real estate. In audio, not so much. Sound bounces off of surfaces. The harder the surface (walls, ceilings, windows, tables, counters), the more you'll sound like you're talking from the bottom of a well. Echo is tough to listen to and edit. "Audio quality can really help a podcast stand out," says Guy Raz. "Most podcasts sound like a person talking in a bathroom—an echoey room. They may have spent $200, $300 on a good USB mic, but that's not enough. You have to do a little bit more work to make it sound great." It doesn't have to cost a lot—but, as Guy points out, good audio quality can be "a game-changer. If the audio fidelity is good, you remove 90 percent of the distractions, and it creates that intimacy that you're looking for."

Try recording in a smaller space with soft surfaces (curtains, throw pillows, cushioned furniture, fabrics, carpet, wall hangings)

3 Kind of exaggerating, kind of not. The coat-recording thing's become something of an NPR cliché, but clichés become clichés because, over the years, hundreds of NPR reporters and podcasters have ducked under their peacoats in the heat of creative fervor and deadline pressure. (Literal heat, too: It's a sauna under there, and it's tough managing mic, tech, script, and vocal delivery—so I don't recommend it except in a pinch.)

to absorb sound and dampen bounce. At minimum, set up your mic so it's not close to the wall.

For a solo podcast, try making a sound-dampened home-recording space. When *Invisibilia*'s Yowei Shaw was starting out, she worked with veteran audio pro Jeff Towne to rig up an itty-bitty-but-effective recording niche in her tiny-and-echoey bedroom. Sitting just in front of her open closet (clothes as sound-dampeners—who knew?), and setting her mic in a folding cloth cube lined with acoustic foam (findable online), she was able to do her indie audio making. This approach assumes little outside noise, though.

Experiment with recording in the least sound-reflective space in your home and try out ways to sound-dampen it. Maybe hang up a blanket (another tactic of Yowei's). Another option she suggests: Find a fellow podcaster to loan their quiet home. High-end: Rent a studio. It depends how DIY you need and want to go.

For location interviews, ask beforehand about a quiet room (now you know what that really means). Some low-level background noise (not music!) can lend atmosphere if it's part of the world you're creating for your audience. In a home, nix the kitchen (hard surfaces! humming appliances!). The living room might work—soft furniture, carpet, drapes, and such.

Last-ditch? Try inside a car (engine not running), mic held close, properly angled for p-pop prevention (read on). You'll sound kinda boxed-in (opening the windows a crack might help), but it beats unfixably noisy vocal tracks.

Before You Go and While Setting Up

First, play with your gear to learn how it works. Then, run a test that mimics a short version of your show—including a mock interview if you'll be doing those, maybe roping a friend into sitting in as an "interviewee" to help you get comfortable—to rehearse setting up, listening to the sound, and adjusting your equipment (or your recording environment) to figure out fixes.

Consider bringing a buddy with production chops to your first recording sessions to help you set up, work the equipment, listen for humming appliances and p-pops, and show you how to troubleshoot stuff to save editing headaches. If you can't, then definitely do a trial run at home with setup and sound tests.

When you're ready for the real thing, go over your script or outline before you go. Read your script aloud and mark it up (see chapter 5 for tips) for emphasis and breath breaks. Give copies to your cohost(s) so everyone's literally on the same page. But beware of the dreaded-and-difficult-to-edit-out paper rustling that can ensue! If you go electronic, use a tablet.

Why tablets and not laptops or desktop computers? Because those devices have internal cooling fans that click on and off at random. Your mic can pick up that whirring sound. Some computer programs are notorious resource hogs that cause your laptop to heat up so much the fans click on a lot,[4] so close all tabs except the one with your script on it.

Charge all batteries ahead of time and make sure everything's plugged in nice and snug and in the right places.[5] During the session, if your headphones pick up audio trouble, first check to see if all your connections are secure and batteries juiced. Oh, and make sure you've got enough storage on your dang phone if you're recording on it.[6]

If you want to keep your episodes to a specific length, and/or cover several subjects in timed segments, bring a stopwatch and set it where everyone can see it. If you use your smartphone stopwatch, set your phone on airplane mode and silence the ringer.

For location work, your first job when you get there is: listen. Scope out a good recording space or place (see "Location, Location, Location" on page 142). Didn't say perfect. Do the best you can. Can you hear TVs or radios? Computer keyboards, printers/scanners, copiers, or cell phones clicking, clacking, pinging, ringing? Noise from espresso machines, fans, or open windows? Be nice, but ask for that stuff to be turned off, silenced, closed—and/or close doors. All this will make the recording sound better, so ask in that spirit. For noise you can't do anything about, set up so your mic points away from it.

You might need to shift furniture a bit for a seating setup. Whether it's opposite each other or at right angles, be close enough to shift your mic toward your interviewee (if you're sharing) with minimal handling and keeping proper mic placement.

Got your gear set up? Now, put your headphones on!!!!!![7] Audio makers have to hear acutely. You need headphones for that.

On a purely practical level, listening on headphones means you can easily tell whether or not you're recording. Say something. Anything.[8] Can you hear yourself in your headphones? Then you can proceed.

Okay, time to set levels. If you've ever had to turn the volume up or down in a podcast to hear better or more comfortably (not because of the sound in your environment), you've experienced a level problem. Loudness is what our ears hear. Levels are loudness expressed

4 Looking at you, Google Chrome.

5 My friend Toni once recorded an entire phone interview on her digital recorder with the mic plugged into the headphone jack instead of the mic jack. On the playback, she heard herself asking her interviewee, "And *then* what happened?" followed by . . . silence.

6 Reminder: WAV files are bigger than you think. Depending on your phone plan, you might need to delete some apps, or some photos of Gramma at Dollywood. Priorities!

7 Can you tell I mean it? Can you tell how often people think they can skip this? But you're not gonna make me come down there, are you?

8 "Test, one, two, three"? Anything but *that*.

as an audio signal. You want the entire episode to be at a comfortable listening level, and each track level balanced with the others.

If you're recording plain ol' human speech, we suggest targeting –15 or –12 dBFS,[9] depending on what number you see on your meter. On a loudness meter, if you're using one, target –24 LUFS.[10]

Now, do a little mic tutorial with your guest(s). If everyone has their own mic, explain how to talk into the mic: to keep it slightly below the chin, keep it close—about four to five inches away—and at an angle to avoid p-pops.

Next, do a test: Just record a few minutes. You talk; ask your guest to talk (see "How We Warm Up," page 148). Play it back to check your equipment and listen for audio problems. P-pops? Check mic position and protection. For sibilance, try repositioning the mic, maybe angling a little away from the mouth. Listen for background noise. If recording remotely, ask your guest to move closer to their earbud or headset mic, and recheck.

Do not skip this step! Imagine recording the whole dang session and finding out later the air conditioner ruined everything.

Last but not least (and more like during), tune up another important instrument: your voice. Do your vocal warm-ups from chapter 5, or try the others that follow. Do lip trills and meows en route. Hum while you set up. To minimize time editing out embarrassing lip smacks and other mouth noise mics can pick up, snack on a Granny Smith apple or bring some apple juice (better this than water),[11] stay away from coffee and milk products,[12] and suggest your interviewees do the same.

Roll Tape!

Final countdown stuff:

PUT. ON. YOUR. HEADPHONES.[13]

On your audio test, did you hear background noise like ventilation, traffic, or other vibration? If so, flip on your mic's—or your recorder's—high-pass filter switch, if it has one.

As soon as you hit Record, "slate the tape": State the date, your location, your interviewee's name (actually, have them say their own name for correct pronunciation), and a bit about the topic. Remind everyone of the agreed-upon purpose of the session.

Don't be afraid to ask a guest to repeat something they flubbed or if they umm'd too much (same goes for you). It's easier to edit out flubs if you stop and repeat the sentence, not just flail on. Let guests know at the start you might do this and not to sweat it.

9 dBFS: decibels relative to full scale. (Like THAT means anything. But you *had* to know, didn't you?)

10 LUFS: loudness unit full-scale. Yeah, I know. Clear as mud. I'll revisit LUFS a teensy bit more in chapter 11.

11 The tartness cuts through any phlegm in the throat and mouth.

12 Phlegm factories. You'll sound like you're drowning in suet.

13 Have I mentioned this? I seem to recall I have.

As a recap, here's a checklist to keep handy:

- ☐ Silence your phone and ask your interviewee to do the same.

- ☐ Set levels before you roll tape!

- ☐ Turn on high-pass filter if needed!

- ☐ Headphones on!

- ☐ Slate the tape (ask interviewees to say their own names).

- ☐ Don't sweat stumbles and flubs—go to the nearest starting point and repeat.

- ☐ Speak or read a little slower than usual—remember, your audience can't see your lips moving.

- ☐ Mind your breath control (plosives and sibilance!).

While Rolling: Get Your Technique Down—and Listen, Listen, Listen

Do these things while you're recording, and you'll make your producer (probably you) and your editor (um, yeah) sooooo happy!

— **Practice proper mic placement.** Okay, you've set everything up great—now keep it that way! The mic should be four to five inches away from the mouth, to one side, and a little below the chin. I say this in one sentence, but I could write paragraphs on why it's so important. Or go ahead, learn the hard way.

— **Keep mic handling minimal.** You bought a mic to improve your podcast. So let it do its work: Stay outta the way. When holding the mic, use a light grip, let your elbow and wrist move the mic, and be quiet when handling the cable.

— **Add mic protections if needed.** A good-quality foam cap or mesh screen can reduce p-pops, and a fur windscreen helps with wind buffeting.

— **Lead the dance.** If you're interviewing multiple folks, cue them in.[14] Catch a guest's eye, address them by name, shift the mic (if shared), and ask the question, keeping eye contact. For a roundtable, designate who leads, along with monitoring time and guiding everyone to the next topic.

14 Later, you can fix cross-talk somewhat if you recorded on split tracks, but it's not a complete solve.

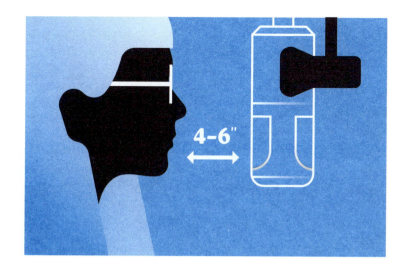

— **Listen for static, crackling, or breakup.** Distortion can happen if the sound levels are blowing past what your setup can handle—for example, bursts of loud noise or laughter. Try adjusting levels to allow room for these sound peaks. Setting levels at -15 dBFS can work in many settings, but watch and listen while rolling—you might have to adjust on the fly. Distortion prevention is key, since you can't do much to fix it (except in phone tape) in editing.

— **Assess how the voices sound.** Do they sound muffled or far away? Check mic placement: Is it close enough? Think how annoying muffling is on a personal call. Don't expect listeners to tolerate it. Stop and fix it. It's usually something simple, like you're talking into the back of the mic. Could happen[15] to anyone.[16]

15 Has happened.

16 To me. A LOT.

— **Keep alert for odd stuff.** Humming, chirps, ticks, static? Could be interference—anything from computers to lights to power lines and more. Try a different location. Shift equipment. Swap in another mic. Turn off cell phones and fluorescent lights. Equipment culprits include worn, piled, or overlong cables, or cables too close to power sources.

How We Warm Up

If you ever get the chance to guest on an NPR podcast or radio show, the producer will sit you down, adjust your microphone, head to the booth, put on their headphones, and ask you what you had for breakfast. They don't care about your açai bowl. They're trying to get a sense of how you'll sound, your volume (level check!), and whether you'll pop those plosives that send their gauge needles into the red.

Every podcaster at NPR has their own pretaping vocal rituals, and it rarely includes a litany of breakfast foods.

When he appears on a podcast, *All Things Considered*'s Ari Shapiro busts out the opening verses of *Beowulf*. In Old English. Show-off.

> *"Hwät! we Gâr-Dena in geâr-dagum þeód-cyninga þrym gefrunon, hû þâ äðelingas llen fremedon."*

Personally, I use a line from an old Bugs Bunny cartoon, "Baseball Bugs," that I memorized as a kid. It's an excellent p-pop test, and I'm a notorious p-popper:

> *"Watch me paste this pathetic palooka with a powerful, paralyzing, perfect pachydermic percussion pitch."*

Meanwhile, *Pop Culture Happy Hour*'s Linda Holmes just talks for a minute about what her dog, Brian, has done that day, what he ate, whether or not he barked at the neighbor, and so on. (Note: He's usually barked at the neighbor.)

What is the runaway most-used level check among NPR podcasters?

> *"Peter Piper picked a peck of pickled peppers. If Peter Piper picked a peck of pickled peppers, how many peppers did Peter Piper pick?"*

Everyone from Guy Raz to Gene Demby busts out this p-pop-testing tongue twister on the regular. *PCHH*'s Stephen Thompson adds his own spin, finishing off by intoning, "This…is NPR."

Finding the Story in the Sound

Beyond technical stuff and vocal tracks, what about the sounds that make the world come vibrantly alive? Sound shouldn't overpower your story, but it should help you tell it.

ACTIVE SOUND

Think of active sound as a voice in your story. It tells your audience where they are. You can use it to segue into and out of scenes, signal a location change, preface someone talking, or reinforce their point.

What sounds would help listeners picture the scene and feel like they're there? What's the one sound that, if removed, would make the scene unrecognizable or generic? What sounds will capture the themes you're aiming for? Is it steak sizzling as it hits the skillet, test tubes clicking in the lab, playground swings creaking and kids shouting, dancers' feet thumping to a mazurka, the zipper on a dress going up (or, ahem, down)?

Be a sound sleuth. A sound bloodhound! Record a sound in different ways—solo; with your interviewee explaining what they're up to; keeping the mic close (the norm), more distant, or moving to capture a series of sounds; capturing individual sounds (a match being struck). If you want music in the scene to establish atmosphere, record it while it's on—then ask that it be turned off during the interview.

Don't stage sounds that didn't actually happen. But you can ask for a redo if you aren't sure you captured a sound, or you suddenly realize it'd be great to have a clear sample on tape to use "in the clear" (audio speak for a standalone sound, not under a vocal track). Nick Fountain says: "You can ask people to do a sound twice if you didn't get a sound in the clear: 'Hey, I want just that one sound. Can you give that to me again, just that one sound?' And if it happened in the moment, ethically, I am totally fine with asking someone to redo it."

Get more different sounds and more minutes than you think you'll need. They might come in handy for storytelling or mistake-fixing in editing.

And keep in mind these tips:

— In the field, deconstruct the sound of the scene
and record the elements.

— Avoid clichés when using scene sound.

— Look for and record movement.

— Find transitional sound—something that changes.

— Avoid music in the background at all costs.

— Get close, stay close.

— Patience is key!

AMBIENT SOUND

You know what your bedroom sounds like at night, before you fall asleep? Maybe you can't quite describe it, but it has a sound.

Ambient sound is the unique atmosphere in a location. You want to collect it as a track of its own and use it under your vocal tracks to help your audience orient ("Oh, that's the scientist in her lab; that's the patient in the hospital"), and to help smooth out, or mask, seams in your edits.

Deciding how much ambi[17] you need is like deciding how much shrimp to serve at a party: You can never have too much. Get one minute *minimum* per interview in the field so you can be pretty sure you've got clean track without handling noise. Keep your mic positioned just as it was in the interview, and on the same settings.

To give yourself the most options while editing, collect ambi from multiple vantage points: farther away, midspace, and close up on particular sounds of things happening in the space.

NARRATION

You can also *say* what you're seeing, smelling, hearing, tasting, or touching. You can record yourself on-site narrating what's going on:

> In a booth by the window, in a booster chair, a little girl is trying to eat a red velvet cupcake that's as big as the two hands she's holding it in. It's all over her face and on the floor. Her mom is laughing, taking pictures, trying to mop her up. The cupcake is winning.

> Wow. The lion cub's fur looks soft, but it feels wiry. Like it would shuck off the rain. And there's this incredibly solid bone structure underneath. You can really feel this is a wild animal.

Narration can help you assemble a story if you're taping an event or clarify what your audience is hearing: "The crew heaves the lobster traps on deck" [crash, slosh]. Narration combined with active

17 Look at you, getting up to speed with the lingo!

Phoners Without Hang-Ups

EVERYONE does phoners because we can't sit down face-to-face for lots of reasons.[18] But phone tape can be full of all the cruddy sound I've described. You've been on personal calls like this. Imagine listening to someone's muffled, staticky, tinny voice for, like, an hour.[19] Then add spotty internet connections with internet-based calling (such as Skype or Zoom).

Prevention and damage control won't work miracles, but they're the name of the game, since chances are, you'll be using phone tape to varying degrees.

For starters, see if you can find a sound-dampened room.

One method, a tape sync, involves you recording by phone while your guest records their voice on their smartphone,[20] sends you the tape, and you assemble both together. If both parties have their own recording gear, you can each record a high-quality track of your own end of the conversation and then combine them.

For optimal mic position on smartphone recording, hold it near your cheek, similar to when you're on a call, or about four inches in front of your face.

Using an internet-based service? Make sure your interviewee has the software/an account, if needed. They should use a headset or earbud mic—run a sound check to see if they're close enough.

If the quality's really bad and it's not too long, you could paraphrase or repeat that material.

18 During COVID-19, NPR became the all-phoners, all-the-time network.

19 Nah, it was just a few minutes. Just *seemed* like an hour.

20 This was the NPR go-to protocol for phoners for years and years, until landlines started going the way of the dodo.

---

sound can amp up drama: "The runners hit the home stretch in a pack. It's the final kick. The crowd's on its feet. It's anyone's race."

You can also ask your interviewee to say what they're doing, mixing, chopping, gathering, lifting, sewing, tuning, or clipping; where they're going, walking, hurrying, or climbing.

You could even record scene-description notes and impressions on your smartphone—kind of like an audio sketchbook—for added detail when you're revising your script or editing your tape.

Before and Just After You Wrap

Woohoo!! You did it! Now, hang on. Before you close up shop, listen back to your tape: Have you got what you need? Including plenty of ambi?

With your smartphone, take some pix or video for reference during editing. Record or jot down final impressions (if you haven't already), those standout moments and sensory details you want to remember: "The nursing home halls smell like disinfectant and cooked green beans." "After the service ended, the smell of candle smoke wafted over the pews." "The baby laughed and tangled her fingers in her grandfather's beard."

Remember to thank your guests or interviewee, and tell them you'll let them know when the episode is published.

Now you can kick back and congratulate yourself on a job well done!

The Ten Commandments of Recording

To help future sessions go smoothly, we leave you with NPR's Ten Commandments of Recording:

1   Thou shalt always get a minute of ambience.
2   Thou shalt keep the same mic placement when recording room tone.
3   Thou shalt not walk on the end of sound bites. (Which is to say: Shut up. Let the interviewee talk, and don't fill up silences with "Uh-huh," "Yeah," "Right, right," or "Interesting!" You'll need those silences when pulling things together.)
4   Thou shalt always wear your headphones and keep them holy.
5   Thou shalt shun the evil hums: fluorescents, computers, fridges.
6   Thou shalt not interview people with music playing in the background.
7   Thou shalt always have the person say their name for proper pronunciation.
8   Thou shalt check thy tape before thy departure from the scene.
9   Thou shalt mic closely.
10 Thou shalt get another minute of ambience ... just in case.

Notes from the Pros: Get Ambi Aplenty and Get Creative with Transitions

Nick Fountain, producer, *Planet Money*

Get a *lot* of ambi. You want some close-ups. And get transition sound. One of the easiest ways to transition between scenes rather than having to write, "We went down the road and whatever, whatever," is to do some transition ambi. So the trope of this is: car door slam, gravel, gravel. Or: ring, ring, "Hey, are you there?" In a pinch, you can use them. But there can be more creative transitions. I was doing a story on postal policy and I asked this guy, "Hey, we're checking for p-pops. Can you just say postal policy ten times fast?" And he said, "Postal policy, postal policy, postal policy, postal policy." It was funny, and it was different.

CHAPTER 10

Acing the Interview

Ever eavesdropped on a conversation?[1] Been captive to the one-sided blurts of cell phone talkers?[2] Other people's chatter can be deeply inane. They'd think the same of our own prattle, blather, and nattering. Which proves my main point: An interview's got to be more than two people yakking about stuff *they* think is fascinating. The best podcast conversations center on those questions you asked in chapter 2: Who's your podcast for, and why should they care? If you let those answers drive your interviews, you're more likely to have revealing conversations that keep your audience coming back for more.

Quality and authenticity matter, too. It's about striking a balance between preparation and spontaneity, so you and your guest sound like yourselves at your best—but *real*.

Good interviewers do that. To explore how, this chapter reviews some key strategies from NPR pros and gets a special assist from Jesse Thorn, host of *Bullseye with Jesse Thorn*, who shares insights as an experienced interlocutor and a perennial student of what makes for a great interview.

Ground Rules

Interviews are podcast staples. They can add variety and complexity to a solo or a review show. They let you bring in knowledgeable voices on new topics, creating opportunities to expand your audience. And they're essential to story-driven podcasting.

[1] C'mon.

[2] Oh, *this* you'll admit to.

Terry Gross is a brilliant genius, but she is always glad to highlight the guest and what is great or interesting about them. She also always asks for examples, always brings the conversation to specifics and stories when it could be vague. Jerry Springer really respects everyone he talks to and cares about them and their story, including folks other people might laugh at or scorn or pity. He just goes in and tries to give them a chance to be heard.

—Jesse Thorn, host, *Bullseye with Jesse Thorn*

The biggest rule to remember for successful interviewing? The "golden" one we learned as kids: Treat your guest as you'd like to be treated. It's the best way to help them relax into the candid give-and-take of a good interview. And it's the right thing to do.

Also crucial to remember when creating content for the public are the standards of journalism, accuracy, and ethics all truth-seekers should follow. Speaking of which: If you skipped over chapter 8—which covers the legal issues related to speaking with or about other people, from interviewee releases to privacy issues—go back and read that now. It's important info you need to know before interviewing someone. Also see chapter 12 for more tips on accuracy. NPR publishes its standards of journalism in the *NPR Ethics Handbook*, but here's a pertinent bit to set the tone:

> Everyone affected by our journalism deserves to be treated with decency and compassion. We are civil in our actions and words, avoiding arrogance and hubris. We listen to others. When we ask tough questions, we do so to seek answers—not confrontations. We are sensitive to differences in attitudes and culture. We minimize undue harm and take special care with those who are vulnerable or suffering. And with all subjects of our coverage, we are mindful of their privacy as we fulfill our journalistic obligations.

The Preinterview

As an interviewer, you never want to get caught flat-footed, finding out only once your guest is behind the mic that they don't have the information you expected, or that talking to them is only slightly less painful than pulling teeth. That's not a good use of anyone's time (your audience's included). Enter: the preinterview—a step you shouldn't skip unless your guest is so well known or has so many clips online that you've got a clear idea of what they'll deliver, or they're too busy for a preinterview and it's book 'em or lose 'em. "We do a *ton* of preinterviews," says *Embedded* host Kelly McEvers. "Just trying to suss out: Who's the person who might work?"

Of course, this starts by contacting the person (via phone or email) and asking if they're willing to be interviewed for your podcast. When making an initial request, be clear about your aims. Say or write some version of this:

> My name is [your name], and I host [or produce] a podcast called [name of podcast]. I'm researching an episode about [name or describe the topic in a sentence]. I found your name during my research [or say who referred you]. I was wondering if I could have a short conversation with you to learn more about your experiences and knowledge. Then, depending on the conversation and if you're willing, I will schedule a time to record an interview with you for the story.

Bottom line: Before you record anything, make sure the person knows you'll be recording and how that recording will be used.

If they say no, politely thank them and ask if there's anyone else they think you should be talking to. You never know what doors will open. Word to the wise: Unless the episode hinges on booking one particular person, have several possible candidates in mind (as chapter 7 advises, make a list of potential interviewees when researching your story). This can make your pitch stronger (since you can tell each person about the other people you're thinking of talking to), and you can pivot to other guests if your first choice says no, the fit's not right, the scheduling doesn't work, they become tongue-tied on tape, or they cancel at the last minute.

If they say yes, then schedule the preinterview.

At NPR, we tend to do preinterviews pretty close to when we'd tape the actual interview—often the day before, or sometimes the morning before an afternoon taping session. Usually the preinterview isn't taped, but if we do tape it, we let the interviewee know we're doing that. We're also very clear that this preinterview is purely informational, and we make no guarantees about whether the person will actually be interviewed for the show—that is, unless we're certain by the end of the preinterview that we want to book the person for an interview.

Your preinterview should help you assess the following:

— Do they add to what your audience needs to know?

— Does their personal or professional experience help to flesh out the topic?

— Do they introduce a new, important element?

— Do they take the story in an unexpected but pivotal direction?

Oh, and:

— How well do they communicate all that?[3]

While you want the preinterview to be in-depth enough to get a sense of what they have to say—and to give them an idea of your episode so they can decide if they'd like to participate—you don't want to get into a conversation that's so deep it drains the juice from the actual interview. You just want to ask enough and hear enough to find out whether there is enough for a meaty interview. What's their point of view? How will that shape your story? Kelly McEvers describes how her team evaluates the preinterview: "We're sort of in a collaborative, curiosity mode, thinking: *What do we really want to know here? What are we missing? What are we not understanding? Well, that didn't surprise me. That really did surprise me. What about . . . ?* And then: *Is this just a short anecdote? Half an episode? A whole episode?*"

Although you should let your guest know what to expect from the recording session, don't promise them the world (or even a few continents). Give them a sense of your line of questions and interests without promising what you'll ask. Tell them approximately how long the recording session may be, when you think it'll be published—and assure them that you'll send a link they can share when that happens.

If you're booking them to talk about their new album, film, book, or play, then that'll be a focal point. But if it isn't the reason for the booking, say you'll "try" to mention it—but you don't have to promise to rave about it (though you can say you loved it, if you did). You could let them know you'll be asking about their creative process; influences; what was easy, difficult, or interesting about the project; a behind-the-scenes story. That sort of thing. There are lots of ways

3 If you're doing a three-minute piece for *All Things Considered*, you value people who make their point in a few sentences, then stop. For a podcast, where you're not working against an unforgiving clock, it's okay—maybe even desirable—to talk to folks who like to talk. Maybe even yammer. It's a judgment call. What do you value more, pithiness or personality?

to make an interview interesting for your audience, respectful for your guest, and beneficial to you without saying or doing things you don't feel are aligned with the goals of your show.

In the preinterview, don't be afraid to (courteously) ask your sources for their sources. Also, clarify their willingness to let their full name be used. NPR requires reporters to get the full names of interviewees who are going to be featured on-air, both for legal reasons and to make fact-checking easier (but: you do you).

Booking and Planning the Interview

If you're satisfied with the preinterview and would like to set up the formal interview, let them know that you'd like to book an interview and, if they agree, move into planning-the-actual-interview mode.

Put the person at ease about the process. For starters, get their name right. Ask for pronunciation if you aren't sure. Jot it down in a way that'll help you remember. Ask for any professional title or other identifier they want used, as well as their preferred gender pronoun. This is part of accurate reporting and respecting your interviewee for their time and contribution.

If appropriate to your show, ask guests for a bio that you can draw on to introduce them; that way, you both know the information will be accurate. Also if appropriate, ask for info on where listeners can find their latest film, book, album, and the like.

Sometimes people get all tangled up about taping an interview and start sounding stilted and unnatural. Or they spout jargon (because they think they "should" or maybe it's just how they talk). Your job: Angle them toward what would help your audience understand what they have to say. As *All Things Considered* editor Jessica Deahl writes: "I often tell prospective guests to imagine they're explaining the subject at hand to a really smart high school student."

If you book the interview, plan together where and how it'll happen. Scope out the technical side: Could you both be in a studio (ideal, but rare)? Use a recording app? If a phoner, how good is the sound? If an internet platform, how's their connection? If on location, talk about a recording space (see chapter 9). Make time to record active sound if needed, and kick around ideas—what sounds would be associated with this person's world? Add them to your sound list.

Some podcasts pay interviewees for their time. It's NPR policy not to pay those we interview for news or features—but on *PCHH*, for example, we do pay guests or "fourth chairs," those we invite to the table to take advantage of their expertise. Generally (very generally) speaking, the difference is whether the person you're interviewing is considered a source (no pay) or a contributor (small fee).

Try to get everything you need in that interview session. That way, the active and ambient sounds associated with that interviewee's voice will be consistent in the final piece, creating an easier editing job for you and a more seamless listening experience for your audience. If you need more tape and can't return to the location, make sure your script signposts to your audience that this professional fisherman you'd interviewed aboard his boat is now talking to you by phone—nary a splash to be heard: "We wondered.... So we called Joe Jenkins on one of his rare days off to find out."

Allow more time than you think you'll need. Sami Yenigun, supervising editor for *All Things Considered*, helped start the podcast *What's Good with Stretch & Bobbito* as a producer. "For a half-hour show," he says, "we might record a two-hour-long interview or an hour and a half, maybe."

Preparing Your Interview Questions

We asked Jesse Thorn about the interview prep process for his show, *Bullseye with Jesse Thorn,* which interviews notable pop-culture figures about their life and work. Now, you might be a bit more structured than Jesse in planning out your questions, at least until you get your sea legs as an interviewer. Some approaches are highly focused: "Audie Cornish is astonishingly clear-eyed," Jesse notes. "She knows what she needs to know; she knows the context; she goes and gets it." Others are more freewheeling. A lot depends on the kind of show you're doing. Either way, the only way to know what storylines might be of interest to your audience is to dig in, do some research, and get a sense of exactly that: your guest's story.

During the interview, Jesse allows for curiosity, spontaneity, and naturalness. Because he's prepared and brings a lot of knowledge to the session, he can move the conversation in interesting directions in real time. His preparation allows him to keep his structure loose enough so that the interview can develop in the more organic way of a "real" conversation—by not feeling compelled to fill silences with the next scripted question, letting an unexpected emotional moment play out, or gently "poking back" at a crotchety guest (see "On Spontaneity in Interviewing" on page 167). "The kind of supercharged secret to doing a good interview is

Notes from the Pros: Prepping for the Interview

Jesse Thorn, host, *Bullseye with Jesse Thorn*

If I find media I want to incorporate or ask about, I send it to my producer, who's pulling clips [that is, short audio and video clips that might be discussed and played during the interview]. My producer will give me a list of clips before the interview.

If there's a book, I usually read it over the preceding week or so. If there's a movie or a show, I see it when I can. I read as much as I can. Usually a few dozen things. I'll try to listen to or watch at least one interview. That gives me a feeling of what it's like to talk to them.

In general, I'm trying to think about a general outline for the interview—like, "We'll talk a bit about the new thing first, then circle back to childhood, then through the biography." Or whatever. And I'm trying to be curious and think about why they make the choices they do and what I find myself wondering about.

knowing as much as possible about the person you are going to interview—spending a lot of time reading about them and studying them as best you can," says Guy Raz. "Not because there aren't going to be things to learn during the interview. To the contrary, that's how you get moments of serendipity. When you know a lot about a person and ask detailed questions, you're essentially saying, 'I honor you. I respect you. I have taken a lot of time to learn about you. I'm here to learn even more.' When it's clear to them that you've spent a lot of time preparing, there's no way they won't respond with generosity, stories, recollections, insights. One of the mistakes I think a lot of podcasters make is in kind of showing up and saying, 'Let's hit the Record button and just see where this goes.'"

And your actual questions? You want them to be open-ended, not yes/no questions. In a way, you get to be both audience and host, asking the "why" and "how'd that work out" and "what happened next" questions your audience is likely wondering about.

Before You Hit Record

Review your "Sound Collection Worksheet/Checklist" (see page 141), and bring this with you to the interview, so you don't overlook anything. If you're going on location, use your Field Equipment Checklist (page 141) to make sure you bring everything you need. Run through all the tech setup advice in chapter 9: Confirm mic placement and protection, prep the room for optimal sound, run an audio test, make sure background noise isn't ruining your tape, and give your guest a little mic placement tutorial while testing for sibilance and p-pops. And set your levels—get a natural-sounding sample of your guest's speech by asking an everyday question, like what they had for breakfast.

Bring your interview questions or notes.

Do a little vocal warm-up ahead of time (see chapters 5 and 9 for ideas and examples). Or at least repeat "red leather, yellow leather"—a classic warm-up that sends the tongue on a quick tour around the hard and soft palate (. . . see?). Have some voice-refreshing apple juice or water on hand. Your guest might appreciate a choice of these.

Once the technical nuts and bolts are handled, turn your focus to the human being whose mind and heart you hope to tap into. How do you get the most from this session?

I think Ira Glass is always very deeply interested in other people's feelings. It is absolutely sincere, and he just asks about them. Reggie Ossé—or Combat Jack—knew everything about the subject he was interviewing people about. Everything. So he always had a little anecdote or a little insight that opened things up.

—Jesse Thorn, host, *Bullseye with Jesse Thorn*

Make the person feel comfortable with a blend of friendliness and low-key authority about what you're doing. While setting up—and maybe walking around and shifting furniture to optimize sound quality and find the best place to record—make small talk. Ask about the trip to get there (yours or theirs) or the place where they live; something innocuous that gets a conversation going. "I try to put them at ease when I meet them," Jesse says. "I say hello, shake their hand, smile. Let them know we're gonna talk for an hour or so. It'll just be talking. We'll make them sound great. For most guests if there's something that might be sensitive, I'll let them know it isn't live, and if there's something personal they don't want to talk about, to just let me know."[4]

Also let them know that they can take their time and double back if they flub a sentence, or if they figure out a better way to say something. Gently remind them that you'll be editing the interview, so even if you talk to them for half an hour, the actual interview will run shorter—possibly much shorter.

Some people might ask if they can hear the interview before it runs. If you're podcasting the NPR way, the polite-but-firm answer would be no, that's not journalistic practice. If they're asking because there's something specific they're not comfortable talking about, then you might want to get that concern on the table, and discuss together how or whether to approach it, before you roll tape.

Roll Tape! Er, Hit Record!

You're rolling! For the record, slate the tape with the date, the time, your name, podcast name, your location, and recap the episode topic and the focus of the interview to refresh your guest's memory and remind them of why you're both here together.

Then ask your interviewee to introduce themselves—to say their full name and where they live—and something about themselves: maybe their professional title, what they do, or their connection to this story.

If your guest is doing something—cooking, making something, fixing something, playing an instrument, using a tool, interacting with an animal—ask them to describe what they're doing for listeners. You can also prompt them a bit: "What's your trick for cracking eggs into the skillet one-handed like that?" "Can we talk about those double back flips? How the heck do you train for that?" (These can be sound collection opportunities, BTW—the sound of that cracking eggshell, sticking the landing!)

This is all part of following your natural curiosity. It's okay—important, even—to jump off from your script into reactions and questions that come up in the moment, and then circle back to the central themes or questions you planned. "I listen when they talk and react to what they say," says Jesse Thorn. "I don't try to control the conversation except to the extent that I need to do so to make a radio show." Putting yourself in the tape makes you sound human,

4 If you plan to do one of those dramatic entrances where you're taping your arrival, let the person know ahead of time to expect a gear-toting, headphone-wearing audio geek showing up with tape rolling (ditto for the phoner version).

Notes from the Pros: Be You

Nick Fountain, producer, *Planet Money*

We really like when our reporters are being humans in tape, responding and interacting with guests as normal humans would—laughing, being empathetic when empathy is called for. There's this joke about *Planet Money*, which is like in the orientation, we tell you that anytime someone tells you a number in an interview, you repeat the number back to them with the appropriate emotion. Because numbers mean nothing to people out of context. So if someone said, "I just bought this house for fifty dollars," you should say *"Fifty dollars???"* [sounding incredulous]. But if somebody says, "I'm on my last fifty dollars," you'd say, "Ohhh, fifty dollars . . ." [sounding sympathetic]. Trying to put numbers into context is hard, and it's something we have to do a lot here. And you can do that in your voice.

reflects what your audience might be thinking or wondering, and can help your audience put information in perspective.

Then again, it's one thing to react, interact, and put yourself in the tape. It's another to lead your interviewee toward what to say. If something isn't clear (scientific lingo or industry jargon), you can ask, "Could you explain that a bit, to make sure listeners understand?" Or say, "Whoa, that went by really fast. Could we break that down?" What you don't want to do is put words in their mouth: "So, what you mean is [say what you think they mean]."

Try to get at how a situation, an event, an insight, or an achievement unfolded or feels to the person living or experiencing it. People tend to tell you about destinations, not journeys. They'll tell you the conclusion (the finished song, the research results) but not the story (what sparked the idea, how they set up the experiment, the failures and problems they overcame along the way). It's okay to ask, with curiosity and candor, if they could back up and unpack something they just breezed past that contained a world of interesting stuff. "There's nothing wrong with stopping somebody—like, 'Wait, wait, hold on. Let's wind the tape back. Okay. How did you . . . ?'" says Guy Raz.

Ask questions about process—emotional, intellectual, or physical. Process is action; action is story; stories engage and teach us. Ask about motives, thought process, methodology, emotions in the moment: "Why do you think it turned out that way?" "What led you to that decision?" "Is there a story of a time when that happened?" "How did you learn that?" "I'm trying to picture that—how'd it all go down?" "Did something happen to make you feel that way?" "You sound so calm as you describe this. How did it feel when it happened?"

Remember, even though you're running this interview, you're not controlling it. Your job is to encourage candor. That can mean letting go of the reins sometimes. Jesse Thorn says: "If the interview is rolling and they're holding back, I maybe ask them something friendly and surprising, something that makes me look dumb, maybe something silly. If they're really polished but not revealing themselves, I might ask them a question that requires a heartfelt answer—like, I dunno . . . 'Are you afraid of death?' Mostly, though, I just know that if I talk to them in a nice human way, they'll usually come around to responding in kind."

Jesse's tactic for breaking through an interviewee's polished veneer is important. You'll find that when people are asked about something they've been asked about many times, they revert to an internalized script. Not necessarily because they've been

Notes from the Pros: Don't Prejudge

Yowei Shaw, cohost/editorial lead, *Invisibilia*

Sometimes when you're doing an interview and somebody is explaining something that you've been trying to understand, you get really, really excited. This has happened to me several times, and I think to myself, *Oh, my gosh, that interview was amazing*. Then you listen to the tape, and the interview is a total dud. It was just your emotional response in that moment.

But then, recently, I was interviewing this expert, and they were really putting me in my place, and that did not feel good. I thought, *I can't use this interview, it's horrible*. Then I listened back, and it was great tape. Because it was electric. It was dynamic. The expert was putting me in my place, and that's fun to listen to. More than an expert just telling you calmly this thing they've said a million times. She was really trying to communicate something to me, and she was angry at me for not getting it.

media-trained or are hiding something. It's just how our brains work. Our memories, after all, are stories we tell ourselves about the events we've witnessed. Your job as an interviewer is to do enough research to recognize when your interviewee starts launching into an anodyne anecdote and gently course correct. Ask a question at a slant. Ask them to go back and dig deeper. Ask something that forces them out of the narrative groove (read: rut) they've dug for themselves, and re-see the thing you're asking about, not the mythology they've built around it.

Don't get flustered if you stumble a bit—and reassure your guest, too. You'll edit out major glitches, but you want your podcast

On Spontaneity in Interviewing

Jesse Thorn, host, *Bullseye with Jesse Thorn*

I interviewed Betty Davis, who is a legendary—and legendarily reclusive—funk musician. She was on the phone from Pittsburgh, patched through by her label since she didn't want anyone to have her phone number. She was very polite, but very fragile-sounding. She hadn't done press in a few decades, and hadn't even picked up her ASCAP checks until a fan tracked her down and hand-delivered them. She gave me a lot of one-sentence answers to my questions. It was really, really hard, but I remember thinking of something I'd read in Jessica Abel's and Ira Glass's comic *Out on the Wire*, which is that if you don't say anything, people will fill the space. So when she finished her sentences, I just waited. For a long time, sometimes. Like five or ten seconds, which is *forever*. And every time, she added to her initial remarks. And that saved the interview.

I also remember a time when I played a clip for actor Michael K. Williams of a dance track from the 1980s—this song where he'd appeared in the video. It was his big break. And I thought maybe he'd be happy to hear it, kind of amused, but he started crying. And he was in a studio in New York, so I couldn't really tell if he was sad or hurt or happy or whatever. But I just let him do his thing. Because I didn't need to control the moment. I gave him some time, and he shared some incredible memories.

Another time I went to a fancy hotel in West Los Angeles to interview musician Bill Withers. At the time he hadn't really done any press in, like, fifteen years. He was older and incredibly smart and a little grumpy. And when I sat down, he kind of started giving me the business. Because whatever—I was a young white guy there being presumptuous enough to bother him, a guy who really had nothing to gain from the interview. And I remember at some point he was giving me a hard time, and I kind of poked back at him, and he laughed, and after that it was one of the best interviews I'd ever done. I think just because he was like, "Oh, this is a person, too. He's not an idiot. He's here because he cares, and maybe he's even interesting to talk to."

to sound as if your audience is listening in on an interesting-but-real conversation, which naturally will have some "ums" and "ahems" and a hitch or two.

Before you wrap, make sure you get a couple of minutes of ambient sound. Just let your guest know you need to record how the room sounds, with no talking.

Then review your Sound Collection Worksheet/Checklist one last time: Did you get all the active sounds you need?

All done? Say thank you, and follow up with a thank-you email, too, with the publication date if you know it—or say you'll let them know, and send the link when it's available. Make sure their contact info and any special notes are on file so you can get in touch again—you never know! And once you're on your own after the interview, *Throughline*'s Rund Abdelfatah advises, "Note the things that really worked or excited you so you don't forget."

And there you are. In the end, good interviewing is about doing your homework, being prepared, and then letting go of that and trusting that your natural inquisitiveness will lead you in the right direction and you'll come away with an interview that's as interesting for your audience to listen to as it was for you to create. As Jesse Thorn says, "Be curious. Ask open-ended questions. Remember that whomever you're interviewing—whether it's Buzz Aldrin or Michelle Obama or Little Richard—is a person just like you are a person. And enjoy yourself!"

CHAPTER 11

It's All in the Mix

Look at you. You've collected sound, done interviews, and recorded spellbinding narration or riveting repartee between you, your cohost(s), and your guest(s). You did it with correct gear setup and testing. Proper mic placement. In a space as optimized for sound as you could make it. Courteously and ethically. With headphones *on*.

You rock.

Now, what do you *do* with those hours and hours of sound...in all those different files...containing, let's surmise, more than a few p-pops, lip smacks, odd and intrusive background noises, and verbal bloopers?

You've got raw sound, but what your audience wants is a compelling story, smoothly told.

Enter audio production and editing.

First, a lingo lesson. You'll hear the words *production* and *editing* tossed around interchangeably, but technically, as true audio geeks know, they aren't the same. *Audio production* molds the sound. It's what makes it, well, sound good. It's mixing (sometimes salvaging) audio. Adjusting levels. Cleaning up p-pops and rumbles. Cleverly making it look like no one talked over anyone else, flubbed a line, or sniffled. Using sound, ambi, or music to mask edits.[1] And more. You'll learn about that in this chapter.

Audio editing molds the narrative. It's about cutting together all of these strands currently on separate tracks—vocal tracks, active sound, background sound, ambi, music—to create one sound thread that tells a story. That's tackled in chapter 12.

The goal of both: to keep your audience immersed in the audio world you've worked so hard to build. Although we're dividing them for purposes of explanation, sound and story are welded together.

[1] When your podcast finally walks the red carpet in its strapless designer gown, you don't want anyone muttering that it's had work done.

As Jessica Reedy says, "People think we just record our show and put it out without any editing. That there's no reverb, or whatever. That they sat down and this is how it sounded. Which is not true."

Production and editing can overlap. And depending on the complexity of your podcast, the size of your operation, and the looming specter of your deadline, they might be done by several people or just one; over many increasingly picayune passes or in a handful of passes that accomplish both processes in an organized frenzy.[2]

A little roughness around the edges of a podcast evokes an artful, artisanal feeling. But "some irregularities"—that phrase you see on labels of handmade anything—shouldn't be a euphemism covering a multitude of avoidable sins. Glaring errors and low audio quality yank listeners out of your story, giving people who took time to click and listen good reason to press Skip or even (pearls: clutched) thumbs-down. Don't let them!

Audio production ensures that all your hard work doesn't go to waste. That said, not everything is completely—or even at all— fixable.[3] Audio production will help you. It can't save you.[4]

Some people dig this process. Others not so much. In which case, this might be a stage to outsource to a qualified pro. If you're the hand on the dials (keyboard), know that practice will sharpen your ear and your skills. This chapter describes how NPR producers suss out and fix the most common audio glitches to get you started on the right foot.

What Producers Listen For, and How They Listen

Certain goals and best practices apply across the board. Here's what producers strive for:

— Naturalistic, intelligible speech (with normal-sounding cadences, inflections, pauses, volume)

— A natural-sounding setting (appropriate background sound that doesn't overwhelm the vocals)

— No distracting noises (buzzes, pops, tinniness, bassiness, Sid the dog going buck wild at the sight of a squirrel, etc.)

2 I've watched Jessica do this. Monsta on the dials.

3 Crackly distortion (other than on phone tape), sibilance, overcompression (see "The Eight-Step Mix" on page 174), certain types of interference, off-mic speech, and low-bitrate audio (that tinniness you get on internet conference services) are, variously, impossible-to-difficult-to-needing-special-tools-or-teams-of-hardbitten-professionals to fix.

4 This is why I banged the drum on good sound collection habits in chapter 9. You're welcome.

As for practices, here are some general pointers:

— **Get your eyes off the script or the screen; focus on your ears.**
It's tempting to read the script or outline while you listen.
Or to get obsessed with what the gauges are telling you. But
pros edit *first* with their ears. They know that their brain can
miss audio problems if they're reading along. Listeners won't
have the script in front of them, of course, so put yourself in
their … earbuds. Use the gauges to *confirm* and *measure*—not
influence—what your ears tell you.

— **Use your headphones *and* your speakers.** Your headphones
pick up harder-to-hear audio "dirt" (p-pops and the like) and
help you check for seamless edits. Speakers can help you check
overall balances: Is the music too loud under that voice?

— **Ideally, listen as many ways as you can—since that's how
your audience will listen.** On earbuds, laptops, crappy
headphones, good ones. While driving, walking on the street,
cooking. Especially listen for levels: Can everything be heard
that needs to be?

— **Make a hit list of major trouble spots.** Mark the time where you
hear them. Some pros do this while recording, but you can do
it when you play back a session. While you're at it, mark where
you hear lengthy pauses or gratuitous yakking (the latter often
before you get down to business). Those are for-sure edits.[5]

— **Create time-saving templates.** Are there repeating elements
in your podcast (parts of your intro or outro; interview tracks)?
Set up a template that automatically applies certain audio
settings (once you know what they are) to new recordings as
you save them; this saves time. That head start doesn't give you
a pass on editing, though. You've still got to listen and adjust.

After you fix one thing, you might hear another problem you
hadn't noticed. Don't overtinker, though. It's a time suck; plus, too
much editing will make your audio sound unnatural.

On your final passes, listen to transitions (where something
changes: vocals end and music or sounds begin, scenes shift, or
you made an edit). If they're hitchy, they'll distract your audience.

[5] *Unless* … those pauses are
story important. Maybe you
want your audience to sit
with someone's hesitance or
thoughtfulness. You might
keep pauses for good storytelling reasons—as Jesse Thorn
did in his interview with
Betty Davis.

Here's a trick to check the balance of your mix: Make note of the level you're listening at. Then turn it down so low that you really have to pay attention to grasp the words. Can you understand them all? Do any parts pop out or recede? Those might need balancing.

Especially if you're working alone, fatigue can set in. You might make errors or lose perspective. Try to get away from the dials for a while—sleep on it, if you can—and come back when you're fresh.

The Eight-Step Mix

Here is an eight-step walk-through of the mixing process. This is adapted and expanded from a model originally developed and written by Rob Byers for NPR Training. Try it out, adapt it to your needs, and create a workflow that works for you and your podcast format.

STEP 1: ORGANIZE

Organize your mixing session, setting up a project that's properly labeled, with similar audio grouped on individual tracks. This involves arranging the tracks, organizing the audio clips, and cascading the tracks.

Arrange Your Tracks

This order is a common layout for audio storytelling:

1 Host audio
2 Actualities and guest audio
3 Ambience and room tone
4 Music

Using the same layout for every project makes it easier to navigate and collaborate with others. As you'll see, it also makes it easier to set levels, equalization, and compression.

Organize the Audio Clips

Make sure that each track includes only clips that are alike. Each clip on an actuality track should be from the same person and interview. Each clip on an ambience track should be from the same scene, and so on. This way, each different voice or scene gets its own track.

You may have to make more than the four original tracks to accommodate all your clips. Name them appropriately and avoid generic titles like "Track 1" or "Audio 1." Use descriptive names like "Larry" or "AMBI market."[6]

6 You're going to want to come up with a clear and consistent naming scheme for your files. Like, yesterday. If it's just you, you can let your freak flag fly, and get real cute with it. But if there's more than one person putting your tracks together, this will save a lot of time...and passive-aggressive emails.

Cascade the Tracks

Once you've named the tracks and grouped together similar clips, organize them visually so that they cascade diagonally from top to bottom, left to right. If the "Sara phoner" actuality is heard in the story before "Tracie phoner," then the "Sara phoner" track should be above the "Tracie phoner" track. Cascading clips make the project much easier to navigate and mix.

STEP 2: ROUGH IN LEVELS

Before you can assess whether any voices need fixing with equalization and compression (steps 3 and 4), take a moment to adjust the level of your tracks so that every voice track is roughly at the same level. Don't try to get things perfect at this point. It's okay for transitions and fades (see the following) to be rough.

Learning About Levels

In chapter 9 we talked about setting levels when recording. It's time to check and adjust those levels across your tracks—so your audience doesn't to have to adjust your podcast's volume during an episode.

Levels can refer to the complete mix or to how each track balances with the others. Both are crucial. To check levels, listen at different volumes: Is everything intelligible, but nothing's jumping out or dropping out? As Jessica describes: "Some of it is: 'Glen is too soft here.'[7] And if you were listening on your iPhone, you'd have to turn up the volume to hear. Sometimes, you futz up the levels to make something sound natural that didn't record perfectly."

Your loudness meter can guide you, but rely on your ears: Turn off your screen, close your eyes, and listen to the whole dang thing.

STEP 3: DETERMINE IF YOU NEED EQUALIZATION

At this point, deal with each track one by one, in isolation. Use the Solo button to isolate tracks (not the Mute button).[8]

The first thing to tackle is equalization (EQ). Solo the first track and play it back. Do you hear any unnatural tonal issues like rumble, hollowness, harshness, or sibilance? Are any frequencies jumping out at you?

If so, insert an EQ plug-in on the track and use it to reduce the problem frequencies. It's also a good idea to preemptively use a high-pass filter to clean up low-end rumble.

An EQ Education

EQ plug-ins help even out tone by balancing frequencies (tinniness/brightness = too high; muddiness/boominess/bassiness = too low). Brightness or muddiness can happen in phone interviews and internet conference or calling services, or they can be caused by gear problems, low battery, or not being plugged in properly.

Generally, audio editors have an EQ that'll work for audio stories. A parametric plug-in is versatile and useful. Ideally it'll also have high- and low-pass filters (like high-pass filters on mics, remember?),

7 Jess, quoting my fifth-grade bully. As is her wont.

8 A brief note about Solo and Mute buttons: They achieve similar outcomes and have very different purposes. Solo is intended to temporarily isolate the selected track and quiet all of the other tracks with one button press. Mute is intended to quiet only the selected track. Use the Solo button for its intended purpose—otherwise, it can interrupt routing and change the way your audio editor behaves.

which can help you eliminate whole sound ranges if need be. Low-pass filters screen out high frequencies and let low frequencies "pass"; high-pass filters do the opposite.

High-pass filters can help reduce rumbles, wind buffeting, some mic handling noise, p-pops, and location noise like traffic, ventilation systems, and machines. Low-pass filters might help with high-end hiss.

EQ doesn't happen in a vacuum. Lower one frequency and the others will seem louder, and vice versa. Go slow; change by increments.

Match EQ Settings in Each Track

If you recorded ambience that matches up with voices recorded in the same location, both need to match in tone. So: If you use EQ to adjust the tone of a voice track, apply the same change to the accompanying ambience track. If there's an environmental issue like rumble or hum in the voice track, it's likely audible in the ambience recording, too. You can fix it with the same EQ settings.

Remember: A plug-in will process every clip of audio on a track. That's why it helps to organize similar clips as in step 1.

When you're happy with the results, keep the track soloed and move on to step 4.

STEP 4: DETERMINE IF YOU NEED COMPRESSION

Assess the voice of each speaker by asking yourself these questions:

— Does the person speak in an even, consistent way?

— Does the speaker sound strong and present?

— If you turn the listening level down halfway, can you still hear and understand every word?

If you answer yes to all, you can probably get by without compression. But if the speaker emphasizes certain syllables and words in ways that make them sound inconsistent or "jumpy" in level, you might need it. Also consider compression if a voice doesn't sound strong or is layered over music.

To do this, insert a compression plug-in on the track and configure it as needed. However, unlike EQ, you don't usually need to apply compression to ambience. But since compression can impact the level of voices, you may need to adjust the level of the accompanying ambience to match.

Comprehending Compression

"OmiGOD, I can't bel*eeeve* you DID that!" Is this person ecstatic or furious? Listeners will soon find out, but for sure, strong emotion leads to natural peaks and valleys in speech—that's why you mark up a script for emphasis, to make certain words stand out and be memorable. But there's such a thing as too much. Sometimes hilly vocal terrain needs some evening out.

Compression basically sets a ceiling on emphasis in words and syllables, so you don't have to fix each instance individually. Peaks that go above the ceiling are made lower. Compression can also reduce the effects of mic-ing someone too closely. The best audio-editor compressors for speech have an adjustable threshold (where it kicks in), ratio (the ceiling—try a 1.5:1 to 2:1 range for dialogue), and make-up gain (a means to boost or "make up" a level that can get lost in compression). You'll also set "attack" and "release" controls—akin to hitting/easing off a gas pedal.

Go easy—it doesn't take much to make speech sound unnatural (try overcompressing some "junk" tape and see). Use it to spot-adjust larger level adjustments. If you're doing a remote interview with another studio, ask them to remove any compressors or other processing—because you can't fix overly compressed audio once it's done.

STEP 5: CHECK EDITS AND FADES

Now do a quick check of all the edits in the piece to make sure they're distraction-free and natural.

Smoothing Out Speech and Sounds

Part of your job is to minimize or "disappear" speech glitches (p-pops, flubs, audible breaths), reduce ear-jarring extremes (bursts of laughter, exclamations), and create an even pace. It's like a face-lift for language. Like a good surgeon, you want to do just enough to make it seem like you weren't there. And make sure your stitches don't show—that's called masking your edits.

Adjust levels to even out sound. Don't get obsessed with individual words. Adjust across phrases and sentences unless a word jumps out.

A high-pass filter might partially fix a plosive by getting rid of the rumbly part. Other fixes are more complex or involve special editing software—so proper mic placement (aka, getting it right in the first place) is your best bet.

Sibilance can be tough to fix. Targeted EQ and compression can help, or a tool called a de-esser—but we suggest you talk to an audio pro.

Doing fades—literally fading out speech, sounds, music—at the "top and tail" (beginning and end) of clips smooths transitions between speakers, between scenes, and from speech to sound or speech to music. Cross-fades sound like what they are: fading down one sound while another fades up. Listen to your favorite podcasts and notice how many fades there are—some superlong and subtle; others so short they're barely noticeable.

Also remove glaring pauses between speakers to make the pace and rhythm of the conversation more even and natural.

Here's where that ambience you carefully collected can come in handy. Use it to soften the beginnings and ends of actualities. Or to mask the seam where you put two tracks together. If you're joining two clips that end/begin abruptly, a little ambi underneath gives you something to fade.

Check Each Edit and Add Fades

Check every edit in the episode. Does the edit sound natural? Are words or breaths upcut: a bit of audio is cut off, or clipped, at top or tail? Are there doubled breaths from putting two clips together? Maybe you removed too much breath between words, andthepersonsoundslike-alatenightinfomercialsalesperson. If you insert a teeny pause between where they took a breath and started the next sentence, you'll naturalize this glitch. Does the tone or cadence change? Is there an audible shift in ambience? Take the time to fine-tune as needed.

Then, the top and tail of every clip should have fades, even if supershort. This is the best practice to avoid abrupt entrances.

This process is easier if you know some of the keyboard shortcuts for your audio editor. Learn the shortcut to jump to the next edit on the track as well as the shortcut to move the playhead back a few seconds. With those two shortcuts, you'll be able to jump from edit to edit, back up a couple of seconds, and listen to the edit quickly.

STEP 6: FINE-TUNE LEVELS

Fine-tuning levels is called *balancing*. Each audio clip needs to match the clip preceding it—not too loud, not too soft. Ambience and music should be audible, but not compete. To create this balance, you need a foundation. Use the host track for that purpose.

Balance tracks in the same order you organized them in step 1:

1   Host tracks

2   Actualities and guest audio

3   Ambience and room tone

4   Music

Instead of trying to mix all of the tracks at once, use the host track to create a foundation for balancing the other tracks. Basically, mix each track from the top down.

First, balance the clips on the host track to one another and get them close to the mixing target.[9] Mute all the tracks except for the host track. Listen through the first clip of audio. Does it regularly hit the target on your meter and sound consistent to your ear? You quickly roughed in levels earlier, so the level should be close—but it might need adjusting. If a sentence or a phrase seems out of balance, apply the level automation tools in your audio editor to that portion. Try to make changes in sentences or phrases (see "Smoothing Out Speech and Sounds," page 178). Once the host track consistently hits the mixing target on your meter and each clip sounds balanced to the clip that precedes it, you're ready to move on to the next track.

Then, balance clips on the next track to the first track. Turn off the mute so you now hear the first actuality/guest track and the host track together. Listen to the last few seconds of the host clip going into the first actuality clip. Do the two sound balanced? Make the appropriate change to bring the actuality in line with the host track.

Now listen through the rest of the clip and determine if a change is necessary. Finally, check the transition out of the clip into the host track to make sure it's balanced.

Repeat this process for all of your guest tracks, unmuting and adjusting one new track at a time.

Once you've balanced each clip to the host track, do another pass and listen to all of the transitions. Double-check balances. Do any transitions and edits need to be masked with ambience? If you can't solve an abrupt transition with ambience, sometimes just a brief pause (think of it like a breath) or a bite of music will do the trick.

STEP 7: BALANCE AMBIENCE AND MUSIC

Tricky step! Ambience and music shouldn't compete with voice tracks, but they still have to be hearable. Try the earlier tip about listening with the level turned way low. Listen in different settings,

[9] NPR's standards are roughly the same across every show so it's suitable for broadcast—at −24 LUFS, which is way quieter than what gets put out on our podcasts. That's because NPR's encoding process builds in another 8 LUFS boost automatically, to ensure they're loud enough for people's different podcast listening habits (in cars vs. in earbuds, for example).

Notes from the Pros: The "Ears Economy"

Yowei Shaw, cohost and editorial lead, *Invisibilia*

> Trade your ears. When you're on your own, you might not have
> a team behind you and with you, making things. So one thing to try
> is offering up your ears to other people on their drafts, and then they
> offer their ears for you. It's like this ears economy.

as your audience would. Listen on headphones and speakers—they'll sound a bit different on each. A middle ground between the two could be the way to go. Also, check the fades on ambience and music.

STEP 8: LISTEN TO THE MIX

Finally, listen to the entire mix on headphones. Listen for anything unnatural. Especially focus on transitions and balances of voice over ambience or music.

That's it! You created a well-balanced mix in an organized and efficient way. The first couple of times you do it this way, it might take a while. It gets easier the more you do it!

One of the best things about the audio world in general and the podcasting world in particular is how much people *love* doing this, how passionate they are about audio making, and how helpful they are about sharing what they know. Especially with tech, there's so much to learn and try, with software always improving or updating. Definitely go online and search out videos, tutorials, and articles. But also just *ask* people. It's a great way to build connections: talk in online or in-person groups about how to edit, what solutions and work-arounds people have used, and what you should try as you learn the ropes. And when you succeed—whether it's figuring out how to set your levels or getting rid of a p-pop the size of Paterson, New Jersey—no one will be cheering louder than your podcasting peeps.

CHAPTER 12

Shaping the Story

At *Pop Culture Happy Hour*, there's a thing we call the "Jess filter." It refers to the exceptional ability of our producer, Jessica Reedy, to transform raw tape into the finished product that makes each of us sound about 40 percent smarter and more confident than we actually are—because our hemming and hawing and speech stumbles are gone.

Ever wanted to rewind something and say it better, faster, or smarter? Then you begin to understand what editors do.

A story editor's job is multipronged and can span the whole life of a story—from the big-picture thinking at the very start of the development process (remember chapter 7?) all the way through to the final editing tweaks for timing and smoothness. "The primary job of the editor is to edit the script for content. Make sure that there are no mistakes, that it's clear, makes sense, it's to time, all that kind of stuff," says *All Things Considered* supervising editor Sami Yenigun.

Big job description.

Like audio production, you learn story editing by doing—and the roles often overlap: "A good producer does a little bit of editing and a good editor does a little bit of producing," Sami says.

This chapter walks through the fundamental processes and practices good editors keep front of mind to create strong stories.

EXERCISE Has Your Story Changed?

In chapter 7, you roughed out an outline or script for your podcast based on your brainstorming, early research, and wish lists for interviews and sounds. Now, you've got all that stuff. So, take a look at what your story actually *is* versus what you thought it might be—and, as Rund Abdelfatah says, "Be open to the story radically changing!"

Consider these questions, jotting down any thoughts you want to capture in your notebook (later in the chapter, you'll have a chance to flesh out your ideas):

— Based on the tape you now have, has the story changed?

— What topics or new ideas have surfaced?

— Have you looked at the story from all sides? Are there different slants or shadings of your original ideas?

— What information or perspectives are missing?

— Is the story as interesting as you'd hoped?

— Does it have enough substance to work at the length you targeted?

— If not, what would help? Or should you set this story aside?

— Is this story headed in a totally different direction? If so, what would you need to pursue that?

— If budget and schedule are tight, is there a natural stopping point for this story?

— Is there a possible follow-up to this story? Say, a part 2 or a series?

I used to tear my hair out [when a story went through a complete rewrite]. But I know that the product this process produces is so superior to what happens if we don't. This is part of how the show works. It's not for everyone, and not for every type of show. But the types of stories that we're trying to do involve many layers. There's the narrative, and we're trying to explore a big idea, so we're often talking to experts, scientists, and researchers. There's a lot going on.

—Liana Simstrom, podcast manager, *Invisibilia*

Editing Foundations: Truth, Fairness, Energy, Naturalness, Clarity

There are certain principles for story editing that apply to any podcast.

Looking at your story components, ask yourself if you're giving people a fair and truthful picture of the subject. You can do a story focused on one person's experience or perspective—but is it clear that this is one person's unique view? That other viewpoints exist?[1] Maybe you could do a callout inviting your audience to share their views: "We'd love to hear *your* experiences with this. Head over to our website community or post on our Twitter. Let's keep the conversation going!" Bottom line: Fairness is about making sure that the audio never feels like it's stacked the deck in one direction or another.

> *We had a situation where Glen didn't like the movie we were talking about. Stephen was kind of neutral. That was the right place to start. Otherwise, everyone else is left defending it. For our show, starting with someone on a more positive side tends to work out better for the conversation.*
>
> —Jessica Reedy, producer, *Pop Culture Happy Hour*

Beware of using sound untruthfully. If birds weren't singing during that park bench interview with the old-timer about the changes he's seen, sitting there every afternoon for fifty years, don't sneak in a loop of chirping chickadees.[2] It's fine to combine or select sound elements within a scene, but not to swap them across scenes or time frames.

> *A conversation may have happened in a less linear way. You can go back and sort of reorganize some of the questions so that it makes sense to the listener. You want to be really careful that you are not editing things that make it dishonest to what the actual conversation was. You never want to cut things in a way that if I played it back for the person I was interviewing, they would say, 'No, that's not an accurate representation of what we were talking about.' That's not to say that your source decides what content goes where; that's not true. We need to have strong editorial control over all of that.*
>
> —Sami Yenigun, supervising editor, *All Things Considered*

[1] Beware of both-siderism, however. "But my next guest says fat-shaming babies is a *good* idea. From the Society Against Sausage-Armed Infants, please welcome . . ."

[2] CBS got busted doing that, actually—putting a fake bird-song loop in golf broadcasts.

Remember what you learned in chapter 7 about the story's driving question and the something at stake? That's where the story arc will come from—the energy that pulls your audience into and through the story. Know what that is, so you can edit to bring out its bones. (You'll use it to write your episode description, too—see chapter 14.)

Are there parts that drag? Don't move the story forward?[3] Are funny, but irrelevant?[4] Watch for those energy leaks.

If you put time markers in your outline or timed your recording (see chapter 7), did you hit your marks? If not, and you decide during editing to go longer on one segment because it's great stuff, then you'll have to shorten other segments, if you want to keep your podcast a certain length.

Now, how much to edit and polish voice tracks? Judgment call, based on the character of your show. Some podcasts need heavy scripting/editing, while others follow a loose-ish outline and keep some speech stumbles. Podcasters traditionally go for nonslickness, but whatever you decide, make sure it fits your show. Definitely clean up or cut major flubs, errors, pauses (unless they add to the story), excessive cross-talk, too many "uhs," "likes," and "you knows," and distractions like coughs, lip smacks, and that phoner guest's yappy Schnauzer who made a brief but memorable appearance at 10:57.

And hey, roundtable discussion podcasts? You're not off the editing hook, either:

> ◁)) *Sometimes at* PCHH *when they talk over each other, if I notice during recording, I'll stop them and say, "Glen, finish your point, and then, Linda, pick up with your next question"—because I know somewhere in there, I'm gonna need a clean edit point, and I can't have them talking over each other. But it's interesting when they're talking over each other. That's part of what makes the show fun and engaging. I'm not gonna stop them from doing that during the things I know I want to keep.*
>
> —Jessica Reedy, producer, *Pop Culture Happy Hour*

Finally, always think of your audience. Are you bringing them with you on this journey? Does everyone understand where you're headed? What about newbies to your topic—should you gently lead them in? Seasoned podcasters debate these questions (as does Sami Yenigun; see quote). As podcast creator/editor, they're your calls.

3 You can sometimes veer off-topic in, say, an interview show *if* (a) it reveals a superinteresting side of your guest that you *know* your audience will love hearing, and (b) you steer back on track. It can't just be a rabbit hole for nerds. Unless your audience *is* nerds. Then, going down rabbit holes is the point.

4 Oof. World of s**t in that single sentence. Yours truly is the crown prince of self-deemed funny "bits" and therefore eminently qualified to say that probably 50 percent never make it into the studio (they don't get past the "Glen filter"), 30 percent never make it past the aforementioned snaggletoothed "Jess filter," and 10 percent actually make it into the show. (What happens to the other 10 percent, you ask? Those I forget before I have a chance to write 'em down. You're welcome.)

There's a really good Code Switch *episode called the "Explanatory Comma," which explores the idea of: Who are you speaking to and what do you need to explain to that audience?*[5] *It came out of a conversation that the hosts had about Tupac Shakur, the hip-hop artist, and there were people writing in asking, "Can you explain to me who Tupac was?" So, there was always the tension: Do we alienate our listeners who know about this person by saying, "Hold on, this is who Tupac is," or do we alienate the listener who doesn't know it by just sort of taking that for granted? That is explored in the piece. We were constantly balancing those two audiences. And wanting to speak to both, I think.*

—Sami Yenigun, supervising editor, *All Things Considered*

5 There's a *Parks and Recreation* episode where Leslie goes on her local NPR station, mentions the Bat Signal in passing, and the host goes, "The Bat Signal, for those listeners who might not know, refers to the children's character the Bat-Man, a strong gentleman who fights crime nocturnally." Yeah that…that was cold.

EXERCISE **Creating Your Sound Thread**

Now that you've got all of your audio pieces, it's time to weave them together into a single, spellbinding thread of sound.

— Revisit "Mapping Your Story" in chapter 7 (page 106). How would you answer those questions now?

— What points should be in your intro to really get folks to sit up and listen?

— What do you think would be the most compelling first bite of tape?

— Look back at the story structures you learned about in chapter 7—chronological, three-act, news feature, detective story—and consider if any fit this story. Who or what is the main character? What "beats" would reveal new info, twists, or surprises along the way? Plot out your sound thread, beat by beat, on a timeline of sorts.

— What do you want listeners to remember? Got it? Okay, then what's the final thought you will leave them with?

— Based on all this, should you change the title of your episode?

Script Tips

To get a general idea of the format for audio scripts, find a podcast online that's similar to yours and view their transcript (usually a button to click). They may not have every little detail of every sound, but they will be good guides.

Outlines for roundtables, interview shows, or review shows can be in a looser format, but you might still want to cue in intro/outro, music, clips, the order of topics or questions, and other features to guide you in assembling the pieces. Include who says what if you've got cohosts, panelists, or interviewees. Include timing and production directions for actualities and sounds to keep your podcast on track time-wise and to be clear about mixing instructions. For example:

<<Monks chanting: Post in the clear for :05, then fade under>>

or

[Monks chanting] (:05)

<<cross-fade . . . >>

HOST: That was the sound of the "Salve Regina," a medieval hymn sung at the end of the day by Catholic monastics.

As you listen to podcasts, keep your ears peeled for how they use fades, cross-fades, montages, and other tools (see "Fades, Cascades, Montages, and More," page 195) to tell the story.

Remember: Your audience can only "see" what they can hear. If it's clear what a sound is, no need to explain it. If there's any chance people might not instantly recognize it, you've got to explain:

<<purring, snuffling sounds>>

HOST: That's a happy baby having dinner. A baby lion, that is. We visited Rory—get it: Roar-y?—the first lion cub ever born at the Greentree Zoo, during mealtime with his mom, Maggie.

To hold interest, try to do something different about every sixty seconds—a change in topic, voice, scene, or sound; a pithy phrase or grabby idea; a surprise, new question, or twist.

Let your actualities do the talking. In the biz, this is called writing to tape: weaving the story together using the interviews, the sounds, the music as much as possible. You're not the center of the action—your actualities are. Unless something needs explaining, let your interviewees speak for themselves. You can set up the topic (what we call "setting the table"): "If you think there's only one way to make a fried egg, think again . . ." But if you preexplain the Egg Man's eccentric approach to sunny side up, it takes all the interest out of *his* explanation.[6]

Editing for Excellence

So, you've got your script, recorded any narration you need to do, and now you're listening to this whole thing to see just how well it all hangs together.

Editors do multiple editing passes, listening for things both editorial and technical, and not doing anything too radical, too soon. "I would listen at least twice or three times with different ears," says Sami Yenigun, referring to his time working as an editor at *Code Switch*.

Then there's what Liana Simstrom describes on *Invisibilia* (One Approach to Editing," page 190). That's . . . a lot. I get that. So for our purposes, let's just think in terms of a first edit, followed by a rewrite, then a second edit—but you should customize this for your podcast format, schedule, budget, and story needs. If your podcast's dialogue-driven, you may want to edit that first, then add in other sounds, clips, and music. But while you work on the dialogue, be thinking about how the sounds, clips, or music you've gathered could move your story forward and "speak" to your audience.

THE FIRST EDIT: START WITH YOUR EARS

We sometimes call this the "ear edit." You're listening like your audience—picking up first impressions, letting your ears tell you what works and what doesn't.

Have your script/outline handy, but don't follow along. What reads fine on paper might sound clunky on tape. Or your interviewee says something cogent on paper, but it's toneless on tape. Or someone closes a door at exactly the wrong moment. It's easy to miss these glitches with eyes glued to a script. Just glance down to mark where you hear problems.

"Typically, I do a rough editorial cut," Jessica Reedy says. "Things that I know for sure I want left out: things I think are boring, the ums, pauses. The main thing I've learned is if, in my gut, I'm starting to get bored and wanna go check my email or look at

One Approach to Editing: Long-Form Narrative

Liana Simstrom, podcast manager, *Invisibilia*

We usually go through three rounds of edits. The first is just an edit with your editor. Then you go to the first group edit, with just our small team. Then you do a second group edit, which is our team plus new listeners outside the team, preferably experts in the area we're exploring.

Then it goes to fact-checking and gets produced. It gets scored and sound designed while it's getting fact-checked. Then the scored version goes out as an audition link to a bigger group. Because there's no way for us to become experts in all of the things in the story, we try to make sure that we're putting it in front of people who know more about those things than we do. Then, there's usually maybe one more round of editing, sending it to a smaller group and asking people to limit feedback to just sound design—tweaks. Then it goes through a final pass by our host. Then it goes to our technical director and our engineers for mastering. And then we publish.

Part of what makes *Invisibilia* the show that it is, is that we have a highly collaborative editing process. It's part of the ethos of the show. It might represent how you would do something if you wanted to iterate many times and seek many, many people's input.

Twitter while I'm cutting the tape, then I know it probably should go." Sami Yenigun's focus: "Does this conversation make sense? Can I follow this as a listener? You're editing for clarity and making sure that the listener does not get lost in the chronology of what's happening."

Trust your ears. If something doesn't sound clear to *you*—and you're about a thousand times more familiar with this story than your audience will be—it's a sure bet you need to fix it. Some first-edit questions to ask:

— Does the intro grab interest without giving away the whole story?

— Is it clear in the first couple of minutes what's at stake or what the mystery or main interest is?

- If you're getting bored or lost, is it a script issue: sentences not punchy enough; too many adjectives, not enough verbs; dizzying stacks of facts and figures? Or a structural issue: no clear beginning, middle, or end; no rising tension or stakes; too much extraneous detail or unnecessary scenes; scene changes too subtle? Stronger signposting or transitions can help raise the ante on stakes. Cutting can accelerate pace. Figure out which facts and figures your audience has to know up front, which could come later—and which could be cut.

- Ask someone else to listen and tell you if *they* got bored or lost. If so, exactly where and why?

- Are any sounds confusing or hard to identify? You might need to describe them.

- Does the story pass the "truth, fairness, energy, naturalness, clarity" test (see page 185)?

- Were there parts that worked great? What makes them work?

- Is this running long? Time the scenes or segments. Is the editorial balance right: Do main storyline points get more setup/treatment than side trips?

> *We've become diligent about "signposting"—quick asides to reiterate and synopsize the important details, tensions, and characters as we move from beat to beat in a story. They also provide good places to anticipate questions or concerns listeners might have—and inject some of our voices into the story. "I can hear you rolling your eyes, listeners. Here is someone who did something, and you're like WTF because . . . "*
>
> —Gene Demby, cohost/correspondent, *Code Switch*

Listen for surprises. Stuff maybe you didn't even realize you had. The tremor of emotion or weariness in an interviewee's voice. A mischievous laugh. The little, savoring lip smack as the chef tastes his creation—one lip smack you *don't* want to edit out! The lilt of hope when a scientist describes a turning point in her research.

These audible "tells" that would pale if described in words are the emotional truths that make audio unique and magical.

Okay, grab your ear edit fix-it list and go revise before the second edit.

**THE SECOND EDIT: SHARP EARS, SHARP EYES...
SHARP KNIFE**

This time, follow along more on your script and make line edits—but keep your ears peeled to confirm your suspicions. Some questions to ask now:

— Is the writing skating into cliché, or are there grammatical errors? You want your script to sound the way you talk, but not have cringe-worthy metaphors or grammar mistakes that undermine your credibility.

— Are there flubs or muddy audio needing retracking (rerecording)? Set up those sections beforehand; then you (and your cohosts) can listen and match how it was said so it doesn't sound obviously retracked—but say it correctly this time around.

— Will your audience know what things mean? For example, in a podcast about musical theater, lingo like dance captain...swing...blackout? Or, in a cooking show: deglaze the pan...julienne the carrots...make a roux? Last chance to add explanations.

— Are there twists, turns, and surprises? Always be thinking of ways to perk up the audience's ears, even if it's just a change in your tone, a funny aside, or a guest's unexpected chuckle. Sometimes adding a rhythm sound under an informative-but-sort-of-boring interview bite can keep momentum going and bridge us to the place where we learn why this info is important.

— If you're using music, are you using it in ways that aren't obvious, but to slow or accelerate the pace of the story or to highlight emotional nuances?

— Does every scene and sound reveal something?

One Approach to Editing: The Interview Show

Sami Yenigun, of his time as a producer on *What's Good with Stretch & Bobbito*

We first note big-picture stuff: "This interview really takes off around fifteen minutes in; here's too much chitchat about what they had for lunch in the first ten minutes." Or: "We start talking about this person's new album before we even understand what their old work sounded like. So we need to shift things." Then I listen for the moments that made my head turn; my ears perk up. Then I go back and try to cut it into a conversation that makes sense. The editor takes a listen to that conversation. I make any fixes that the editor has. Then we publish.

Now's when you get ruthless about cutting—because, as Sam Sanders tactfully points out, "The only person wanting to hang onto every word you say is your mother"—but not *so* ruthless that the story goes dead on you.

Brutal objectivity isn't easy. But you're wearing your tough-love hat now. We at NPR have an assist: the NPR One app, which lets us see precisely, painfully, where listeners drop off our beloved podcasts. "For episodes where I left something in that I wasn't sure of, I would sometimes look on NPR One and see a dramatic drop-off," Jessica says. And she'd realize: "I should have ended it two-and-a-half minutes sooner." You, too, can have such teachable moments, as Jessica notes: "Apple does have analytics that show you this now."

You might discover you like the challenge of picking up a second here; two seconds there; whittling your podcast down to a razor edge with cuts so seamless that eventually even you forget it didn't just come out that way the first time. There are all kinds of cool tricks. "Sometimes you can add a breath or an 'um' as a way to transition to a new point," Jessica says. Another trick: "Sometimes when I know I'm gonna make a lot of transitions between people's points, at the end of the taping, I'll have the panelists all record a neutral 'yeah' to drop in to sound naturalistic when I have to edit out a back-and-forth where they get to the point thirty seconds later, and I want to shorten that, but I need an acknowledgment in order to do that."

Notes from the Pros: On Cutting with Head and Heart

Kelly McEvers, host, *Embedded*

When we first started *Embedded*, we were doing, like, fifty-minute episodes. There's no way those episodes should have been that long. One thing that's great/dangerous about podcasts is that they can be whatever length. We err on the side of cutting the crap out of everything. I think that'd be one of my biggest pieces of advice: Whatever you think sounds good, cut it by another 20 percent to 40 percent. You can fall in love with your tape. Under more intense interrogation, it can—often should—fall away. It's painful. But it is really good advice.

Jessica Reedy, producer, *Pop Culture Happy Hour*

When I was an intern at *All Things Considered*, I'd do practice cuts on the two-ways[7] I booked. The producer who did the real cut was kind enough to listen to it and give me feedback. Theo Balcomb was great about listening to my stuff. I remember a two-way about cooking. My cut saved all the practical steps. And she's like, "No, you did this wrong. You kept all the boring stuff and not the evocative, 'Oh, it smells so good in the kitchen'—the interesting stuff." That really stuck with me.

7 A conversation between two people, often host/interviewee.

Fact-Checking: The Step You'll Be Tempted to Skip

Fact-checking may happen at various points in a podcast's production process. Just make sure it happens. For important legal reasons (see chapter 8). But also because having credibility with your audience is crucial.

If you aren't sure you understand what an interviewee meant, don't write what you think or guess. Ask and get clear. Think before you use phrases like "the only," "the first," "the largest."[8] They just up your chances of being proven wrong. Don't be afraid to politely ask your interviewees how they came by their info—not because you assume they're untruthful but because it's easy for facts to get unintentionally changed in transmission. Especially don't assume something's true because the internet said so. Double- and triple-check. That includes verifying spellings of names, titles, and business and school names. Get pronunciations right.[9] Verify dates. Test web addresses and phone numbers. And here's a tip: Don't ask someone's age; ask for their birthday (in case they have a birthday before you publish). Once again, our *NPR Ethics Handbook* can help (see Resources, page 266)—especially the "Accuracy" section.

> 8 Superlatives are sexy, and they do add drama in the short term, but they're a lazy way to do it. Plus, they just plant a flag on your episode that attracts the internet's teeming throngs of "Well, actually. . . ." If you can convey why something's important without resorting to a simple superlative, do it.

> 9 Pro tip: Search for celebrities by name along with the word "*junket*". You'll find video of them doing press for one of their projects where they're helpfully instructing one of the seventy-eight journalists they've talked to that day about how to pronounce their name.

Editing gets easier the more you do it—and the more you do your podcast. "As everybody gets more experienced and more in tune

---

Fades, Cascades, Montages, and More

Want to set a mood under a vocal track? Try a bed. Jump from one point to another without a hokey transition? Try a button. Show a dramatic contrast? Go for a butt cut. Showcase three or four great, short blurts from interviewees showing different angles on the same topic? Make a cascade or waterfall.

These are just a few of the techniques you'll learn for "getting into and out of tape" as you sharpen your editing chops.

For these and other terms, see this book's glossary (page 262), which is based on the excellent NPR Training guide by Alison MacAdam entitled " 'Butt Cut What?' A Glossary of Audio Production Terms and Definitions." Some—like fade, in the clear, two-way—have already been introduced. Others are new. Enjoy learning the lingo—and then apply it to your podcast!

with what the show really is, you have less fixing to do," Jessica Reedy says.

Don't get disheartened if you keep hitting speed bumps. "I've heard many audio people say this so it's a bit of a cliché, but it's still true. Every story is a new puzzle," says *Invisibilia*'s Yowei Shaw. "If you're having a tough time with a particular episode, just know that is the same experience we are all having as we're making podcasts. Every story has its own particular set of annoying holes and jagged edges, and it's just a matter of creatively rising to the challenge. Podcasting and, possibly, all creative work is about problem-solving."

It can help to remember that your product isn't about you. As Kelly McEvers says, it's about delivering a meaningful experience to your audience as best you can: "I'm not trying to say, 'Look at me.' I'm trying to say, 'Stand in my shoes and look at this.'"

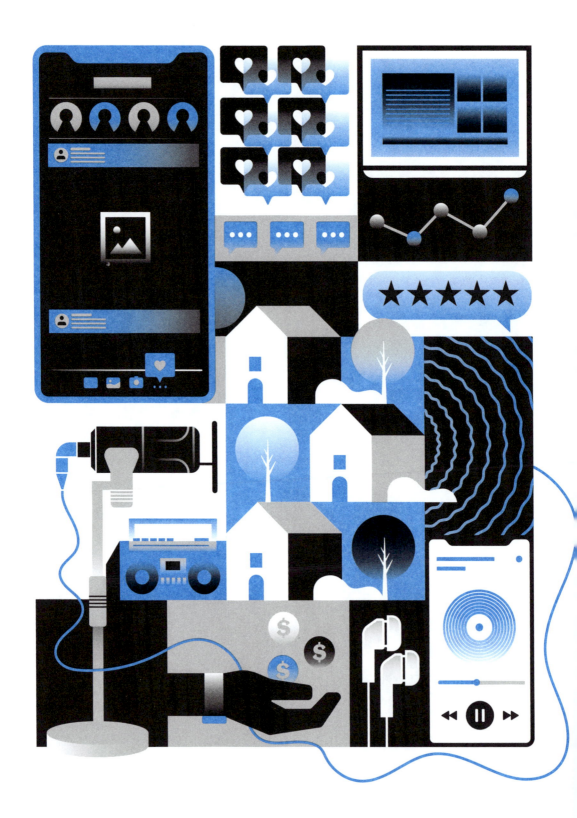

SHARE

Your Podcast Goes Public

You did it! You've conceived of, planned, and created a podcast. Now, how do you get it to others besides yourself and your cocreators? This final part drills down on everything from how to run a listening session to building your platform to spreading word about your podcast and attracting new (maybe paying?!) listeners to your work.

Part 4 dives into the run-up to publication—from writing show notes (a big deal; it'll help your promo efforts hugely) to prepping the files to pulling together your logo and your social media campaign. It provides a rundown of features and issues to consider when looking for a hosting service. It covers options for growing your podcast and your platform, including ways to turn your hard work into income.

It includes the best baseline practices, questions, and considerations, and it points you toward ways to learn more. And this is all done—promise!—without your having to sit through a single meeting about "analytics in the audio space"[1] (which produce firm, clear guidelines...that change a few weeks later).

[1] Okay, I said I wouldn't use this term, and I used it. Yes. Fine. But only three times. *Three times!* In a book about podcasting. I'll bet you've forgotten the others by now, anyway. So then, do they truly count? Hmmm?

CHAPTER 13

Me, My Platform, and I

You know those two guests who are crashing on the couches in your brain's spare room? The ones who have long overstayed their welcome?

We're talking about FOM (fear of marketing) and their dirtbag friend DOM (dislike of marketing). We bet you're tired of their inane chatter:

FOM: I'm not good at this. There's so much to *do*. It's over-*whelming*! Wah wah *wah*.

DOM: All that hard sell, the focus on me, me, me. It's just not ME! Blah blah *blah*.

Time for them to move on. You're out of coffee, OJ, fresh towels, and patience. Out!!

Here's the thing. Marketing's nothing more and nothing less than sharing your genuine excitement about something genuinely worth being excited about. You've worked hard on your podcast. You have something of quality to offer. Your enthusiasm is real. Wouldn't you want to tell your friends about something you think they might enjoy?

The marketing I'm talking about is rooted in that realness. Yes, there are strategies and tactics—which are described here and in the next chapters.[1] But it's basically about sharing information geared to the other person's interests or needs and suggesting, "How about giving this a try?"

Platform: What Is It, Anyway?

The term *platform* gets thrown around a lot. It's just a jargony way of describing someone's public presence, profile, or outreach. Think of it like an actual platform—with planks made of different

1 News flash for the DOMs and FOMs who refuse to pack their bags and move on, oblivious to your polite-yet-increasingly-pointed hints: This marketing stuff's not as forbidding as it may appear. Just wade in and pick it up, bit by bit. Make an ongoing project of reading, learning, and talking to people about marketing in general and about entrepreneur and podcast marketing in particular. Ask what others do to spread the word about their work—podcast or anything else. You might be able to adapt it to your needs. It's a whole new way to be creative.

components. These used to be limited to TV, radio, print (newspapers/magazines/journals/newsletters), and film, but the internet has rapidly expanded the options. Now, there are internet-unique platforms like social media (Facebook, Twitter, Instagram, Pinterest, TikTok, and others), websites and blogs, and video platforms such as YouTube.

Which ones might be part of your platform? Any or all. Only wrong answer: none.

 My model of promotion and marketing leaned pretty heavily on social media for a few reasons:

1. *It was free. And that very much fit my budget.*

2. *It gave my cohost, Josiah Branaman, and me a space to promote the podcast without clogging up our personal social media with podcast links—which would only stand to annoy our friends and family.*

3. *It gave us a central location to direct people who did want to engage with our content.*

—J. C. Howard, producer, *TED Radio Hour* and *How I Built This with Guy Raz*

Your Platform: Personal, But Not Personal

You may not consider yourself a marketer, but you act like one all the time. When you meet new people, you say who you are, give them an idea about what you do, take an interest in what they're up to,[2] and in general try politely to get to know folks and let them know a little of what you're about. You're making a positive impression on others. That's good marketing in a nutshell. It's about building trust.[3]

That trust increases, let's hope, each time you make contact. And at some point—we know not when—there's a tipping point where the other person likes you enough to do something on your behalf. Get coffee with you. Invite you over for a cookout. Share a job lead. They're willing to spend time, energy, and maybe even money on you.

Professional engagement is personal connecting writ large. The internet amplifies it with a mega-megaphone. Instead of meeting for coffee or being a guest at someone's cookout, you're a guest in their email inbox, on their social media, or in their ears, and they eventually decide it's worth their time and effort to check out your podcast. Your

2 Or, you know, *fake* an interest in what they're up to. Works either way!

3 I know, I know, suddenly this is sounding like Norman Vincent Peale all up in here. But keep reading, I'm going somewhere with this.

hope? That you leave them saying, "I liked that person's newsletter/blog post/podcast. I'd like to know more/read more/listen more."[4]

In our social life we don't expect big commitments right away.[5] So don't expect big commitments right away when trying to engage people with your podcast, blog, social platforms, or other products or services. Maybe they "like" one of your social media posts. Maybe they opt in to get emails from you. Maybe (*woo!*) they download your podcast. Maybe *maybe* (*woo X2!!*) they decide to follow it. All good, all eaded in the right direction.

Want to do it smartly? Manners matter. Be welcoming. Be nice. Say please and thank you. Don't spend too long bending their ear, their attention span, or their patience. No overshares. No TMI. No humblebrags. Ask about them, don't yak about you.

The Public You is basically the Personal You. With your shirt tucked in.

Marketing You Is All About ... Not You

Make marketing about being helpful to others, and it puts a whole new spin on your spin. You're not selling yourself or your stuff. You're trying to help someone see how what you provide might be helpful or interesting to them (yup, those pain and pleasure points you pondered in chapter 2). This has a ripple effect on everything— your mind-set, what you do, what you say, and how you say it. Here are some basic guidelines:

— **Talk their talk.** From your website to your e-blasts to your episode descriptions, talk like your target audience. Not to the point of being someone you're not. But study what they're reading and how they discuss your topic on social media. They'll be more comfortable if you speak to them in familiar language.

— **It's not about what you do, but what your audience needs.** How can your podcast help? Alternatively, if you're podcasting to interest people in your products or services, how can your offerings help?

— **Do stuff for people.** As Sara Horowitz writes in *The Freelancer's Bible:* "Think give, not get." Contribute to the community. Spend time on the platforms related to your subject. Then start becoming a contributing member. Participate[6] in comments threads. "Like" posts. Repost or

4 In olden-timey days, you'd hand your calling card to the butler, who'd deliver it on a silver platter to the person you were visiting. Nowadays, you just *bamf* right into their inbox. Much more efficient, though the silver platter industry is cratering.

5 I'm speaking in generalities here that do not apply to, for example, this one dude in the nineties who, on our *second date*, invited himself to my family's Thanksgiving like I was Charlie Brown and he was Peppermint Freaking Patty.

6 *Participate*. Not dominate. Mark the difference. Many don't.

retweet stuff you like that other people are doing, tagging them so they're looped in. In the process you'll get on the hosts' radar, gain credibility from your knowledgeable contributions, and become more influential. As a result, others will be more likely to help you get word out about your podcast—recommending it, inviting you to guest-post on their blog, or even inviting you to guest-host (hey, you can dream).

— **Have freebies.** That might just be your podcast (for now, or maybe forever—if you just have a message you want to get out, or if your goal is to build relationships with potential clients). Or once you've got a following, maybe make recent episodes free, but restrict your back catalog for paying subscribers (for more on paid versus free, see chapter 16). Or you might "tease" some of the podcast content in a blog post with a couple of takeaways from your interview with the famous Mac-and-Cheese Mama about her secrets for making *the* most comforting comfort foods—and include a link where they can download the complete episode. (Do they want the actual recipes? Those are in her book, which you mention in the podcast—and include a link in your show notes.)

— **One dang thing at a time.** Ever sent an email where you asked three questions and people answered maybe one? Folks are busy. Don't expect them to catch every fine nuance of your prose. Social media is, well, "social." Blurt-like. In e-blasts or other communications, keep it short, clear, concise, with just one idea or request.

— **More conversation, less promotion.** Don't be one of those people who only calls when they want something: You only post on social media to plug your episodes, or you only email to ask people to follow you or sign up for whatever. Be someone who asks questions and invites conversations about the subject of your podcast and hosts a space where info or fun, interesting stuff gets exchanged. Make your platform a place where it's appealing to hang out. That's how you build "stickiness" (when people visit and stay a while—which helps your visibility in internet search). Which builds trust. Which builds loyalty. Which builds an audience.

— **Start an email list.** If you've got good info to share related to your podcast topic (not just earnest exhortations to check it out!), build an email list. Invite people to sign up by asking if they'd like to hear from you with news and info about this subject. It's superimportant to make sure you get their permission. And always include an "unsubscribe" or "unfollow" option. Add a sign-up link in your email signature, on your website, and in your show notes. In your podcast outro, invite listeners to head over to your website and sign up. People who agree to be on your list are like beautiful fish in your home tank versus fish randomly swimming by in your social media streams. Don't overfeed them or flood the tank with constant selling or verbiage. It's a smart way to be in contact with a core group you know is interested in your topic and your work.

What if you've only got time for a blog *or* an email newsletter? Do the newsletter—it's a direct conversation with people who want to be there.[7] Be sure to announce new episodes to your email list— not just "Hey! New episode here!" with a link, but some enticing tidbits about what you think they'd find interesting about it. It's the difference between banging the dinner gong and yelling, "Come and get it!" and putting a couple of fragrant, fresh-baked pies on a picnic table with a nice, big jug of iced tea. *Yeah.*

When I write the *PCHH* newsletter, I try to channel the tone of the show—loose, conversational, breezy—while keeping in mind that at its core, *PCHH* is a recommendation engine. That means studding the newsletter with links, and not only to the current "What's Making Us Happy This Week" items. I also link to pieces we've written, interesting articles I've come across, a funny Twitter account, and maybe a meme that hasn't gotten beaten to death yet. There's a reason I do that, beyond my own indefatigable selfless- ness. I'm trying to build a relationship.

The thing about newsletters is: The number of subscribers doesn't tell you how many people are actually reading it. Neither— even though many continue to tout it—does the "open rate" because many email programs automatically "open" newsletters. Instead, pay attention to things like how many people click on the links you include (and which ones!), and how long they stay on your site. That's what matters—that's engagement.

7 Also, it's not 2011 anymore.

We have a newsletter that has about fifty-thousand subscribers, and we do an issue, basically, of the newsletter to correspond with every episode. That usually has more details about what's in the episode, where they can find more information, and the original artwork that we commission for every episode.

—Liana Simstrom, podcast manager, *Invisibilia*

Deciding Where to Put Your Energy

When choosing social media platforms/spaces, go where your target market is. If they're not on Pinterest in large numbers, you don't need to be, either. But if they are, then why aren't you?

Start small and grow. See what's doable. How much time do your efforts take? Are they actually growing your audience? Better to scale up by degrees than to spread yourself too thin and have to scale back.[8]

EXERCISE **Where Are They, and What Do They Care About?**

Remember the exercise in chapter 2, "Where Does Your Audience Hang Out?" (page 26). That asked you to list the media your podcast's target audience is likely consuming in order to come up with a kind of 3D portrait of them. Revisit and expand that now (or hey, do it for the first time!) to help see your listeners' interests and consumption habits from every angle you can. Make a list of the following:

— The magazines, newspapers, and books they're reading

— The websites and blogs they're visiting

— The social media they use the most

— The podcasts they're listening to

— The platforms they use to stream or download content (books, music, news, you name it)

The online versions of these magazines and newspapers have comments threads to explore as audience research. The authors of the books they're reading are on social media, which can yield useful insight as well. (Plus maybe those authors would be good guests on your podcast?)

8 Because you know how impressed *you* are when you click on someone's social media to learn more about them—only to find that their last post was...six months ago.

Learn what people are worried about, wondering about, working on, clicking on, debating, liking, laughing about. Make a list. Can you angle your efforts toward those pleasure and pain points? Find ways for you and your content to join in?

Knowing what your audience wants and cares about, where they "live" online, and what holds their attention is important because you want to be not just a player, but a stayer. You want to be known for worthwhile conversation, solid substance, lots of fun—a positive, recognizable presence around your topic, whatever that may be. That's how you develop a core following that's more likely to follow your podcast.

Why a Website?

In a podcast directory, you're one among millions. On your website? You're number one. It's *your* house. Built and decorated your way. It might be a simple, clear-and-attractive page with info about you, your podcast, why it's worth listening to, where people can download it, and how to contact you, with your social media buttons. Or it could be a house you add onto as you grow. Use it to point people toward where they can find your podcast. Post your show notes and transcripts (see chapter 14). Set up a discussion group. Include tabs for products, services, or merchandise, including stuff you might develop out of your podcast (books, T-shirts, mugs). Have a way for people to contact you directly, to sign up for your mailing list for news and updates, or to donate (through PayPal or other online platforms).

On a website, you're in control of the story. You get to say what your podcast is, what makes it special, who created it, what others have said about it, and anything else we should know. That's super-important because you want people reviewing your podcast to have a place where they can look you up and find that story. Potential sponsors, too. Someone who first "meets" you on social media might check out your website and be intrigued enough by your witty and informative show notes to try your podcast. Someone who downloads your podcast might head to your website for the show notes or other goodies you mentioned in your outro. That's how your website and your podcast can each attract traffic, cross-pollinate each other, and deepen your connection with your audience. "[Our] podcast relied heavily on the personalities and opinions of my cohost and myself," says J. C. Howard of his start-up podcast. "So if I were giving my former self advice, I'd suggest to start a website. Maybe include pictures of myself and my cohost, have a few separate or joint blog posts, some form of bonus content people weren't getting somewhere else. Though my former self was kind of a know-it-all, so who knows if he'd listen."

Having a web presence where there's regular activity—where you post updates and content about your podcast as episodes launch—helps build community among existing listeners, but it also helps new listeners discover you online. More on that in chapter 14.

Your podcast hosting service might offer a website for your podcast. But for full control over the features, the ability to build it out as much as you want, and to make sure it'll still be there should the host go the way of the internet dodo, your own site is the way to go.

Can you host your podcast itself on your website? Well, maybe. But audio files are large, and as you publish more episodes and get more downloads (let's hope!), the load can exceed what web hosts will support, or you might end up having to upgrade. More likely, you'll have a podcast host, and then embed a player on your website.

EXERCISE Knowing and Growing Niche Communities
Chapter 2 helped you identify your main audience, the people in the middle of your target. But don't forget about secondary, tertiary, or niche audiences, especially those working in fields related to your podcast, and that special community you are now part of: fellow podcasters. These potential listeners could be crucial to spreading word about your podcast.

1   Given the topics your podcast covers, what professionals and practitioners are connected with these subjects? Who would be helpful for you to get to know and network with—as potential experts to approach for interviews and/or as a potential audience?
2   Now, where to find them? What books, magazines, journals, and blogs are they reading? Here again: What discussion groups are they in? Where do they hang out and converse on social media? What conventions are they attending?
3   Make a list of podcasters whose work you admire or who are working on subjects related to yours. For instance, say you're podcasting about organizing and decluttering, then identify existing podcasters doing interior decorating; if you're doing nature or wildlife, seek podcasters doing camping and hiking.

Pick all types, from scrappy-but-not-crappy start-ups to established veterans and big names.

These are podcasters to have on your radar. If their work is good quality and they're building a following, what are they doing to be successful? Are there things you can learn from them about building a better podcast? About smart ways to promote?

Keep track of what they're up to, follow them on social media, share their posts, and comment supportively on their work. You could even contact them and write a fan letter to tell them how much you enjoy their podcast. Be sure to thank them for any help or insights offered and look for ways to return the favor.

You never know where these relationships might lead—at the very least a nodding acquaintance in social media that might get their followers curious about your work. But if you hit it off, maybe you'll find yourself guest-hosting or interviewing, or swapping ads (see chapter 16). Even collaborating on special episodes, teaching a webinar together, or hosting a live event.

Podcaster and Proud

Once you're ready to fully take on this podcasting thing, then it's time to start integrating your role as a podcaster into your life. Have business cards made up that include your podcast logo.[9] Beef up your email signature with a line and a link (for extra credit, update it with each new episode: "NEW! Latest podcast: [link]"). Use that one-liner you came up with about your podcast when you meet new people and they ask what you're up to.

Don't be afraid to get your lanyard on: Talk to other podcasters about groups to join and events you might attend. You'll be staying current in the industry (which is changing faster than you can say, "Wait—that's a whole thing, now? Since when?") while growing your podcasting network—a helpful hive mind of nerdy audiophilic souls. In the run-up to the event, look at the event's social media and the speakers', too. Post about event happenings with the event hashtag and speakers' handles. It's a way to share podcasting info and enthusiasm and make industry connections. Others might appreciate your support and share your posts.

Become a Hub

Getting people interested in your podcast is, obviously, a major goal. That's what's in it for *you*. But flip the camera and focus on

9 Yes! Still! Trust me. Oh sure, *you're* extremely online, but not everyone you're trying to reach will be.

what's in it for your audience, as you've been doing throughout this book, and you'll find a more effective way to roll.

If you're doing nonfiction podcasting, whether it's humor, how-to, or high-level thought leadership, you have an opportunity to become a hub for quality content in your chosen niche. Make your platform and your promotion about providing something people can trust and benefit from. Be someone who learns about these topics and shares news, articles, ideas, and stuff worth knowing. In the process, you'll connect with others who share those interests and are putting out good content, too. And you'll be connecting with people who want to receive it.[10] All of that can come full circle to help you and your podcast. That's the quid pro quo[11] of conversation and connection that the internet lets us achieve across the globe. You want your website, your social media, your "spaces" online to be a welcoming hub where there's good conversation going on.

When you approach your platform and promotion with a hub mind-set, you've actually got a shot at not only having a successful podcast but using it to make a contribution.

I get it—you're a humble, self-effacing soul, and the idea of tooting your own horn makes you think of slick salesmen in polyester suits and pinky rings who do that finger-guns thing. Or tech-bros in their trade-show lanyards, hawking their services at passersby on the exhibition floor. That's why I hope this chapter makes the process of building and marketing your platform less intimidating. More than anything, it's about being willing to persist. Getting traction takes time. You might publish episodes for half a year or so before you start seeing real improvement in audience numbers. Be patient. Stick with your marketing efforts and production values. Keep refining your skills and putting your best pod out there. Most of all, stay true to your purpose for podcasting, and think of marketing as the energy that will put this shining thing you love out into the world.

10 Your podcast will attract people who share your taste, so they'll come to trust your recommendations. Keep that in mind, and don't steer them wrong. One of my favorite podcasts has a host who's kinda high-minded (read: snooty), and when they read ad copy for like a frozen-dinner company or whatever, I can hear their teeth gnashing.

11 Podcast like a quid *pro* quo, not a quid *amateur* quo.

The most important thing about launching a great podcast is not having the right microphone, or the right training or the right "voice." Yes, those things are important. But the real question, and it is the same question you must ask yourself if you want to be a novelist or a painter or any kind of artist: Do you actually have something to say? *Ultimately, art is not about technique and it is not about the ego of the artist; it's about passion and authenticity. If you are willing to walk over broken glass to say what you have to say, because it is* that *important and original, chances are, people will listen.*

—Shankar Vedantam, who developed *Hidden Brain* at NPR

CHAPTER 14

Countdown to Launch

It's getting real, now. Your podcast is a thing—okay, a digital thing, a mind-bogglingly unique mashup of 0s and 1s—but a *thing* that didn't exist before. It's time to plan its debut.

This chapter walks you through key checkpoints—some for the launch of your brand-new podcast (that is, podcast logo, podcast description) and some for each episode in your podcast's hopefully long life (as in, episode description, transcription, show notes). Even if you decide not to pursue some ideas, they'll be on your radar for the future.

In other words, this covers the content-prep side to launch. But be aware there is also a tech-prep side that involves prepping your files and setting up your distribution process, so you can actually publish your podcast. That stuff merits a chapter of its own, so check out chapter 15 to get your distro on. For more ways to promote and grow your podcast, see chapter 16.

Give yourself a couple of months for the launch phase, breaking it into manageable steps—these aren't processes you want to rush through, especially at the beginning.

Quality First (and a Tough Question)

Here's the tough question: Is this podcast *the one*? Meaning: Knowing what you now know about making podcasts, do you feel this piece is strong enough to share in the big world?

Now's when some honest, informed feedback comes in handy. Enter the listening session.

HOW A LISTENING SESSION WORKS

At NPR, we gather a formal focus group to react to our content. Yours doesn't have to be über-formal; it just has to encourage truthful-but-friendly feedback. Here are the guidelines we at NPR suggest:

1   **Make it fun.** Invite your podcasting peers. Order pizza—and get the feedback done before the fourth bottle of wine gets opened. If people are far-flung, do it over an internet conference line, and everyone slurp on-screen.

2   **Encourage honesty, clarity, and kindness.** Ask people to go deeper than "I liked it/didn't like it." Request specifics about what people did or didn't respond to and why. Talk storytelling, editing, audio quality. You can even stop the tape at certain points and ask what people think will happen, or what's interesting, confusing, or missing.

3   **Ask how it makes people *feel*.** What's their takeaway thought, insight, memory, emotion? Is it what you hoped and intended?

Aaaand...if people *don't* give you the takeaways you'd hoped for and intended, what then? Well, take a breath, sit yourself down, and have a think. Is it fixable? Or are there production-quality or story issues that go too deep for fixability, at least until you get a bit more podcasting experience? That is, you need to decide whether to put in the time and effort to fix this episode or whether to consider this your "practice pod," don't publish it, and try again with a new, maybe less complex topic.

If "move on" is the answer, take heart. So what if this was your practice pod? As *Invisibilia*'s Yowei Shaw says, sometimes it's about "making a lot of bad things first and getting it out of your system, making sure to listen critically to your work, and seeking out other people's constructive feedback." "The key is to keep experimenting," says *Throughline*'s Rund Abdelfatah. "Let the things that don't work guide you to the things that *do* work. We are all learning as we go. That's half the fun of it!"

If you decide to try revising and fixing, remember: Perfect is the enemy of...whatever that phrase is. It's definitely the enemy of publication. Creators rarely consider their work *done*. There's always something you'd do differently. Here again, feedback can help: Are most of your listeners running into problems with major issues like story arc (or the lack thereof), confusion over basic points, or not getting most of the takeaways you thought were clear? No matter how eager you are to publish, these are issues to fix, since they mean the execution or the premise aren't landing with listeners. But if the feedback is more nitpicky—say, quibbles over a joke, or an ambi sound, or the length of an interview—don't let perfectionism slow your momentum.[1]

 There is no such thing as a perfect episode.

—Sam Sanders, correspondent/host, *It's Been a Minute with Sam Sanders*

PREP YOUR MATERIALS FOR LAUNCH

After weighing the feedback and making any changes, ask yourself: Are you still proud and excited to share this podcast with the world? If so . . . let's go! First, revisit the marketing target you drew (see "Exercise: Target Audience," page 22). Picture the person in the bull's-eye. Average age? Likes/dislikes? Interests? Yearnings? Worries? Wonderings? How does your podcast fit into their life? How would you describe it to them to pique their interest? Keep this image in mind as you prep your materials for launching and pitching your podcast.

Revisit Your Intro and Outro

This is your last chance to make sure your intro and outro capture and keep ears—see chapter 7 for ideas. Listen to popular podcasts. Notice what they do to (a) identify their "brand" and grab your interest up front (podcast name, host name, one-liner), and (b) hold your interest in the outro: inviting you to sample tasty extras on their website, send input for a future episode, review the show, share it, follow it, and more. *Always* thank those who helped—and the audience for listening.

Some podcasts start and end every episode exactly the same way—the same script, music, and so on. Many listeners value this consistency; it works on a subliminal level to reassure them that they know what's coming. You may decide, however, to keep things looser, to reward listeners who don't hit the fifteen-second Skip button when your intro starts.

Mostly, though? Keep it pithy.

1 The one and only reason you definitely *should* delay is if you have *any* question about *any* fact. If you can't verify something, do *not* put your podcast out in the world. Take the time to get it right.

Think About Ad Space from the Get-Go

Maybe it's hard to imagine your podcast being popular enough to attract advertisers or sponsors. Or maybe that's not your goal. To both, I say: You never know.

Paid ads can run at the beginning, middle, or end of a podcast. If your podcast really makes it, you might go back and insert ads in previous episodes[2]—*if* you've set them up so you can later edit out some content and drop in the ad. The stuff you edit out might be your next-episode promo, a promo of your business services, or ad swaps (see chapter 16). Just something to think about now, so you have the option to do this down the line.

2 The industry jargon for this is "dynamic marketing," which some hosting services offer.

Get All Legalities in Order

If you haven't already checked to see if a podcast of the same name already exists, the name has been trademarked, or if your podcast might be confused with another podcast, do it *now* before launching the first episode. Also, confirm that you have any needed clearances or releases from interviewees, for music, or for anything used to create your show logo, and that you are including the required credits. Don't know what I'm talking about? Go read chapter 8.

Set Up Your Pipeline Before Launch

Have several episodes done before you publish your first one. "Done" means edited and uploaded for distribution. Why not publish the first episode the very second it's ready?

Because look. The Podcast Muse doesn't just swoop down and smack your head with her glittery wand, filling it with fascinating episode ideas that are then lovingly assembled by elves.[3]

3 Sole exceptions: podcasts about fudge cookies, labor conditions in toy workshops, and race relations in Middle Earth.

Setting up your pipeline before launch gives you time to get new episodes going, while still publishing on a regular schedule. It's time to lay claim to being an audio maker. Like any creative process, podcasting's a blend of staying loose *and* being disciplined: loose so ideas can flow; disciplined so you can drop into that groove fast and easy, with a system for developing ideas to see if they're episode-worthy.

Wait to launch until that development system is ready: So, reach back to that Idea Bank we talked about in chapter 4. Grab your calendar and schedule brainstorming sessions. Chart a development process for promising ideas. These creative habits feed your podcast pipeline.

Create Grabby Episode Titles

When you're looking for a new podcast to listen to, it's the episode title that nabs your attention, right? Now you're the nabber, not the nabbee. You want your title to grab the eyeballs of someone in the hypnotic grip of scrolling on their device—flipflipflipflipflip—and convince them your podcast's worth clicking on.

Convince them fast. As Colin Dwyer and Stephanie Federico wrote in an NPR Training article: "Pretend an elevator door is shutting and you want to tell someone on the other side about a story."

Without being too cryptic ("Huh?"), too cute ("Yuk"), or too sensational ("Riiiight"), you want to activate an emotion. Touch a pain point (concern, questions, needing help) or a pleasure point (humor, de-stressing, entertainment). Spark curiosity (demystify something; offer a different, new, or helpful view; present a contrarian idea, an enticement, a surprise). Make sure it matches the tone of your episode.

Brainstorm with or bounce your ideas off of friends or podcasting buddies. What grabs their attention? Why?

Here are my analyses of some NPR podcast titles:

Life Kit, "Anxious Thoughts? 5 Tips to Help You Sleep": This hits a pain point and offers help.

Short Wave, "What Would It Be Like to Fall into a Black Hole?": This piques curiosity about something you'd think would be impossible to know.

Alt.Latino, "The Meteoric Rise of Latin Urban Explained": This demystifies a phenomenon, and the word *meteoric* makes us feel we shouldn't *not* know about this.

Pop Culture Happy Hour, "Huzzah! We're Russian to Finish *The Great*": This signposts what's being reviewed and the takeaway—with a garnish of *PCHH*'s signature personality.[4]

Make sure you date your episodes. Most episodes are also numbered, as some directories require it. Definitely number them if you're running a series that people need to hear sequentially for it to make sense.

4 Every week, *PCHH* producers Jess or Mike send a Slack message asking for possible show titles, and we (me, mostly) send a slew of terrible, punny heads. For Disney's *Onward*, about a pair of elf brothers working through grief, I sent: "We Get Elf-Involved with *Onward*"; "Elf-Help"; "Our Bodies, Our Elves"; "Risks of Elf-Harm"; "What's It All About, Elfy?"; "Get Over Your Elf"; "The Lord Helps Those Who Help Them Elves"; "Hi, Fantasy!"; "Heal, Thy Elf"; "Half an Elf Is Better Than None" and "Hail, the Van-Quishing Hero!" They picked...none of the above and went with "*Onward* Explores a Sibling Riv-Elf-Ry,' which I think is even sweatier than any of mine, but whaddyagonnado.

Draft Your Podcast and Episode Descriptions

Time to write your podcast and episode descriptions. Here's your chance to speak directly to your audience about why it's worth their time to listen. Try these exercises to get rolling.

EXERCISE Your Podcast Description

1   Read each podcast description below and consider these questions:

—   What does each description "promise"?

—   What emotional experience will listeners have?

—   What will they learn, discover, or enjoy?

—   Each description has its own tone or vibe. Describe that.

—   What words or phrases accomplish these things? Highlight or circle them.

> *Life Kit*: "Everyone needs a little help being a human. From sleep to saving money to parenting and more, we talk to the experts to get the best advice out there. *Life Kit* is here to help you get it together." [Gets right to the point—we're here to help; look to us to provide navigation through the stormy seas of modern life. Places the listener's needs front and center, from the jump.]
>
> *Short Wave*: "New discoveries, everyday mysteries, and the science behind the headlines — all in about 10 minutes, every weekday. It's science for everyone, using a lot of creativity and a little humor. Join host Maddie Sofia for science on a different wavelength." ["Everyday mysteries" is the *perfect* phrase to describe what *Short Wave* does—reveals the science that's always furiously paddling its feet below the surface of the water of the world.]
>
> *Alt.Latino*: "*Alt.Latino* is a spotlight on the world of Latinx arts and culture through music, stories, and conversation." [Admirably concise—both a mission statement and an invitation, which is the whole idea.]
>
> *Pop Culture Happy Hour*: "*Pop Culture Happy Hour* is a fun and freewheeling chat about the latest movies, television, books, and music." [The word *chat* is doing a lot of heavy lifting

here—it's a nice, economical way to say "roundtable discussion." "Fun and freewheeling" makes a promise that we strive to keep every episode—but it also signposts what to expect in the tone of the show.]

2   Go back to the one-liner you drafted in chapter 2 (page 35). Does it need revising or tweaking? Write your final podcast one-liner here, along with any other keywords, phrases, and ideas.

3   Knowing what you know about your podcast now, brainstorm and develop a two- to three-line description. Some directories have word-count limits, but as a general rule: Keep it pithy. Fold in any keywords or phrases that fit. Get feedback from friends on the final wording.

EXERCISE   Your Episode Description

1   Read each episode description below and answer these questions:

—   What pain or pleasure point does the description hit?

—   How does it address why listeners should care about this topic?

—   How does it arouse curiosity?

—   What words or phrases accomplish these things?

—   Essentially, answer the question, "Why should I bother?"

Life Kit, "Anxious Thoughts? 5 Tips to Help You Sleep," March 26, 2020: "Difficulty sleeping can cause anxiety, which often leads to more trouble sleeping. *Life Kit* host Allison Aubrey talks to sleep experts about how cognitive behavioral therapy for insomnia can bring relief for people with chronic sleep issues." [This lays out the pain point—the way insomnia feeds on itself, and the feeling of being trapped. Then it *immediately* follows up with an intriguing potential solution, backed by science.]

Short Wave, "What Would It Be Like to Fall into a Black Hole?," May 27, 2020: "Black holes are one of the most beguiling objects in our universe. What are they exactly?

How do they affect the universe? And what would it be like to fall into one? We venture beyond the point of no return with Yale astrophysicist Priyamvada Natarajan into a fascinating world of black holes—where the laws of physics break down." [This makes a simple statement about the subject and plants questions in the listener's brain they'll want answered.]

Alt.Latino, "The Meteoric Rise of Latin Urban Explained," February 28, 2020: "The story of Latin America has always been reflected in music. We asked a music writer, a college professor, and reggaeton pioneer to help us understand the history and nuance of Latin Urban's dominance in pop music." [This clearly tells listeners that the episode will break down a whoppingly huge subject by looking at it from three different perspectives. The word *nuance* conveys that this episode will embrace complexities from a place of knowledge, not pretend they don't exist.]

Pop Culture Happy Hour, "Huzzah! We're Russian to Finish *The Great,*" May 20, 2020: "Hulu's new series *The Great* bills itself as 'An Occasionally True Story.' And it's a big story: a sweeping epic about Russia in the 1700s, full of palace intrigue, sex and violence, and the rise of Catherine the Great. Elle Fanning plays Catherine, and Nicholas Hoult also stars as the sociopathic emperor Peter. The show shares a lot of thematic DNA with the 2018 film *The Favourite*—it was created by one of the film's screenwriters, Tony McNamara. And it's more than willing to scramble history in the service of a good story." [This tells folks who may not be familiar with the subject some basic, table-setting info: stars, story, setting. The tone signals, softly, that we liked it, so this episode won't be a pan.]

2 Next, consider your episode. Back in chapter 7, you pondered a *lot* of questions about your developing story. Now, take a few of those and answer them for your finished product:

— What's the focus of your story?

— What's new or surprising about it?

— Is there *one question* it answers? That is, what's the "driving question"?

— Where is the tension? Or ask, What's at stake?

— What would you say to make this story relevant or interesting to people who don't already care about your subject?

— How might people benefit from your story?

3 Now, brainstorm and draft your episode description—the shorter, the better!

Once you've drafted the episode description, add ways to stay in touch: your contact info, social media and website links, a link to join your email list, how to follow to your pod, plus thanks to advertisers or sponsors (with website links)—all potentially helpful for SEO (see "Keyword Salad"). You don't *have* to do all of these in every description, but it's a good idea to have at least your contact info and

---

Keyword Salad

Keywords and search terms are words and phrases that people tend to use when searching online for certain subjects—as determined by the endless chugging of internet search engines. They can be helpful to have in your website and descriptive materials because, if people type in those terms, theoretically, your podcast might be more likely to pop up in the results. That means you're improving (*optimizing*) the chances of someone finding a link to your podcast and maybe clicking on it. The more clicks your stuff gets, the more search engines "notice" the attention you're getting, and the better your rankings in search results might be. Thus was born the term *search engine optimization,* or SEO.[5]

But see those "mights" and "maybes"? Overreliance on keywords can backfire if you don't keep up with the changes in how the internet search algorithms work, and overdoing them can get you rejected by Apple Podcast's server (as I caution in chapter 2). Use keywords when they fit what you want to say. Certainly use phrases and terms related to your subject. (The Battle of the Bulge/World War II…Coco Chanel/haute couture…Frank Sinatra/Rat Pack). Some programs allow you to find out what other keywords were searched for by people who searched for your podcast, which will be useful. And it's smart to use your keywords consistently across your platforms (website, social media, and all others). Just know they're only one marketing tool of many.

5 This is us, sticking our toenail into SEO. With social media marketing, it's a huge subject, with countless books and newsletters devoted thereto. We recommend you read up on internet marketing, and specifically applied to podcasting. It's a learning curve we're all on together.

a short rundown of the topics you discuss (include titles of books, movies, and more), so people can look them up. You can put more detailed info, including links, in your show notes and newsletter.

Gahhh—Did You Remember Artwork?

What's about the size of a nickel, but worth a lot more? Your podcast art! That's the size your podcast logo will be on a lot of devices. But that picture's worth a thousand words—or at least, say, a few hundred.

For many, graphic design can be a rabbit hole, but whether it leads to heaven or hell depends on your graphic design knowledge, budget, schedule, and that idiosyncratic thing called "taste." If you don't have design experience, however, I don't recommend doing this yourself. You don't need to break the bank, but this is a brand statement you'll be using in multiple ways. Talk to fellow podcasters whose logos you like—who did they work with? You might find a new-grad designer with reasonable rates, creative energy, and a vested interest in building their business by making you a happy client.

If you've got design chops, you might be able to create your own logo using templates online. Here are some general guidelines:

— Above all, art must be readable. View it at the "nickel"-or-smaller size. Not *instantly* legible? Reviiiiise!

— Sans serif fonts tend to be more readable on-screen than serif fonts. But do what fits the feeling of your podcast. Script fonts are usually too elaborate.

— Keep words and fonts to a minimum. Generally two to four for the former. One to two for the latter.

— You might be surprised how many of NPR's podcast logos don't use artwork. It's amazing how striking a strong type composition against a strong color can be.[6]

— Look for high contrast between background and type.

— If you use art, keep it bold and simple. And get whatever permissions/licenses/clearances you need.

6 While you're at it, pick a (*resigned sigh*) "color story" that you're prepared to stick to. It seems silly, but branding is a thing you have to think about now, big-time-podcaster-creator. That means establishing a look that's unique, recognizable, and consistent.

— Make certain your logo conforms to the specifications of the major directories (such as Apple Podcasts).

— While you're at it, check your podcast name to make sure it won't get rejected for violating directory name rules.

— Consider how it'll look in marketing materials, business cards, your website—you may need to adapt a rectangular version a bit.

Post Free Episode Transcripts

Publishing free transcripts of your episodes on your website broadens your reach. It makes your content available to those with hearing or auditory processing issues, who are less fluent in your language, or who want a written version for reference (including you!).

Transcriptions are smart marketing because search engines pick up on the words and phrases relevant to your podcast—beyond what's possible with your episode title and short description (see "Keyword Salad" on page 221).

Some transcription services use voice recognition technology. Some use human transcribers. There are free and paid options. Type "podcast transcription services" into your browser. See if your podcast hosting service offers transcription. Or hire an individual— ask your podcasting community for recs. Or do it yourself. Always proofread transcripts for accuracy—*especially* if you go with voice recognition. That's even more important if your podcast has multiple speakers or audio-quality issues, or is complex in other ways. If your show's scripted, use the script as the transcript base, adding sound or other cues in brackets, and removing notes to yourself or others.

Set up a style guide so you or anyone proofreading your transcripts can make them consistent in format, plus a running list of names for correct spelling.[7]

Oh, and Show Notes

Think of the good stuff that didn't make it into your episode. Geeky details, interview outtakes, advice tidbits, research sources. What a waste for these goodies to end up as forgotten outtakes.

Show notes to the rescue!

Post them on your website to take your audience deeper into your topic and to give them another chance to engage with you.

Show notes can include guests' bios, websites, social media, and links to their work. Always include a way to contact you. How about an invitation to sign up for your email newsletter? And (eventually) links to previous episodes on related topics?

Down the line, you could link to your crowdfunding or donation page, promote your snazzy podcast merch, or include advertiser or sponsor links.

Think of these extras as an opportunity to whisper in your audience's ear just a little longer.

Prep Your Promo

Okay, breaaaathe.... You're doing great! Just a few bits and pieces to go. Rest assured all of this launch marketing will become second nature eventually!

SET UP YOUR SOCIAL MEDIA AND EMAIL CAMPAIGNS

Search engines "notice" your social media posts and activity. So be ready with your social media campaign: prepublication "teasers"

7 Because how many times do you want to look up how to spell Pyotr Ilyich Tchaikovsky or Antonín Dvořák?

about how excited you are to be launching your podcast, the Big Announcement after it drops, suggestions to check out show notes or bonus content, relevant news or info related to your topic (as in, a podcast for runners gives you the opportunity to be a hub for info about proper training, gear, injury prevention, and more). Other ideas: Post short audio clips, show quotes, and recording session pix of you and your guests.

You can't handle social media for audience-building the way you do your personal social media: posting whenever you feel like it, whenever something strikes you as noteworthy. To build an audience, you need to commit to regular content that keeps them interested. Trust me: A schedule will help you stay on top of this. You can create a schedule in your calendar or on a spreadsheet, or use a social media management tool (Hootsuite is one example) to prepare posts on specific dates and times.

Of course, you can't just endlessly flog your podcast. You wouldn't do that in real life, would you?[8] Always focus on why someone should care: "Ever wonder what became of Batman's original Batsuit? Find out on our kick-off episode of *Everything Batman*!"

8 "But enough about *me*. What do you think of my podcast?"

Are Audio or Video Trailers for You?

Social media professionals call 'em assets, but we can dispense with the jargon, as we're clear-eyed, no-nonsense types, you and I. The logo you come up with should be formatted so that you can share it in a variety of ways: as a Twitter banner, as an Instagram story, as an email signature, and more. But you know this.

If you've got a bit more time and resources, consider the next step—a teaser trailer. Doesn't have to be fancy—you could simply take your logo and attach a brief (!), short (!!), not-long (!!!) clip from your episode to it.[9] Make sure the clip in question is powerful—funny, sad, intriguing, incendiary, whatever—but most of all, make sure it's representative of your podcast.[10] Then send it out on social media. Doesn't have to go viral. What you're looking for are shares, hearts, "likes," comments; bumps in your mailing list; upward trends in your number of followers—that kind of thing.

Of course, if you've got mad video editing skillz, don't sleep on them. Get creative, include lots of quick cuts, but not so many that the clip is confusing—remember, people won't know what to expect when it pops up in their feeds, so walk them through things at first, then razzle-dazzle 'em toward the finish.

9 *Audiogram* is the term of use. Sling it around at your next podcasting conference.

10 And short. Dunno if I mentioned that.

Be sensitive to tone—Facebook, Twitter, Instagram, and so on each have their own demographic and vibe, from word choice to length to preferences for use of visuals, slang, and emojis. Customize your posts.

Make sure to announce new episodes to your email list, with a link. This loops in those who are less active on social media or who aren't podcast followers.

PRESS: ON!

Suppose your alumnae magazine wants to announce your new podcast. Or you're giving a talk and the organizers need your bio, photo, and a podcast description ASAP. Or you're reaching out to interview someone who needs a bit more info about just who the hell *you* are and why they should share their theories about the internecine links between late-stage capitalism and *Saved by the Bell*.[11] Wouldn't it be great to have all the info anyone might need in one place, so you could just fire them a link and get back to creating more content? That's a website press kit, which also makes it easy for someone writing a review of your podcast to flesh out their write-up.

At minimum, a press kit includes your podcast title, show logo and description, host bios, social media links, and links to directories. And *always* how to contact you.

Other ideas: host photos, media reviews, listener reviews, links to recommended episodes, audio/video clips, an option to join your email list, an option to follow you. Is there an origin story behind your podcast? How about a Q&A? Candid pix? Downloadable logos of various dimensions and file sizes?

A press kit is often a work in progress that you develop as your podcasting grows. But you're in this for the long haul, and you want your podcast to find as wide an audience as it can, yes? Then put together, and publish, the tools that will give your listeners—present and future—a place to satisfy their curiosity and contact you. You can also draw on this content to assemble custom PDF packages, plus analytics and pricing, to pitch sponsors.

MEDIA PITCH LIST

Once you've published a handful of episodes you're really happy with, consider doing your own outreach to media. This takes time and doesn't reliably pay off, so for now just make a list of potential media pitches. For instance, podcasters who have a largish podcast network behind them might submit their newborn podcast

11 I mean: *I'd* listen.

Pitching Your Pitch at the Right Pitch

When you work at a media organization like NPR, your inbox consists almost entirely of pitches. I devote a few minutes every day to deleting hundreds of pitches that have nothing to do with the areas I cover. The ones I do pay attention to, and follow up on, have a few things in common:

— **Pitcher, know thy catcher.** You might think "Cover the waterfront!" is an effective strategy. It isn't. Mass email blasts that aren't meaningfully targeted only result in mass email deletions. Narrow your list to those who cover the subject of your podcast.

— **Respect the subject line, and keep it pithy.** Personally, I like it when senders are up front at the top, and call a pitch a pitch, without any coyness.[12] (For example, "PITCH: *Make Mine Mamie* Podcast Debuts, Unpacking All Things Eisenhower.") This helps immensely when I'm surfing and sorting through reams of emails.

— **Be the BCC you (don't) want to see in the world.** If I see a "To:" field filled with a string of other people, this just signposts a mass email, and thus, one unlikely to be tailored to me. Use the BCC field so we can both pretend, and preserve the mystery.

— **Frontload that sucker like it's a VW Beetle (which has its trunk in the front, is the idea here).** Gimme the details I need—podcast name, drop date, your name, frequency, and contact info—in the lede graf. Don't make me search for it.

— **Tone it up, then tone it down.** I want to know why you're so enthused about your podcast and its subject. The tone of your pitch email should testify to that enthusiasm: friendly, open, and excited, even. Excited is good! But keep it professional, and keep it short. If your pitch is longer than two paragraphs, I start to wonder if you have the necessary focus. It's a pitch, not a whole ballgame.

— **Twice is nice.** Personally, I appreciate a follow-up email asking if I saw the pitch. Often, that second email serves its intended purpose by reminding me of an email I meant to flag but got distracted before I could. Two emails is perfect, three is pushing it, and four or more is *Fatal Attraction*.[13]

12 Coyness in a paramour can be enticing; coyness in a publicist is grating.

13 "I'm not going to be *ignored*, Dan!" But, see: You are. You will be. Is the thing.

for media reviews in industry publications. And it can be helpful for other media to know, too: Your podcast on running might be of interest to websites and print magazines on running, health, and fitness, or your alma mater might put it in their alumnae news.

Liftoff!

Woo!! You uploaded your podcast (or you will soon; see chapter 15), the pub date arrived, and this baby is born!! Sit back and pop the cork.

Well, yeah, do that—but do it while wearing your marketing hat.[14] Once your podcast is available online, Marketing You swings into action, sharing the news and building connections, goodwill, and word of mouth.

Going forward, here are some marketing habits to get in the habit of:

— **Spread the word and the appreciation.** Email any guests the episode link and your thanks for being on the show. It's right and smart—they might share the link, post it on their social media, and help get the word out. Do this with anyone who gave time, energy, advice, or help. The PR person at the zoo who helped arrange your interview with the keeper caring for the baby hippo. The owners of the stores where you found the vintage clothes you talked about (you put their names and websites in your show notes, right?). Show your appreciation on social media, too, thanking and tagging them. They might like, share, retweet. This is how you build word of mouth.

— **Share good news.** Did someone publish a review of your podcast? Do a Q&A with you? Publish a guest blog post you wrote? These can be social media posts that don't flog your pod but share exciting developments about it, with thanks to (and tagging) those involved.

— **Tease your content.** Post a guest's great one-liner (funny, wise, weird, provocative), tag them, and include a link to the episode.

— **Don't spread yourself too thin.** Remember what we said in chapter 13 about going where your audience is? Don't waste time on social media platforms where they don't hang out in large numbers. Focus promotion on your core audience first— the bull's-eye of your target market—then strategize reaching

14 It's sort of like the Sorting Hat, only instead of sorting you into a Hogwarts house, it murmurs to you enticingly about leveraging your verticals and suggests ways to incentivize influencers through content innovations.

secondary and tertiary markets. You might get more press traction targeting niche publications, organizations, or groups likely to be interested in your topic than spinning your wheels vying for attention from a major general-audience outlet. Use your personal connections first, then make a plan to expand.

— **Drill down in a few areas; measure results.** If you try too many marketing things at once, you'll burn out *and* won't have clarity on what's working and what isn't. Focus your energy—for example, by diving deep into a couple of social media platforms for a certain period while doing less in others. This lets you see if what you're doing makes a difference in downloads.

— **Website and social media traffic are good, too.** Traffic helps your search rankings—which is always good. So, downloads are everything, but not *everything*. Maybe people visited your website because they were intrigued by your post: "Did you know how much a single poop of a baby hippo can weigh? We didn't, either." They read the show notes, which contained the fun and funky outtakes from your interview with the zookeeper, and left, but you never know—maybe they'll tell friends and come back to catch the full interview on your podcast later.

And that's . . . it? Actually, it's just the beginning. Of something you've worked long and hard for. You are no longer someone wanting to do a podcast "someday." That day has arrived. Your podcast is a reality. Savor it and celebrate how far you've come. Now it's time to share and grow.

CHAPTER 15

Let the Pod Go Forth

Why put your heart, soul, tears,[1] and sweat into your podcast if no one can find it? Publishing your podcast involves a combination of factors, including the type of file you upload, how it's prepared, and where that file "lives" on the internet.

For the latter, many people choose a hosting service, which makes the podcast available to podcast directories (also called podcast aggregators or podcatchers). Those are the apps you, I, and millions of others download to play our favorite podcasts or to stream stuff—Apple Podcasts or Spotify, to name just two (type "podcast directories" into your browser to learn what's out there).

Whether you handle every detail of this process yourself or team up with services for help along the way, you have the ultimate sign-off. So let's dive into the essentials of audio formatting to help you turn your good audio into good internet that's easily shareable.

The Prepping Handbook (for Your Files)

To publish effectively and with maximum reach on the internet, you need the right kind of files, set up to get easily slurped into your listeners' devices. The faster, more glitch-free, and more digitally compatible this process is for everyone, the better.

FILE TYPE: WAV BYE-BYE

Isn't it annoying when you can't email an attachment because it exceeds the server's size limits? Imagine your podcast files being so ginormous that they hog space on your listeners' cell phones or tablets. This wouldn't endear you as a digital guest and you wouldn't be invited back. This is why, although you probably created your episode as a WAV (Waveform Audio Format) file, you'll

[1] Not you. No tears from you, reader of this book. But, like, those other people? Nonreaders of this book who start podcasts? Joe Rogan, say? Waterworks, from that guy. Great salty torrents, famously.

need to convert it to an MP3 file for distribution. WAV files capture high-quality audio, but they're too big for the portable devices most people use for podcast listening. MP3 files are "compressed"—some audio data is dropped—to reduce the file size.[2]

THE YUGELY IMPORTANT, SOMETIMES-FINICKY RSS FEED

Your goal is for people to be interested enough in your podcast to follow it, so new episodes just automatically show up on their devices. That happens via an RSS (Really Simple Syndication) feed. Think of it like a digital pipeline that "feeds" your podcast to followers. Podcast directories require them.

The internet is teeming with Poindexters eager to walk you through setting up an RSS feed. It's a simple process that involves creating a podcast-only account (the RSS feed used for websites won't do the job). Or you could subscribe to a hosting service that'll do it for you, based on info you provide called metadata (title, description, cover art, categories, length, and more). Once the feed's set up, you just add info for new episodes as you publish them.

RSS feeds don't work sometimes for various reasons. Could be a typing error or a tiny problem in the code.[3] A feed validator (look them up online; some are specific to podcasts) can test for broken feeds. Other glitches: a feed that's not accessible, one that takes so long to load that it times out, one that doesn't have all the episodes due to limits on the number of items, or one with problems migrating between hosts.

When snafus happen, service providers are generally quick to pounce on them and provide solutions. But that's back-end tech stuff—*you* need to focus on your listeners. Release a corrected version of the episode in question as soon as possible, and record a humble acknowledgment of what went wrong at the top. This helps turn listeners' frustration into listeners' appreciation.

FILE TAGGING TO BRING ALL THE EARS TO THE YARD

Imagine if your dog were lost, and when describing the pooch on your "Lost" poster, you said: "Lost dog! Owner heartbroken." You wouldn't get many calls. But if the poster said: "Lost dog! Yellow Labrador puppy, approx. 6 mos. old, 65 lbs. Very friendly. Not a thinker, but carries self with a blithe, recherché insouciance. Will probably have a gross wet stick in his mouth he fished out of a

2 This causes MP3s to sound a bit tinnier and flatter than WAV files, yes. But the (slight) sacrifice is worth it if it saves your listeners some phone memory.

3 You listen to podcasts. You know that hiccups (*oh god I woke up and found seven years' worth of* Planet Money *in my feed I mean I love the show but that's a lot of delightfully engaging content about the dismal science first thing in the dang morning*) are not an uncommon occurrence. Technology! Suck it up!

gutter. Name: Sid (also answers to Put That Down!). Call: xxx-xxx-xxxx." Top it off with a fetching photo, and you've upped the chances that people who care might actually be able to search for and find your dog.

That's what file tagging does for your podcast. You're giving information (metadata) to internet search engines to tell them what your podcast is about. *That*, let's hope, helps your podcast show up when folks type search terms into their browser, looking for the kind of thing your podcast provides.

Your metadata includes the stuff you've seen about a million times on a search engine results page (SERP)—the headline-like entry (title); website link; the pithy one- to two-line description. You can add other info, too. Tagging your files puts you in better control of the pretty-much-uncontrollable internet by choosing the words, phrases, and info *you* want associated with your podcast. What search words or phrases does your audience find relevant and appealing? This is your chance to speak directly to them on the über-billboard of the internet.

The portion of your description that actually shows up in search results is supershort—often around just 155 to 160 characters—so answer the "what's in it for me" question right up front, as alluringly as you can.

You can do tagging using an app like Apple Podcasts on your computer, through your digital audio workstation (DAW) as part of exporting the final file, or when uploading files to many hosting services.

The Host with the Most

Your episodes need a place they can call home. Generally, that's not likely to be your website. The size of audio files, plus (let's hope!) the demand for them, can be too much for the bandwidth of many web hosts. And the care and feeding of a podcast catalog can be a tech- and time-consuming process.

Enter podcast hosting services; two well-known examples of many are Libsyn and Blubrry. For a monthly fee (I'll cover "free" in a sec), podcasters upload their files, and the service handles the RSS feed and distribution to directories, provides metrics on downloads, in some cases takes care of file formatting and sizing, and can make the process of setting up descriptions, cover art, and posting on social media more straightforward, plus other features. You can then embed the host's player on your website.

Sounds good, right? It is, or can be. But as with any service, it's important to be aware of the features different hosts offer and seek the right match for you.

So, the "free" thing. There are some free hosts. That model might work if you're keeping things small-scale, but read the fine print. Some hosts delete podcasts after a certain number of days, they may add advertisements (without your okay or participation in profit), and you might be caught flat-footed if the business up and folds. You also want to be sure you can move your files to a different host if you decide to.

Some hosts have a free level, with limits: how many hours you can upload per month, monthly bandwidth, and a few other features. This can be a way to test-drive a service before you go with a paid level—but first find out if it's simple to migrate your files to a different hosting service, and also whether it's a month-to-month plan, so you aren't committed long-term if you want out. And make sure any service you use submits your podcast under your name, not theirs, so you can easily check your stats.

Hosts without a free option might let you try them for a little while for free, if you ask, to see if the fit works for you.

Hosting services may tout their download speed (fast is good—duh) but that's the tip of the services-and-features iceberg.

Pricing's generally tied to how much you're storing on the site and how much downloading is happening (that is, bandwidth). You'll want to find out if there are limits on the number of hours or total megabytes (MB) you can upload every month[4]—maybe no big deal for a short or less frequent podcast, but possibly an issue for one that's long or has an ambitious publishing schedule. Also: How long can you store your episodes before they're deleted? The answers may be reflected in price tiers.

Or pricing might depend on the number of monthly downloads. That could be a factor if you're fast-growing, but other features the host offers (support for monetizing? video hosting?) might be worth the trade-off.

It can be challenging to weigh up the features. It can feel like online dating.[5] Here is a list of questions to ask, followed by a Podcast Hosting Service Checklist (see page 238). Use these to help you comparison shop.

— **Easy to use?** If you're not that into tech,[6] make sure the host's features are user friendly, and be sure to ask about their support.

[4] Rule o' thumb? Sixty minutes of a spoken podcast equals approximately 50 MB—*but* this depends on a lot of file factors, so it's really a broad generalization o' thumb.

[5] Joy.

[6] True story. I once heard an ad for a website-building service that bragged about its "drag-and-drop interface," and I am so tech-averse I heard "dragon drop interface" and thought to myself I had to build a website because, come on, how cool does *that* sound?

— **What about website (yours, theirs) and show notes?** Got a website of your own? Find out if the service has a player you can embed on your site, or what other features they have that would let you publish within your site. No website? Then see what they offer in terms of a website on the platform. Take a look, too, at how well show notes are displayed.

— **How good are their nuts and bolts like tagging, categories, and listings?** Check the host's tagging and categories often for any changes, as different hosts tend to change how they tag the files and juggle categories around to chase trends. For example: Do they include episode numbers? (They should.) Do their categories conform to what Apple announced in June 2019? (Quick test: Does "True Crime" appear in their dashboard. No? My dear, this will not do!)

— **What analytics do they provide?** As to analytics (tracking downloads, for example), find out what kinds of stats you get, at what price, and how granular they are—do they drill down into geography, devices, directory?

— **Are they IAB certified?** It's best if your host's stats are IAB certified. This means that the Interactive Advertising Bureau (IAB), which has come up with standards for how this should be done—downloads being pretty much advertisers' only way of knowing whether anyone *might* have heard an ad they placed in a podcast—has vetted and approved the host's methods. This is different from being "IAB compliant," which means that the host believes they're complying with IAB rules, but the IAB hasn't vetted them.

    If you run ads (or intend to), your advertisers will want to know the number of downloads in a given time period, and IAB certification carries credibility. Also, find out what kind of demographics the host can provide (always helpful to know—especially if you pursue advertisers down the line). Being able to download the data is a plus, too.

— **Can they grow with you?** Hosts might offer growth features: ways to set up memberships, provide premium content, and monetize your podcast.

— **Do they change your bitrate?** Some services change the bitrate[7] of your MP3 files if your files exceed certain limits. This may be okay by you or not; could be fine for voice-driven audio, but not your preference for music- or sound-driven audio. Or they may charge you for higher bitrates.

— **Is (good) transcription offered?** Some hosts offer transcription (see chapter 14), so vet that if you'd find it of value.

— **How easy (or not) is it to leave?** In case you want to change hosts, find out if you can migrate your files via the dashboard, not via support.

Here's a partial sampling of other features you might find (or look for, depending on your needs) as you shop: chapter markers, call-to-action buttons in the player, no limits on who can manage the account, multiple episodes visible in the player, plug-ins that let you operate from your website, dynamic ad insertion, controlled timing of publication in different directories, and … more.

You don't need to have every bell and whistle. Just shop around, based on your needs and preferences, on the kind of podcast you're doing (format, length, focus), and on your goals for growth.

Podcast Hosting Service Checklist

While the list on page 238 isn't 100 percent comprehensive, it should help you track and compare various features. Customize it to include the features that are important to you.

When decision time comes, ask yourself: How does this service fit my needs right now? How would it fit my needs as I grow? Consider what growth means to you: Is it more episodes (storage), more complex/longer episodes (file size), more downloads (bandwidth), more promotion and audience engagement (additional features; analytics)?

If you're pretty sure you'll hit major growth benchmarks in the next six months, then check out hosts where you can level up to the next tier(s). If podcasting's more of a pastime, a modest hosting plan might do fine. Also check out what services are being used by other podcasters who are doing podcasts similar to yours, or who are in a similar phase of growth.

7 *Bitrate* is a measure of the speed your files upload or download.

And before you sign on the dotted line, it's important to read the terms of service to make sure you're comfortable with them. They will need you to grant them a license to make your podcast available through their service, but watch out for other terms that could allow them to monetize your content in ways you don't approve of—for example, by inserting ads or sublicensing your content without your consent.

The checklist on the next two pages—which you can adapt as a spreadsheet or use as the basis for keeping more informal notes in your notebook—could be useful in keeping track of what various hosting services offer.

Dancing with Directories

Go wide, go long when submitting your podcast to directories. Given how hard it is to get your podcast noticed, you want to put it out there (known as syndicating) as broadly as you can. You definitely want to submit to Apple Podcasts, a longtime dominant force. Music streaming services such as Spotify and internet radio like Stitcher and iHeartRadio are putting podcasts in front of a new crop of potential followers. And those are just a few. Do research online to learn about directories. If you have a hosting service, they take care of syndication. Check out online tutorials if you're doing it yourself. Usually, once your first submission is accepted, then it's easy to upload new episodes.

It can feel kind of intimidating to wade into all this, but remember your goal of wanting your good work to be found—and how satisfying it'll feel to know you've done right by your podcast in finding it a good home. Remember, too, that you're not alone. You'll find lots of ideas, tips, strategies, debate, and help out there from fellow podcasters who, just like you, are trying to sort things out. So, do your homework, ask questions, match what you learn with what you believe your podcast needs, read the fine print, and forge ahead.

Podcast Hosting Service Checklist

FEATURES	Host	Host	Host
Free tier/features			
Free trial?			
Bandwidth limits (*if any*)/price tier			
Storage limits (*if any*)/price tier			
File alteration			
Time limits for carrying episodes			
Breadth of distribution to directories			
Tagging and categories up-to-date?			
Ease of use			
Quality of website hosting (*if desired*)			
Ease of interface with my website/embedded player available			
Integration of social media			
Audio transcription/ price			

Show notes display quality			
Audio-to-video conversion			
Types of analytics offered/price tier (*Demographics? Downloadable?*)			
IAB certified			
Subscription and/or monetization features?/price tier			
Support/help services			
Pricing			
Month-to-month?			
Policy/process for migration to another hosting service			
Do the terms of service allow the host to monetize your content without your approval or consent?			
Opinions of other podcasters			

CHAPTER 16

Grow for Me

This chapter is a kind of postlaunch "Orbiting 101": ideas to help you promote your work once your podcast is out in the teeming pod-i-verse.

Of course, you already know that the best marketing strategy is a good podcast, since no promo gimmick can make a listener stick around if a show's a mess. But you *do* need to do more than just hit Publish. So here we go.

Every podcaster has only so much time, energy, and money for marketing. For your podcast, there are lots of things you *might* do, but which *should* you do? That's the aim of this chapter: to give you options, not orders. The best approach to marketing is to frame out your goals and priorities (and then keep revisiting them), and avoid getting overwhelmed or pulled off-course by bright, shiny trends or what other people are doing. Start with the exercise below!

EXERCISE Gut Check—Define Success, Define Growth

In chapter 2, you defined what "podcast success" means to you. Was it to build community around an idea you believe in? To form your influence and outreach on a particular topic? To point people toward your products and services? To become a podcasting pro?

In the chapter 2 exercise "Know Thyself" (page 38), you thought about how you defined "podcast success." Has your answer changed now that you know so much more about your podcast? Your goals and priorities will shape your marketing decisions. So grab your notebook and go a little deeper: list your priorities and goals in order of importance.

As you read this chapter and plan your podcast's growth, always ask yourself: *How does this help me aim for my goals?*

Metrics: How You Doin'?

Honestly? It's not so easy to tell how a podcast is doing. Still, the number of unique downloads (how many single users download the file in a twenty-four-hour span)[1] does give you a picture of trends: Are your listeners growing, decreasing, or holding steady?

If you're trying to see if a particular marketing gambit had the hoped-for effect, you'll probably be disappointed. Downloads also can't tell you whether someone even listened to the dang podcast or stalled out partway through. Oh, and sometimes one person downloads an episode multiple times for various devices—so there's, you know, that.

Understand that your efforts gather force over time. Just because you don't always see results doesn't mean that your marketing isn't working on some level you can't clearly measure. This isn't about having blind faith. No: Look for numbers headed in the right direction.

You can roughly guesstimate your dedicated listeners by looking to see how steady the number of downloads is across episodes and in the forty-eight hours postpublication. As a separate stat, you can look at who's "following" you on streaming services like Spotify.

Other indicators: more social media followers, more "Likes," higher website traffic, more names on your mailing list. These things mean your platform's growing, which helps with search results and your visibility overall.

Got an email list where you blast out links to your podcasts when they launch? Track (a) the number of people who open those emails (that also gives you an idea of how enticing your subject line is)[2] and (b) the number of clicks on your podcast links. The goal is for as many people as possible who open your emails to *also* click on that link!

Build Audience Engagement Through Feedback and Audio Callouts

Audience feedback can give you info that download metrics just can't. But it can also be a tyrant. Ask ten people what they think of your podcast, you'll get eleven opinions.

1 We're hoping your hosting service is IAB certified (see chapter 15), for added cred.

2 But remember: Many servers open emails automatically, so this number is not a hill to die on.

Sometimes the episode you hated making becomes extremely popular with listeners. Sometimes the one you loved and toiled over is one of the episodes no one really notices. And without fail, hate mail will always exist, whether your episode was great or awful, so just get used to it or ignore it.

—Sam Sanders, correspondent/host, *It's Been a Minute with Sam Sanders*

How much should you listen to feedback? Ideally, you want to find that sweet spot where your podcast is what you want it to be, *and* it's what your audience wants, too.

Do you see some patterns in the comments? Are they picking up on something you missed? Consistently identifying the same blind spots? If someone sends you negative feedback, answer with thanks. If you can do something about it, great, but either way, let them know you appreciate their honesty and the time they took to contact you.[3] After all, don't *you* like it when your input gets respectfully listened to?

Another great engagement strategy is audio callouts: asking listeners for ideas and info.

There are tons of ways to do callouts and feedback requests. They just need to fit the tone of your podcast. Make sure to give clear instructions for contacting you, whether on social media, website, email, or phone (that routes automatically to an affable voicemail!). Some examples:

"We're doing a poll about what cooking techniques you want to know about. Like, exactly how do you spatchcock a chicken? Boil eggs for perfect results every time? That kinda thing. Go to our website to take the poll and let us know."

"A number of you took us to task for [name what happened]. And you know what? You were right. We goofed. We didn't get this right and should have reported this more fully. Thanks for keeping us on point with our goal to provide quality, accurate, and balanced coverage. Please keep telling us how we're doing."

"Do you like what we're doing? We'd love it if you'd leave a review. Or tell a friend about us!"

3 Use your judgment here. If the commenter is just trolling you—using, say, profanity, invective, personal insults, bad-faith arguments—just understand that they're dealing with something, and there's no reason in the world you should have to deal with it, too. But if they're angry about something specific, consider taking the time to respond with gentle kindness, the way my pal Linda Holmes does. She often writes things like, "Sorry this wasn't for you! Here's what we were aiming for." An astonishing amount of the time, this leads to a sincere, civil, deescalated exchange, and often an apology.

You've only listened to about a million podcasts, so you know there are lots of ways to do this. Get inventive about what would work for your topic and entice people to interact and respond.

And of course, create engagement on your website and social media. Start chats, dedicated pages, and feeds. Post there *not just to plug episodes,*[4] but to share info, ideas, and good stuff relevant to your topic. Producer J. C. Howard learned this lesson in his start-up podcasting days: "We released the show weekly and might have okay engagement on publishing days, but didn't do very well at engaging folks between episodes. Looking back I broke a cardinal rule: Never make your promotion feel like promotion. Since the social media feeds were active mostly when I wanted something from people, I think that inspired fatigue instead of engagement. Sure, we might tweet a couple things or comment here or there otherwise, but that probably felt more like trolling because of the inconsistency of actual engagement. The irony is, while I was finding my voice on the podcast, my social media was blending into the background noise that is social media."

Ask questions to get conversations started. Cheer people on in their successes. Commiserate with their concerns. Post snapshots of your world—pix of you at your mic while having a bad hair day...a script scrawled with notes...periodic cameos of your scene-stealing cat, whom your audience has gotten to know for her habit of head-bumping your mic during sessions.

Search engines notice this activity. Plus, you're upping the value you're bringing to your audience, building trust that you hope will translate into loyalty to your podcast, and becoming that happening "hub" I talked about in chapter 13 (really important for other reasons I'll get into in a minute).

The Five Sacred Buckets of Marketing[5]

Kristin Hume, senior director of brand and marketing at NPR, has some great tips based on how NPR gets the word out about its podcasts. She says that launch strategies typically fall into "five buckets." Some you pay for; others you invest sweat equity in. Note: These aren't mandates. They're ideas for you—the CEO of You, Inc. and its podcast—to consider based on your resources and the right fit for your show. C'mon, let's peer into some buckets!

BUCKET #1: PR AND COMMUNICATIONS
The goal here, Kristin says, is to "announce the launch of the new podcast" and "think about how to make your host a subject-matter

4 Seriously. Just saying "new episode!" is not engagement. Nor is it remotely engaging.

5 Nothing sacred about them. I just liked juxtaposing "sacred" with "buckets."

expert." That launch should include a press release—see "Press: On!" and "Media Pitch List" on page 226.

Are you thinking you're not an expert? No worries. It doesn't mean you can't market yourself as the spokesperson for your podcast. You chose your podcast topic because you're passionate and pretty knowledgeable about it. And because you aim to be a hub for people interested in it. Maybe your hub is about useful information supplied by guest experts, and it shares ideas, trends, and vetted resources. Maybe it's humorous, persnickety observations on the contrariness of life. Maybe it's meaningful community around a sensitive subject. Just know what it is and pitch yourself in a way that is honest and makes you feel good about it.

As part of your promotional efforts, offer yourself as a guest on other podcasts—ones that are similar to yours in profile and have overlapping topics and audiences (for more on this, see "Exercise: Pitching Podcasts for Guest Spots and Ad Swaps," page 247). Guesting is a double-win. It (1) introduces you to new potential listeners, and (2) builds your experience as a go-to guest on your topic (which you can then mention in future pitches to other podcasts).

And why not invite hosts of good start-up podcasts to be guests on *your* show? Then promote on social media, tagging them and such. This helps you create an episode, builds your network, and might result in a return invitation.

Another way to promote is through podcasting festivals, events, and conferences, which can offer great learning and networking opportunities.[6] You never know how these connections might develop into partnerships down the line. And you'll be talking about your podcast with one of the best potential markets: people who *love* listening to podcasts.

BUCKET #2: PAID CAMPAIGNS

"We take two strategies with our paid campaigns," Kristin Hume says. "We do paid marketing within the platforms where people get their podcasts." For example, on Spotify or in the iHeartRadio network. With those, "you're reaching lovers of podcasts in the mind-set of looking for new podcasts."

The other strategy is targeted marketing on social media "to insert the podcast into conversations on the topic it's on."

Depending on the platform, you can designate specific types of users, age groups, hashtags, and interest areas and buy ad space to

6 Some events are schmoozier than others. Some attract scrappy start-ups like yours; others attract lanyard bros from the big networks who say things like "leverage your verticals!" a lot. At this stage, value scrappy over lanyard-y.

create targeted ads: "For example, with *Code Switch*, we had a lot of success with hashtags about race and identity."

"We use audiograms a lot on social media; they really help," Kristin says (see "Are Audio or Video Trailers for You?," page 225). But "social media is a visual medium. And we've done low-budget video, frankly. We shot one with Sam Sanders, and it was just him addressing the camera, a quick two-minute script. I think video is better whenever you can do it."

Paid campaigns can be "tricky" budget-wise, Kristin says. But if you have, say, five to ten thousand dollars to spend, paid social media marketing can put "your podcast in front of about half a million people."

Even if your budget's in the double or triple digits, check to see what those dollars could buy you and decide if you want to test some ads. Paid media in social marketing has potential for what Kristin calls the "amplifier multiplier effect": People can comment on an ad, "like" it, and share it. You never know where it might go.

BUCKET #3: AD SWAPS

This is a great (read: affordable!) cross-promotion option for start-up podcasters that NPR has had good success with. Basically, you barter ad time with fellow podcasters. As with guest appearances, find good-quality, similar- or modest-sized podcasts on topics related to yours. Contact them. Tell them how much you enjoy their podcast (don't pick one you wouldn't want to promote!). And say, as Kristin puts it, something like: "We have this amazing podcast, we're really excited about it. If you'll run a promo in your podcast promoting it, we'll do the same for you." If they say yes, you exchange thirty seconds or so of ad copy for the host to read or an audio trailer. Specific terms are pretty much up to you, but it's smart to agree on a promo end date.

Ads can be placed "preroll" (before or right after the episode begins), "midroll" (somewhere within the episode), or "postroll" (right before or after the credits). You'll notice that a "midroll" ad tends to cost more than a "preroll," which costs more than a "post-roll." Three guesses why.

After family and friends' recommendations, hearing ads for podcasts in other podcasts is the next most frequent way people learn about new podcasts.[7] So definitely check this out. Spikes in downloads around the time the ad launches can indicate that your pod found some new ears, but even small increases that you can't necessarily explain can have a positive cumulative effect.

7 Surprising, no? But true. Which makes this such an attractive . . . um . . . bucket.

EXERCISE Pitching Podcasts for Guest Spots and Ad Swaps

Successfully convincing other podcasts to have you as a guest or to do ad swaps starts with identifying the best podcasts to approach. Search out shows with a similar profile (if you're a start-up, look for start-ups) where the audience or topic would overlap with yours, but you'd add something a little different and potentially interesting. Example: Your podcast *Hacks for Hikers* might marry well with podcasts on nature, travel (hiking hacks geared to location, season, experience level, budget), birdwatching ("Ten Best Hiking Tips for Birdwatchers"), photography ("Best Hiking Gear for Photographers"), cooking ("Beyond Trail Mix"), and even parenting ("Hikes with Tykes").

In chapter 13, the exercise "Knowing and Growing Niche Communities" (page 208) asks you to list the podcasters you admire. That's a great place to start, but cast an even wider net now and list as many podcasts as you can find with audience or subject crossover potential. Start a list in your notebook, listen to a good sampling of each podcast, and make notes about how your topic(s) and theirs might dovetail.

When your prospects are lined up, email them and respectfully (and succinctly) make your pitch for what you want. Use your one-liner to describe your podcast and say a bit about notable guests or successes your show has had (if you have any truly impressive metrics, drop those in). Explain how your show or topic could interest their listeners. List/float a few ideas or options. Of course, promise them similar, reciprocal promotion (whether with ads or guesting), along with tagging them in your social media, and so on. Always include your contact info and links to your website and social media.

That said, rather than cold calling, the best way to get traction with guest spots or ad swaps is if you've already cultivated a relationship with the other podcast: by following them online, participating in comments threads, mentioning them in your social, and liking their podcast.

Already got a great relationship with another podcaster? Consider leveling up: Cross-promote with an "episode drop," in which you put an episode of each other's shows into your respective feeds. To help your audiences orient, add an intro about why the other show's in your lineup and what you love about it. As with ad swaps, agree on a time frame for this cross-promo.

BUCKET #4: PROMO ON PODCAST PLATFORMS

You know that thing where you tap on your friendly neighborhood podcast app and the home page comes up with a bunch of podcast logos you can scroll through? Well, you can pitch your podcast to be featured there, on distribution platforms like Apple, Spotify, Stitcher, and more. It's free. And, naturally, supercompetitive. But these platforms want people to keep returning to them for content, so they've got an interest in featuring quality work—be it start-up or name-brand—that they think will be engaging to their audience.

Your hosting provider likely has the best contact info for the various platforms, but you can find them yourself on their sites. Your pitch should be

1   brief (one beefy paragraph or two skinny ones);
2   about one specific episode, not the podcast itself;
3   informative/persuasive about what makes that episode
    so good/different/special; and
4   up front about how you'll promote the episode (you want
    to convince them to devote some virtual real estate to you,
    so they want assurance your visitors will click it).

BUCKET #5: CROSS-PROMOTION ON YOUR PLATFORM

"If you have a community anywhere," Kristin says, "how are you getting your message in front of them about this new, shiny, amazing thing that you're doing?"

This is why you build a platform! Now use it to tell the people who already know you about your podcast. Could be your website, your email list, your social media, your professional and personal network. Even your email signature can be a place where you post a link to your latest pod masterpiece. Why work so hard on your podcast and then lose chances to let people know it's out there and how to find it?

Go Forth . . . (and Monetize)?

In the highly unlikely event that someone hasn't already given you this reality check, consider yourself duly reality checked: *Most podcasts never make any actual MONEY.*

Don't get me wrong. You can try to profit from your podcast. Or at least get to the point where it pays for itself. This section will lay out lots of ideas, but as you read, temper any monetary aspirations with a requisite mix of hope and flinty-eyed practicality.

Notes from the Pros: Think Dating, Not Marriage

Kristin Hume, senior director of brand and marketing at NPR

Kristin Hume describes a soft-sell method for encouraging people to engage with your podcast: "If you hear an ad for a podcast telling you to follow it, it's kind of like going up to someone in a bar and saying, 'Do you wanna get married?' Pretty ineffective and it can feel really forward. What we like to do is ask people to just listen: 'Here's this amazing episode we have; listen now.' Make it as easy as possible for people to listen. Then in the show, you can have marketing messages like, 'Hey, if you're a new listener, welcome. We hope you're enjoying this. If you wanna hear more, make sure to follow us.' "

But even if a podcast doesn't bring in income, it can add *value*. It can be a calling card, a passport, a badge of credibility, a profile-elevator, a trust-builder, a megaphone, a mailing-list magnet, a funnel to draw people toward other products and services, or a route to new ventures, contacts, projects, clients, connections, or a public/professional community. Your podcast might not monetize, but it might very well … value-ize.

This section will look at some common monetizing models, and then some examples of ways to build value and/or monetize, based on the time/energy investment needed from you.[8] Ultimately, the value decision links back to your passion for your podcast: "If you get no pleasure out of making your podcast, stop doing it immediately," says *TED Radio Hour* host Manoush Zomorodi. "Growing a show beyond friends and family is very hard. Making money off a show is even harder. Producing a podcast should, at the bare minimum, scratch a creative or intellectual itch. Only you can determine the value in that."

8 These ideas are meant to spark your thinking. Feel free to riff, add, mix, and match—plus look at what other creatives are doing and what might work for you.

Notes from the Pros: Two Hugely Important Points About Podcast "Success"

Guy Raz, creator, *How I Built This with Guy Raz*, cocreator, *TED Radio Hour* and *Wow in the World*

The first thing is: Nobody should go into podcasting with the intention of getting rich. I get probably once a week a request from somebody, some of whom are well known, wanting to start a podcast and wanting my advice. And invariably, I will get a call back from that person six months later and they'll say, "I don't understand. I have 1.5 million Twitter followers or a million Instagram followers, but I'm only getting two thousand, three thousand downloads a week on my podcast. Can you help me figure out why?"

And I say, "Well, let me ask you this question. If you could go to an auditorium once a week and speak to three thousand people about your ideas, and they would rapturously hear them and then tell other people about them, and also maybe engage with you in other ways, would you do that?" And the answer is always, "Of course, I would." Then I say: "Okay. If you took a bullhorn to your street corner and started to just spout ideas through the bullhorn, do you think five hundred people would gather around to listen?" No. But five hundred people listening to your podcast—that's a lot of people. A thousand people? That is a concentrated number of incredibly devoted fans and listeners.

If you can create a program that attracts a hundred listeners a week, I would take those hundred listeners over ten thousand or twenty thousand Twitter followers any day because those people are going to be your force multipliers. They're the people who are going to talk about your show, spread it through word of mouth.

The other really important thing is that a podcast should be seen as part of a general overall ecosystem. If you really love a specific video game and want to create a podcast around it, is it connected to something else? Can you think of it as part of an ecosystem? Do you also have a YouTube channel? Do you also have a blog? Can it also be a book that you will write one day? Can you offer classes where you can teach people how to get better at the video game and maybe charge five dollars?

If you've got, say, a wine store and you want to do a podcast about wine, you might only have a hundred people listening to that podcast, but that's a hundred customers who are gonna go to your store more knowledgeable and more likely to spend more money at your store. Maybe eventually you'll write a little self-published book and you can then say to those hundred people, "Hey, I've got a book. Go to my website and check it out." And probably half of them will do that. Whereas if you put a tweet out to fifty thousand people, not even one-tenth of 1 percent will click on that tweet.

So, the idea of a successful podcast is not about numbers. It's about engagement. And one podcast listener is worth a thousand social media followers because that is a person who is going to really spread your message.

Monetizing Models: From Free to Plea to Fee

Podcasts historically have been free, but that's changing as big companies and entrepreneurial solo podcasters have started experimenting with paywalls. Some podcast services offer a paid subscription model, where listeners pay for ad-free podcasts and/or bonus content.

What about individual podcasters? Traditionally, podcasters wanting to make money through their podcasts have done it with ads. Many still do (more on that later).

Other options include

— donations (with a donation button on your website that processes payments through an electronic payment system like PayPal or Stripe);

— a pay-what-you-wish setup;

— a crowdfunding campaign like Kickstarter; and

— a venue like Patreon, a crowdfunding platform that manages the process for a fee, where individual creatives can try the subscription model with their community, offering stuff to listeners who pay to be patrons.

Interested in building a membership[9] website that's customized to you? Start investigating by searching under "membership website builders" and "membership website software," and look up "content management systems" (CMS) that could support a membership setup.

Whatever you choose, make it easy for people to know where to go and what to do to support your show. Build "asks" for donations, membership, and so on in your outro, show notes, and website. Explain how their support helps you provide quality, what extras await them as members—and that you are so grateful that they're listening or sharing your pod with a friend.

These strategies usually require an existing fan base. So work first on audience engagement with solid production values, platform building, and judicious dips in the five marketing buckets above. Then, especially if asking people to pay for stuff, make sure you can provide it reliably and well.

[9] Technically, a membership is free—members are allowed behind a gate, so to speak, for special access to stuff non-members don't get (and they might buy things)—whereas a subscription involves a fee to join. But you might see these terms mashed up together.

As you build your base, you'll probably get a sense of the growth level you're comfortable with (and of your audience, too: pricing yourself out of what your audience can afford would be a no-no, for example). Do you thrive on building a passionately engaged community, just offering freebies when you've got 'em? Want to keep things low-maintenance with one superlow, broadly accessible payment tier in exchange for some easy-to-provide extras? Do you see your podcast as a way to build trust and encourage interest in other (paid) products and services? Or do you envision a Podcast Powerhouse Plan with multiple price tiers and multiple offerings?[10] Up to you!

10 I salute you, and I'll be at the bar, beer (or four) in hand, when you get there.

MONETIZING LEVEL 1: LOWER EFFORT

Leveraging things you're already doing or can easily provide can make modest gains worthwhile. Even if it's a free membership where people sign in to access extras, search engines notice that traffic to your website. (And why not ask if they'd like join to your mailing list while they're there?) Ideas for this level:

— **Donors thanked by name on your show.** A friend once told me how jazzed she was to see her name printed in the symphony program under "Donors in our audience at this performance." Don't underestimate the power of a personal thanks on your podcast.

— **Existing services or products.** Your podcast on work/life balance could funnel people toward your career coaching service. Your podcast on affordable home makeovers could funnel to your decorating business. Your history podcast could funnel to your books and webinars.

— **Bonus content.** Drive traffic to your website where people can listen to interview outtakes and other goodies that didn't get into the final episode. Or link to superinteresting articles and info you found during your research.

— **Joining the gang.** Maybe your online discussion group is open to those who sign in.

- **Episode access.** Once you publish a bunch of episodes, paying subscribers could have full access (assuming the episodes won't go out of date or otherwise lose value), while nonpayers can access more recent shows.

- **Ad-free access.** Maybe all shows are available, but ad-free to paying subscribers.

- **Early-bird special.** Maybe members or paying subscribers get a sneak peek at episodes.

- **Discounts.** Paying subscribers could get discounts to your classes, services, or products.

MONETIZING LEVEL 2: MEDIUM EFFORT
These strategies might take a little more effort:

- **Inside info.** Show and tell how the podcast sausage gets made. What does your recording space look like? Capture a typical day on location. If comedy's your thing, share how you develop your bits. Fitness podcast? Follow yourself training for your first marathon (blisters/sweat/tears). Is there a story behind the story (like, how that episode on deep-sea fishing required you to face your fear of going out on the water, not knowing how to swim)?

- **Interface with you.** Live-chat about your topic, or do a virtual Q&A. You decide what and how often—but don't bail!

- **Make *them* the show.** Record a call-in Q&A show with subscribers to offer as bonus content.

- **Ask for votes, input, opinions, feedback.** Maybe a certain subscriber level is where you do surveys on possible episode topics, solicit votes on your new show logo or merch design (make sure you're okay with *all* the choices!), and develop a core group of passionate fans who want to play a special role in your podcast process.

MONETIZING LEVEL 3: HIGH EFFORT

The more resources needed, the more exclusive your offerings should be. Some might be separately priced products and services outside of your paid subscription model—but maybe subscribers get a discount?

— **Exclusive original content.** Doing a career podcast? Maybe you do a top-tier-only series on navigating office politics. For a culinary show, what about seasonal recipes emailed to paying subscribers?

— **Products and services.** What could you develop for your audience? Maybe survey your community. Would they like a job search online workshop? An e-book, class, or video series tied to your topic? Developing products or services is labor-intensive. So, just like your podcast Idea Bank, create a New Ventures file. Learn, research, and get clear on how each idea fits your goals and your audience.

— **Live and in person!** Any interface with you from the previous levels could have added value with more involvement from you. A virtual face-to-face has more value than an online discussion group. Both are trumped by you in the flesh at an in-person event. If you get really, *really* good at this podcasting thing, have a team behind you to help with tech and event planning, and get a venue set up, you might even do a live recording session.[11]

— **You, with one fan.** A pick-your-brain session. Could be a phone or video consultation on your expertise, applied to their situation. Could be they want to brainstorm their podcast idea with you!

— **Teach what you know.** What do you know that you could help others learn? Formats and levels abound: short instructional videos, webinars, series, brief beginner sessions, master classes, intensives, seminars, even retreats. Based on your interactions with your audience in social media, chats, and such, what would interest them?

11 Again: See you at the bar.

— Merch.[12] Mugs, T-shirts, stickers, hats, magnets, and more, sporting your show logo or slogan . . . merchandise billboards your podcast. E-commerce is a thang all its own, so do your homework. Helpful watchwords: quality, reasonable pricing, easy ordering, reliable fulfillment. You could keep it simple: a sticker with a thank-you note by hand to new subscribers, or a higher-end thank-you item only to new high-tier subscribers. Or forget e-commerce and just use stickers, magnets, or pins as leave-behinds when you're out and about.

Affiliates and Sponsors and Ads—Oh, My!

Some podcasts lend themselves to affiliate relationships: Basically, you get payment in return for featuring a product or service, if it results in a purchase. Talking about equipment, for example, is a natural fit on a podcast on cooking, home repair, photography, hiking, or tech. Home and office furnishings are natural fits on a pod about decorating or design. You get the idea. It's not income you should count on, but if you like the product and would be touting it anyway, it's all potential upside—plus if you're having trouble getting sponsors as a start-up, it can be a way to monetize and gather persuasive stats.

Be careful about the quality and quantity of these. Make sure you *really* like the product or service. And you must be very clear and transparent about disclosing your affiliate relationship publicly. The Federal Trade Commission (FTC) uses the phrase "clear and conspicuous" and has guidelines against deceptive advertising—and you don't want to risk allegations that you've run afoul of those. (For help and good info on this, see the Resources for a link to the FTC guidelines).

Then there are sponsorships and traditional ads. A sponsor generally pays to be prominently featured in your podcast over multiple episodes. A series on Southwestern recipes might use a sponsoring manufacturer's salsas and hot sauces. A "Smart Summer Fun with Kids" series might showcase a line of educational games. A weekly "Weekend Wanderer" feature could profile local eateries and events, sponsored by the local chamber of commerce. Sponsorship's not an easy pitch for a start-up (a solid base of several thousand listeners, plus as much demographic info as you can supply, helps).[13] But if you make a solid case for having a core audience that fits the sponsor's demographic—which might not have to be that large if your topic is specialized, has strong local appeal, or has

12 I know, cookie. You want to make T-shirts bearing your logo and wacky catchphrases the minute your first episode goes live. So did a lot of other folks before you. Folks who've got six pallets of T-shirts moldering in their garages because they jumped to merch-making before they did any audience-building. Never put the cart before the coffee mug.

13 You were so smart to vet your podcast host for the demographics they supply (see chapter 15)!

a passionately engaged community—and if your production values and publication consistency are solid, you've got a better chance. And soon you'll be on your way to featuring "sponcon"—sponsored content—like a thirsty fitness Instagram influencer hawking protein powder. Caveat: Be prepared to share editorial control and build in extra production time.

Ads read by the host and customized to the episode make for the smoothest audio transition into the ad, can be the most appealing to the audience, and may include the host's own positive experiences with the product or service. Or ads can be prerecorded (voiced by the host or someone else) and dropped into episodes. Either way, you'll work out placement (pre-, mid-, or postroll), length, schedule, and price. Payment may be tied to the number of downloads—you might see "CPM," which stands for the cost per thousand listeners.[14]

As with sponsorships, bagging advertisers isn't easy, but a podcast topic that's very targeted with a solid following that an advertiser wants to reach may carry more value than a podcast on a less relevant topic with a larger audience.

Bottom line: Always be building audience engagement. The bigger and more engaged your audience, the better your prospects for third-party arrangements like these. And when you land deals, put

[14] Lots of podcasts with host ad-reads lay them over a bed of music. It's not for aesthetics. It's to signal to impatient listeners hitting that fifteen-second Skip button when the ad starts and stops. You'd be doing your listeners a favor, but you might get a tersely written email from your sponsor. Use your judgment.

On the Business Side: Words to the Wise

You might be making a podcast just for fun or you might be trying to make money as a business. If you're going to profit, you need to pay taxes on the revenue. Your locality may also have business registration requirements, or you might want to incorporate. If you engage and pay freelancers, you'll need professional help to figure out tax, payment, and contractual issues. If you're going to hire people, you need to comply with wage and employment laws. And if you're looking to deduct podcasting expenses as business expenses, there are tax rules and recordkeeping to know about. Therefore, you may need an accountant or business lawyer to help you get set up.

Do you need to copyright your podcast? Aren't there dirty thieving podcast pirates out there who could steal your idea?

No, and no.

Okay, *fine*. If you're the sort of person who checks that the oven's off three times before leaving the house, go nuts. Just know that under current US law, copyright automatically attaches to a creative work once it's been "fixed" (in this case: recorded). So relax, bunky.

on your bean-counter hat and keep careful records of correspondence, publication schedules, listener data, and written deal terms.

Our final advice sounds contradictory, but it's not. It's what you do with any important venture:

Think forward. Are you keeping up with the industry? It's changing fast. Subscribe to newsletters to stay current with tech, marketing, and business developments. Check into events where you could network, learn stuff, and promote. Stay connected with your fellow podcasters. They're a lifeline of information and how-to.

Is your podcast doing great? What about spin-offs? Your parenting podcast might give birth to a show for expectant parents. Your home repair show might spin off into a podcast on fixer-uppers. Think about what your target market might find appealing at different stages or special times of need. Ready for that leap? Tap into your network, build your team, and grow.

Think backward. How can you optimize the effort you've put in? Are you promoting past episodes? If you have a repeat guest or cover a topic related to a past episode that's still up-to-date, repromote it: Give the episode number, a teaser line, and put a link in your show notes. Is there a topic ripe for a follow-up based on current events?

Take stock of where you are. Keep doing your podcast postmortems (see chapter 4) to boost production quality and schedule consistency. They're your foundation for attracting audience and advertisers. Are you spread too thin on social media and need to focus in? Are you pursuing new leads for ad swaps? What are other podcasters doing? Experiment. Focus on what works. And breathe.

See you out there.

Five Rules to Podcast By

I fell in love this week.

Happens a lot.

My husband's cool with it. We have an understanding. Also: The object of my love is a podcast.

Probably should have mentioned that at the top.

What it's about doesn't matter. I mean, it *does*. But I'm driving at something else. Something that, maybe, has happened to you, too....

I did what I always do with a new podcast paramour: I binged. Tore through the archive, episode after episode. It's all I've listened to for a solid week: working out, walking the dog, folding socks, loading the dishwasher, realizing I'd loaded the dishwasher with folded socks, unloading the dishwasher, you get the idea.

It occurred to me, during a pause in my archival gorging, that what triggered this infatuation was exactly what had triggered all the others.

This profound adoration wasn't directed at the podcast's subject or at the hosts. No, what I love, what I hunger for, what keeps me perpetually searching for new podcasts, is what happens when the subjects and the hosts intersect—the *nature* of those conversations.

It creates in me an upwelling of congenial familiarity, a sense of knowing and being known.

Of *friendship*.

Listening to a favorite podcast engenders a powerful sense of intimacy. You come to know the hosts' tastes, tics, pet topics, overused phrases, in exactly the same way that you know your friends'.

Perhaps most crucially, the voices and ideas transmitted inside your head via your earbuds *roost* there, rubbing shoulders with your own thoughts. No wonder you feel as if you know these people.

You likely feel a sense of closeness with the authors of your favorite books, or with actors whose work you've followed or familiar radio personalities. But radio, TV, the silver screen, and the web bring experiences *to* you, and you let down your mental drawbridge, so to speak, to allow them in. Podcasts? They worm their way right inside your brain.

That's the singular power of podcasts, I think.

Not so many chapters ago, your podcast idea was a dream. We've covered a lot of ground together. I hope that reading this book has helped you pursue your quest of creating a podcast, from tending a barely-there glimmer of a concept to taking steps to make your podcast a reality.

I hope, too, that I've gotten you thinking about what podcast creators do to trigger that enduring intimacy that draws an audience in and keeps them there. I've narrowed it down to a handful of "rules" I'd like to leave you with.

1   **Be authentic.** This is the toughest rule to follow. But if you're trying to hit the precise alchemical formula that will make everyone fall in love with your podcast, the best thing to do is . . . not to try. Listeners can *sense* when something's forced, when you're playing on their emotions or calculating an effect instead of providing a story or creating organic curiosity, inquiry, interest, and passion. If listeners can hear your authenticity, they'll join in with it. (I listed this first, but it's not the most important rule. You'll see why.)

2   **Prepare.** I get it. You don't want to sound flat, rehearsed, stale. But know this: Winging it is not an option, not if you care about what you're putting out there, and if you expect others to care about it, too. If there's anything this book teaches, I hope it's to respect your audience's commitment of their time and ears to give them your best.

3   **But leave room for discovery.** You need to invite listeners in. You do that by bringing them along with your thought process: Listeners want to feel like they're in the room with you. So, yes, prepare. *Absolutely* prepare. Map out story arcs, driving questions, signposts, phrasing. But always remember to show your work, to be open to twists in the road, to reach for insights. The goal is for all of us—creators and audience alike—to collectively find something in the story or conversation that we hadn't planned on finding when we started.

4   **Be yourself, but better.** Yeah, yeah, yeah: Be authentic, be prepared, be open to discovery—the first three are good rules. Learn them and live by them. Run your podcast by them. But the moment you start recording? Forget them. Just be there, in front of the mic, and shine. Because the version of yourself that you need to be on your podcast is, at the end of the day, a *performance* of yourself. Or let's say: a *distillation* of yourself. One that's sharper, cleaner, more efficient. Funnier, probably. Maybe even smarter. Certainly pithier. (Please, for the love of all that is holy, be pithier.) How do you go about ensuring all of that? Simple.

5   **Edit. Edit *ruthlessly*. With *no discernible ruth*. At all. None.**[1] This is it, the most important rule. The One True Answer to Everything. Yes, podcasts need to feel natural—but that's just it. They need to *feel* natural. Not be. *Feel.* That means editing. Using your aural scalpel to cut digressions, dead ends, jokes that don't land, and—if you're willing (and oh, *be* willing)—the ums, aahs, and lip smacks. When in doubt, take it out. It's not dishonest. It isn't slick. It's a service to your listeners. It's a way of focusing your discussion, a precious opportunity to identify and delineate what makes your podcast unique. Do not shirk this. Don't fail your podcast—or your audience. Violate rules 1 through 4 if you must, but never, ever flake on rule 5.

[1] I'm serious. Think the last ten minutes of *Harold and Maude*. That ruthless.

So go now, and podcast. Podcast like the wind, if the wind were a thing with a podcast! Be brilliant, be witty, be warm (not *too* warm, please, guys), be brutally tough on yourself, and have fun.

If you do, so will we.

Glossary of Audio Production Terms

Let's say you are producing an audio story, and you're asked to *dip* the *ambi* under the *track*, *butt cut* the next two *acts*, and then *sweep up* and *maintain* the *ambi*. You got it? If that sentence was confusing, this glossary is for you. Terms for producing and mixing audio go back to the days of cutting real tape with razor blades, but most of them have lived on into the era of digital production. This glossary is largely based on Alison MacAdam's " 'Butt Cut What?' A Glossary of Audio Production Terms and Definitions." While it is not intended to be exhaustive, it will add to your audio vocab and help you talk shop with geeky abandon. Enjoy!

actuality (n) — The voices in a story that are not the reporter's or narrator's. Usually recorded on location or in a studio interview. Also known as *acts*, *cuts*, or *sound bites*.

ambience (n) — The pervasive sound at a location, such as traffic on a road, doors slamming, sounds of a demonstration, birds and wind in a forest, and so on. Can be used as an actuality itself or mixed under narration or other actualities. Also known as *ambi*, *nat sound*, or less commonly *sfx*. However, as for the latter, ambience is always real sound, not fake "sound effects"!

bed (n) — Sound running underneath a track or other audio. Not very dynamic—often music or background noise. Common use for ambience.

butt cut (v or n) — To place one actuality immediately after another, rather than dividing them with copy or ambience. Often used to create a transition point, reinforce a point, or demonstrate a contrast.

button (n) — A short piece of music that creates a transition between two unrelated stories, or stories with contrasting moods and tone.

cascade (n) — Type of montage. Three or more distinct pieces of audio combined by fading one into the next. Also known as *waterfall*.

clipped (adj) — When audio is missing the beginning or end of a sound element or word. Also known as *upcut*.

cross-fade (v) — To fade out one sound while fading in another—in order to make the transition seamless. Usually performed in the background, under other tape. When performed in the clear, a cross-fade can indicate a transition.

dip (or duck) (v) — To fade sound underneath a track or other audio that is at a higher volume.

dub (n, v) — Making a recording of a recording; for example, to record audio from a video.

establish (v) — After sound (usually ambience) is swept in, to maintain its volume. (See *hold* and *sweep*.)

fade (v) — To adjust the volume of sound from low to high or high to low at a gradual pace. Often used as a phrase: fade in, out, up, down, under, and so on.

fade to black (or fade away) (v) — To decrease the volume of a sound until it is inaudible—while still in the clear.

hit hot (v) — To begin playing at full volume.

hit warm (v) — To begin playing at medium volume.

hold (v) — To keep the volume of an audio element at the same level. Also known as *maintain*.

in the clear (adj) — When sound is in the foreground without competition from any other sound. Used for ambience or actualities. For instance, a reporter's sound-mixing instructions might say, "Maintain ambi of gunshots in the clear for four seconds."

maintain (v) — See *hold*.

mask (v) — To use existing ambient sound to cover over bad edits or to smooth transitions.

montage (n) — Several pieces of audio combined sequentially to create a single sound element.

post (v, n) — As a verb, to bring up a sound at a specific point so that it is in the foreground. Used for actualities or ambience; for instance, "Post ambi after politician says, 'I'm fighting for you!'" As a noun, the point at which the sound appears; for instance, "Hit the post."

room tone (n) — Indoor ambience recorded at the place where an interview is conducted or an event takes place. Usually low dynamic level. Can be spread beneath the dialogue track to help recordings from different times or locations sound consistent.

sneak (v) — To slowly fade up or out.

sweep (v, n) — To quickly fade up; a quick fade up.

sync up (v) — To combine two or more pieces of audio so that they line up exactly. Usually done with audio that matches; for example, a tape sync.

track (n) — The reporter's narrative, read from their script. Also known as *voice track*.

upcut (adj) — See *clipped*.

waterfall (n) — See *cascade*.

Resources

In addition to the articles, books, websites, and other sources listed in the Notes, this section highlights a selected list of audio- and podcast-related resources. Use these to build your information base and start your explorations.

ANALYSIS AND STATISTICS

Edison Research
Podcast research: https://www.edisonresearch.com/podcast-research

Podcast consumer tracking report: https://www.edisonresearch.com/the-podcast-consumer-quarterly-tracking-report

Podtrac: http://analytics.podtrac.com

BOOKS

Abel, Jessica. *Out on the Wire*. New York: Broadway Books, 2015.

Meinzer, Kristen. *So You Want to Start a Podcast*. New York: William Morrow, 2019.

Messenger, Ashley. *Media Law*. New York: Peter Lang Media & Communication, 2019.

Nuzum, Eric. *Make Noise*. New York: Workman Publishing, 2019.

Olmsted, Jill. *Tools for Podcasting*. Washington, DC: American University, 2019. http://toolsforpodcasting.openbooks.wpengine.com

LAWS AND REGULATIONS

Federal Trade Commission, "The FTC's Endorsement Guides: What People Are Asking": https://www.ftc.gov/tips-advice/business-center/guidance/ftcs-endorsement-guides-what-people-are-asking

Freedom of Information Act
https://www.ftc.gov/tips-advicebusiness-center/guidance/ftcs-endorsement-guides-what-people-are-asking

US Copyright Office

Performing arts: https://www.copyright.gov/registration/
    performing-arts

Frequently asked questions about copyright:
    https://www.copyright.gov/help/faq/index.html

US Patent and Trademark Office

https://www.uspto.gov

Reporters Committee for Freedom of the Press
Open Government Guide

https://www.rcfp.org/open-government-guide

AUDIO AND PODCAST GROUPS

Association of Independents in Radio (AIR): https://airmedia.org
POC Audio Directory: https://pocinaudio.com
Potluck Podcast Collective: https://podcastpotluck.com

NPR RESOURCES

Ethics Handbook: https://www.npr.org/ethics
Training: https://training.npr.org

PODCASTING NEWSLETTERS, BLOGS, AND WEBSITES

Bello Collective: https://bellocollective.com
Hot Pod: https://hotpodnews.com
The Infinite Dial: https://www.edisonresearch.com/
    the-infinite-dial
Podcast Business Journal: https://podcastbusinessjournal.com
Podnews: https://podnews.net
Transom: https://transom.org

Notes

Quotations from individuals interviewed for the book have been edited for concision and clarity. Citations are keyed to the page on which they appear.

INTRODUCTION: PODCASTING WITH A PLAN

1 *In 2019, the* New York Times: Jennifer Miller, "Have We Hit Peak Podcast?," *New York Times*, July 18, 2019, https://www.nytimes.com/2019/07/18/style/why-are-there-so-many-podcasts.html.

1 *podcasting reached a major:* Edison Research, "Podcasting and Audiobooks Both Attain 50% Reach; Facebook Usage Continues to Drop," The Infinite Dial 2019, March 6, 2019, https://www.edisonresearch.com/infinite-dial-2019.

2 *20 to 35 percent:* Tamar Charney, "How to Hook Your Podcast Audience," NPR Training, March 27, 2017, https://training.npr.org/2017/03/27/how-to-hook-your-podcast-audience.

6 *"If you've got a great idea":* Stephen Thompson, email communication, October 20, 2020.

CHAPTER 1: WAIT. WHAT *IS* A PODCAST?

9 *The narrow, conventional definition:* Jill Olmsted, *Tools for Podcasting* (Washington, DC: American University, 2019), 14, http://toolsforpodcasting.openbooks.wpengine.com.

10 *Some people listen:* Olmsted, 25.

10 *"Podcasts allow for":* Guy Raz, interview with author, October 29, 2020.

10 *In addition to searching:* Olmsted, 16.

11 *Podcasts can last:* Ross Winn, "What Is a Podcast and How Do They Work?," Podcast Insights, updated May 7, 2019, https://www.podcastinsights.com/what-is-a-podcast.

11 *Growth areas also include:* Olmsted, *Tools*, 17, 23.

13 *The male-to-female mix:* Tom Webster, "Three Ways to Survive Podcasting's Existential Crisis," *Medium*, August 29, 2019, https://medium.com/swlh/three-ways-to-survive-podcastings-existential-crisis-fe679f0da603.

13 *These days, women comprise:* Olmsted, *Tools*, 21.

13 *It'll be interesting to see:* Olmsted, *Tools*, 28.

13 *On an episode:* Kevin T. Porter, "Jon Gabrus Has an Educated Dockworker Voice," *Inside Voices*, Headgum, April 28, 2020, https://headgum.com/inside-voices/jon-gabrus-has-an-educated-dockworker-voice.

13 *Coined in 2004:* Ben Hammersley, "Audible Revolution," *Guardian*, February 11, 2004, https://www.theguardian.com/media/2004/feb/12/broadcasting.digitalmedia.

13 *thanks to blogs:* Nicholas Quah, "We're Entering the Era of Big Podcasting," Vulture, September 30, 2019, https://www.vulture.com/2019/09/podcasting-history-three-eras.html.

14 *Indeed, so ready:* "Podcasting Historical Timeline and Milestones," International Podcast Day, September 30, 2019, https://internationalpodcastday.com/podcasting-history.

14 *It survived the Great Recession:* Quah, "We're Entering the Era."

14 *by 2013, Apple had one billion:* "Podcasting Historical Timeline."

14 *Hollywood's looking:* Quah, "We're Entering the Era."

15 *"The best—and worst":* Linda Holmes, email communication, February 24, 2020.

16 *No media "gatekeepers":* Discover Pods, "How to Start a Podcast (The Complete Guide), October 29, 2019, https://discoverpods.com/start-a-podcast.

16 *if we want the direct, dynamic, interactive:* Hammersley, "Audible Revolution."

17 *"There are already a ton":* J. C. Howard, email communication, August 6, 2020.

CHAPTER 2: SO . . . HOW DO I GET STARTED?

19 *"Find something interesting":* Argin Hutchins, email communication, November 12, 2020.

20 *"There are definitely some podcasts":* Danielle Kurtzleben, email communication, August 8, 2020.

21 *"I have a really simple approach":* Guy Raz, interview with author, October 29, 2020.

21 *Are your listeners local:* NPR Training, "Project Blueprint," accessed September 3, 2019, https://training.npr.org/wp-content/uploads/2018/05/2018-Project-Blueprint-SLW.pdf; Tamar Charney, "How to Hook Your Podcast Audience," NPR Training, March 27, 2017, https://training.npr.org/2017/03/27/how-to-hook-your-podcast-audience.

22 *How is your audience feeling?:* Alison MacAdam, "Want to Start a Podcast? Read This First," NPR Training, June 19, 2018, https://training.npr.org/2018/06/19/so-you-want-to-start-a-podcast-read-this-first.

25 *"This seems really obvious":* Liana Simstrom, interview with author, November 7, 2019.

25 *Insights about something:* Alison MacAdam, "What Makes a Good Pitch? NPR Editors Weigh In," NPR Training, January 24, 2017, https://training.npr.org/2017/01/24/what-makes-a-good-pitch-npr-editors-weigh-in.

27 *Podcasts can be segmented:* These segment details are from Kristen Meinzer, *So You Want to Start a Podcast* (New York: William Morrow, 2019), chap. 6; Jill Olmsted, *Tools for Podcasting* (Washington, DC: American University, 2019), 35–36, http://toolsforpodcasting.openbooks.wpengine.com.

28 *"Terry Gross's interviews are probing":* Nicholas Quah, "10 Essential Conversation Podcasts That Shaped the Genre," Vulture, October 4, 2019, https://www.vulture.com/article/best-interview-conversation-podcasts.html.

28 *"I'm looking to move past":* Quotes by Jesse Thorn, email communication, October 18, 2019.

30 *You can do the interview:* Olmsted, *Tools,* 35.

30 *Writing's minimal:* Meinzer, *So You Want,* chap. 9.

31 *"It took about a week":* Gene Demby, email communication, February 11, 2019.

32 *Why a podcast?:* Unless otherwise noted, details in this list are from NPR Training, "Project Blueprint."

32 *"There was one story":* Demby, email.

33 *That said, data suggests:* Charney, "How to Hook."

33 *Who's your host?:* MacAdam, "Want to Start."

33 *Who is this podcast* not *for?:* Alison MacAdam, "Want Razor-Sharp Focus in Your Audio Stories? This Group Activity Can Help," NPR Training, September 24, 2018, https://training.npr.org/2018/09/24/focus-audio-stories-exercise-with-your-newsroom.

34 *You may be attracted:* Meinzer, *So You Want,* chap. 9.

35 *one-sentence description:* MacAdam, "Want to Start."

35 *How do they surprise:* MacAdam, "What Makes."

36 *getting directories like Apple:* Olmsted, *Tools,* 37.

36 *Ask them to describe:* Matthew McLean, "Podcast Names: What Should I Call My Podcast?," The Podcast Host, September 17, 2018, https://www.thepodcasthost.com/planning/podcast-names.

36 *It has to be intriguing:* Charney, "How to Hook."

37 *Straightforward podcast names:* McLean, "Podcast Names."

37 *Make sure that the name:* Stephanie Federico and Colin Dwyer, "How to Write Great Headlines That Keep Readers Engaged: 5 Tips (and Examples)," NPR Training, October 25, 2015, https://training.npr.org/2015/10/25/the-checklist-for-writing-good-headlines.

37 *Apple dominates the downloads:* Olmsted, *Tools,* 107.

37 *you need to be included:* McLean, "Podcast Names."

38 *"both an elevator pitch":* NPR Training, "Project Blueprint."

39 *"Doing something that":* Shereen Marisol Meraji, email communication, November 9, 2020.

39 *what spells "podcast success":* Details in this paragraph are from Olmsted, *Tools,* 34; MacAdam, "Want to Start"; and Meinzer, *So You Want,* chap. 1.

CHAPTER 3: WHO'S ON MY TEAM?

41 *"My advice for people":* Stephen Thompson, email communication, October 20, 2020.

44 *But producers can wear:* Kristen Meinzer, *So You Want to Start a Podcast* (New York: William Morrow, 2019), chap. 19.

46 *And it can be a smart move:* Ross Winn, "How to Start a Podcast: A Complete Step-by-Step Tutorial (2019 Guide)," Podcast Insights, updated November 8, 2019. https://www.podcastinsights .com/start-a-podcast.

47 *When I was an intern:* Jessica Reedy, interview with author, February 4, 2020.

47 *permission is always required:* Jill Olmsted, *Tools for Podcasting* (Washington, DC: American University, 2019), 130, http://toolsforpodcasting .openbooks.wpengine.com.

48 *Shop around, follow the rules:* Meinzer, *So You Want*, chap. 37.

48 *"Surround yourself with":* Shereen Marisol Meraji, email communication, November 9, 2020.

48 *enroll in formal classes:* Meinzer, So You Want, chap. 20.

48 *Businesses may choose:* Details here and below are from Colin Gray, "How Much Does Podcasting Cost in 2019?," The Podcast Host, September 10, 2019, https:// www.thepodcasthost.com/ planning/cost-of-podcasting.

50 *People in audio:* Yowei Shaw, interview with author, December 12, 2019.

CHAPTER 4: HOW LONG WILL IT TAKE AND WHAT'LL IT COST?

53 *"I should judge":* Thomas Lowry, *Personal Reminiscences of Abraham Lincoln* (London: Privately printed for Beatrice M. Lowry and her friends, 1910; repr., London: Chiswick Press, 1929), 23.

54 *might cause their podcast app:* Kristen Meinzer, *So You Want to Start a Podcast* (New York: William Morrow, 2019), chap. 28.

55 *Assign research:* Details in these lists are from Castos, "Four Ways to Stay Consistent with Your Podcast Editorial Calendar," updated May 13, 2019, https:// castos.com/podcast-editorial- calendar and "How to Set Up a Podcast Calendar," Podcast Motor, n.d., https://www .podcastmotor.com/setup- podcast-calendar/ (accessed December 7, 2019).

56 *This is the basic outline:* Adapted from Liana Simstrom, email communica- tion, November 11, 2019.

57 *A podcast publication schedule might:* Details in these lists are from Airtable, "Podcast Editorial Calendar," n.d., accessed December 7, 2019, https:// airtable.com/templates/ content-production/ expsl33kQMTB2vASp/ podcast-editorial-calendar.

57 *Will you do a series:* Kristen Meinzer, *So You Want*, chap. 28.

57 *able to count on you:* Jill Olmsted, *Tools for Podcasting* (Washington, DC: American University, 2019), 37, http://toolsforpodcasting .openbooks.wpengine.com.

58 *Businesses will expect ads:* Meagan Francis, "Are You Ready to Make Real Money?" *Podcast Business Journal*, December 3, 2019, https:// podcastbusinessjournal.com/ are-you-ready-to-make-real- money.

58 *giving yourself ample time:* Olmsted, *Tools*, 39.

58 *a three-part series:* Olmsted.

58 *Just make sure:* Meinzer, *So You Want*, chap. 28.

58 *Your first effort at podcasting:* Discover Pods, "How to Start a Podcast (The Complete Guide), July 2, 2020, https:// discoverpods.com/start-a- podcast.

59 *Do postmortems:* NPR Training, "Project Blueprint," accessed September 3, 2019, https://training.npr.org/wp- contentuploads/2018/05/ 2018-Project-Blueprint-SLW .pdf.

59 *Include your squad:* Ross Winn, "How to Start a Podcast: A Complete Step-by-Step Tutorial (2019 Guide)," Podcast Insights, updated October 1, 2020, https://www.podcastinsights .com/start-a-podcast; NPR Training, "Project Blueprint."

59 *In "Project Blueprint":* NPR Training, "Project Blueprint."

59 *You can promote:* Castos, "Four Ways to Stay."

60 *Keep a file:* Castos, "Four Ways to Stay."

60 *Have some easier-to-do epi- sodes:* Castos.

60 *Make time for mixing:* NPR, "Starting Your Podcast: A Guide for Students," November 15, 2018, https:// www.npr.org/2018/11/15/ 662070097/starting- your-podcast-a-guide- for-students.

61 *that might run you:* Meinzer, *So You Want*, chap. 21.

61 *you need to track:* Amanda McLoughlin, "Accounting for Podcasts," Bello Collective, July 17, 2017, https://bellocollective.com/

accounting-for-podcasters-792bb1f1a667.

62   *Call recording software:* Matthew McLean, "Best Call Recording App for Online Call & Remote Recording," The Podcast Host, November 6, 2019, https://www.thepodcast host.com/podcast-interviews/best-tools-for-recording-a-podcast-online.

63   *maybe invest in engaging:* Meinzer, *So You Want,* chap. 19.

CHAPTER 5: FINDING YOUR VOICE

69   *"Should I make":* Alison MacAdam, "How NPR's Sam Sanders Is Finding His Voice," NPR Training, February 25, 2015, https://training.np.org/2015/02/25/how-sam-sanders-is-finding-his-voice.

69   *"Everyone cringes when":* Manoush Zomorodi, email communication, November 2, 2020.

69   *"Don't be afraid to listen":* Cardiff de Alejo Garcia, cohost, *The Indicator from Planet Money.*

71   *"A lot of low vocal energy":* Jessica Hansen quoted from NPR Training, "Three Tips for Training Your Voice," YouTube, June 19, 2017, https://www.youtube.com/watch?v=cSTqKi7Wuq4.

72   *Vocal folds in:* Arika Okrent, "What Is Vocal Fry?," *Mental Floss,* August 24, 2018, https://www.mentalfloss.com/article/61552/what-vocal-fry.

73   *"From a vocal technique standpoint":* NPR Training, "Three Tips."

75   *The idea is to knock:* NPR Training, "Three Tips."

75   *Jessica Hansen, for example:* Jessica Hansen, "Aerobics for Your Voice: 3 Tips for Sounding Better On Air," NPR Training, June 19, 2017, https://training.npr.org/2017/06/19/aerobics-for-your-voice-3-tips-for-sounding-better-on-air.

75   *Script aloud:* Jill Olmsted, *Tools for Podcasting* (Washington, DC: American University, 2019), 90, http://toolsforpodcasting.openbooks.wpengine.com.

75   *as NPR correspondent Carrie Johnson does:* Alison MacAdam, "How NPR's Carrie Johnson Found Her Radio Voice," NPR Training, April 30, 2015, https://training.npr.org/2015/04/30how-nprs-carrie-johnson-found-her-radio-voice.

75   *"for keeping the voice":* Hansen, "Aerobics."

76   *Plosives (aka p-pops) and:* Unless otherwise noted, details in this section are from Rob Byers, "The Ear Training Guide for Audio Producers," NPR Training, January 31, 2017, https://training.npr.org/2017/01/31/the-ear-training-guide-for-audio-producers; Rob Byers, "The Producer's Handbook to Mixing Audio Stories," NPR Training, October 31, 2018, https://training.npr.org/2018/10/31/mixing; and Jeff Towne, "P-Pops and Other Plosives," Transom, April 27, 2016, https://transom.org/2016/p-pops-plosives.

76   *Equip the mic:* Olmsted, *Tools,* 92.

77   *Go slow:* Olmsted, *Tools,* 90.

77   *hold the phone near:* NPR, "NPR's Guide to Sending Audio," August 15, 2017, https://www.npr.org/2017/08/15/496888150/nprs-guide-to-sending-audio.

CHAPTER 6: THE WELL-EQUIPPED PODCAST

79   *You might already have the equipment:* NPR, "Starting Your Podcast: A Guide for Students," November 15, 2018, https://www.npr.org/2018/11/15/662070097/starting-your-podcast-a-guide-for-students.

80   *"One of the lazier reasons":* Yowei Shaw, interview with author, December 12, 2019.

80   *Then use free sound editing:* Colin Gray, "Podcast Software: The Complete Guide, From Plan to Edit," The Podcast Host, February 7, 2019, https://www.thepodcasthost.com/general/podcast-software; "Starting Your Podcast," NPR.

80   *it's not great for interviews:* Jill Olmsted, *Tools for Podcasting* (Washington, DC: American University, 2019), 49, http://toolsforpodcasting.openbooks.wpengine.com.

81   *For interviews—or:* Matthew McLean, "Best Call Recording App for Online Call & Remote Recording," The Podcast Host, November 6, 2019, https://www.thepodcasthost.com/podcast-interviews/best-tools-for-recording-a-podcast-online.

81   *That way, you can edit:* Olmsted, *Tools,* 49.

81 For example, maybe you sound fine: Matthew McLean, "How Much Editing Should I Do in My Podcast?," The Podcast Host, September 15, 2016, https://www.thepodcasthost.com/editing-production/much-editing-should-i-do-in-my-podcast.

81 Another issue: internet connectivity: McLean, "Best Call Recording."

81 Finally, the audio might sound: Rob Byers, "The Ear Training Guide for Audio Producers," NPR Training, January 31, 2017, https://training.npr.org/2017/01/31/the-ear-training-guide-for-audio-producers.

81 Try software: Gray, "Podcast Software."

82 Some questions: McLean, "Best Call Recording."

83 "I wouldn't go fancy": Yowei Shaw, interview with author, December 12, 2019.

83 "I wish someone": J. C. Howard, email communication, August 6, 2020.

83 going out in the field: Rob Byers, "Which Mic Should I Use? (Mics Part 1)," NPR Training, June 28, 2016, https://training.npr.org/2016/06/28/which-mic-should-i-use.

83 possibly a portable audio recorder: Kristen Meinzer, So You Want to Start a Podcast (New York: William Morrow, 2019), chap. 21.

83 Nothing in audio happens: Unless otherwise noted, the details in this section are from Teresa Chin, "DIY: How to Record High-Quality Sound with Your Phone,"

YR Media, February 26, 2015, https://yr.media/diy/diy-resource-how-to-record-high-quality-sound-with-your-phone; Meinzer, So You Want to Start, chap. 21; Ross Winn, "How to Start a Podcast: A Complete Step-by-Step Tutorial (2019 Guide)," Podcast Insights, updated October 1, 2020, https://www.podcastinsights.com/start-a-podcast/; and "XLR Connector," Techopedia, accessed January 6, 2020, https://www.techopedia.com/definition/31107/xlr-connector.

84 need what's called phantom power: Byers, "Which Mic Should I Use? (Mics Part 1)".

84 for podcast purposes, focus on: Discover Pods, "How to Start a Podcast (The Complete Guide)," October 11, 2019, https://discoverpods.com/start-a-podcast.

84 The key pickup patterns: Byers, "Which Mic."

84 Cardioid mics are good: Byers.

84 a plus if the room: Matthew McLean, "What Polar Pattern Should I Record My Podcast With?," The Podcast Host, July 11, 2016, https://www.thepodcasthost.com/equipment/microphone-polar-patterns.

84 These mics are sensitive: Jeff Towne, "P-Pops and Other Plosives," Transom, April 27, 2016, https://transom.org/2016/p-pops-plosives.

84 It could work if you've got: McLean, "What Polar Pattern."

84 Given the intimacy: Olmsted, Tools, 45.

84 You've got to hold it close: Byers, "Which Mic."

84 this mic is also more resistant: Rob Byers, "Get Great Sound Every Time with This Field Recording Checklist," NPR Training, June 30, 2017, https://training.npr.org/2017/06/30/get-great-sound-every-time-with-this-field-recording-checklist.

84 If you can't get: Towne, "P-Pops."

84 for one-on-one interviews: McLean, "What Polar Pattern"; Olmsted, Tools, 45.

85 But their sensitivity means: Byers, "Get Great Sound."

85 Don't hold the mic itself: Byers, "Which Mic."

85 These stalwart, stationary babies: Olmsted, Tools, 46.

85 Handhelds are affordable: Olmsted, 46–47.

85 You can attach: Olmsted, 48.

85 The mic's not close: Rob Byers, "Audio Production FAQ: Headphones, Levels, Mics, and More," NPR Training, May 19, 2017, https://training.npr.org/2017/05/19/audio-production-faq-headphones-levels-mics.

86 A mic can pick up: Olmsted, Tools, 50; Byers, "Which Mic."

86 A shock mount: Olmsted.

86 Described by Rob Byers: Byers, "Ear Training Guide"; Byers, "Audio Production FAQ."

86 It also helps keep saliva: Discover Pods, "How to Start."

86 *The mesh can be metal:* Towne, "P-Pops."

86 *Inexpensive and effective:* Olmsted, *Tools*, 49–50.

86 *But no pop filter screens out:* Byers, "Audio Production FAQ."

86 *A pop filter is a type:* Byers, "Ear Training Guide."

86 *Then there's the ginormous:* Towne, "P-Pops."

86 *"dead cat":* Olmsted, *Tools*, 49.

87 *Turn it on and it'll help:* Byers, "Which Mic."

87 *some reduction's better:* Byers, "Ear Training Guide."

87 *Many can more or less fit:* Jeff Towne, "Portable Digital Recorder Comparison," Transom, October 17, 2014, https://transom.org/2014/portable-digital-recorder-comparison.

87 *You transfer the tracks:* Meinzer, *So You Want*, chap. 21.

87 *Here are some factors to consider:* Unless otherwise noted, the details in this list are from Colin Gray, "The Best Digital Podcast Recorders on the Market," The Podcast Host, May 15, 2017, https://www.thepodcasthost.com/equipment/best-digital-podcast-recorders; Meinzer, *So You Want*, chap. 21; and Towne, "Portable Digital Recorder."

88 *Becoming a podcaster:* Byers, "Audio Production FAQ"; and Meinzer, *So You Want*, chap. 21.

88 *Don't get the noise-canceling:* Rob Byers, "The Producer's Handbook to Mixing Audio Stories," NPR Training, October 31, 2018, https://training.npr.org/2018/10/31/mixing.

88 *recording and editing software:* Unless otherwise noted, details in this section are from Meinzer, *So You Want*, chap. 21; Olmsted, *Tools*, 96–99; and Byers, "Producer's Handbook."

89 *If possible, find something:* Rob Byers, "The Audio Producer's Guide to Loudness," Transom, February 9, 2015, https://transom.org/2015/the-audio-producers-guide-to-loudness; For the Public Radio Satellite System's list of loudness tools, see http://prss.org/loudness-tools-list. For NPR's free version, see http://prss.org/loudness-tool.

90 *in a helpful how-to article:* Sean Phillips, "Protecting, Cleaning, and Sanitizing Your Gear the Right Way," NPR Training, June 5, 2020, https://training.npr.org/2020/06/05/protecting-cleaning-and-sanitizing-your-gear-the-right-way.

90 *Test it out!:* Details in this section are from Rob Byers, "Ask the Engineer: Don't Fear the Filter," Air, January 31, 2015, https://airmedia.org/tools/ask-engineer-dont-fear-filter; and Byers, "Producer's Handbook."

CHAPTER 7: AUDIO STORYTELLING 101

94 *"I think the most challenging":* J. C. Howard, email communication, August 6, 2020.

95 *other people's voices:* Kevin Wait, "Audio Truth Killers: An Approach to Collecting Better Sound," NPR Training, November 13, 2015, https://training.npr.org/2015/11/13/webinar-avoiding-audio-truth-killers-a-guide-to-getting-good-sound/.

95 *Figure out how every scene:* Alison MacAdam, "The Journey from Print to Radio Storytelling: A Guide for Navigating a New Landscape," NPR Training, December 6, 2017, https://training.npr.org/2017/12/06/the-journey-from-print-to-radio-storytelling-a-guide-for-navigating-a-new-landscape.

95 *readers can scan:* MacAdam, "Journey from Print."

96 *If listeners miss something:* Alison MacAdam, "How to Edit with Your Ears," NPR Training, November 13, 2015, https://training.npr.org/2015/11/13/how-to-edit-with-your-ears.

96 *Too much distance:* MacAdam, "Journey from Print."

96 *Like the yarns:* Chris Joyce, "Campfire Tales: The Essentials of Writing for Radio," NPR Training, March 20, 2015, https://training.npr.org/2015/03/20/campfire-tales-the-essentials-of-writing-for-radio.

96 *"We talk about beats":* Kelly McEvers, interview with author, June 8, 2020.

96 *Stick with one purpose:* Joyce, "Campfire Tales."

97 *grab your audience's attention:* Tamar Charney, "How to Hook Your Podcast Audience," NPR Training, March 27, 2017, https://training.npr.org/2017/03/27/how-to-hook-your-podcast-audience.

97 *not confused:* Alison MacAdam, "How a Long Audio Story Is Different from a Short One," NPR Training, March 9, 2015, https://training.npr.org/2015/03/09/how-a-long-audio-story-is-different-from-a-short-one.

97 *"What will the audience":* Alison MacAdam, "Beyond the 5 W's: What Should You Ask Before Starting a Story?," NPR Training, December 13, 2016, https://training.npr.org/2016/12/13/beyond-the-5ws-what-should-you-ask-before-starting-a-story.

97 *"We use the term* delight": Nick Fountain, interview with author, February 27, 2020.

97 *"We're very, very, very scripted":* McEvers, interview.

98 *might break into scenes:* MacAdam, "How a Long Audio."

98 *you can't really write:* NPR, "Starting Your Podcast: A Guide for Students," November 15, 2018, https://www.npr.org/2018/11/15/662070097/starting-your-podcast-a-guide-for-students.

98 *A basic outline:* Ross Winn, "How to Start a Podcast: A Complete Step-by-Step Tutorial (2019 Guide)," Podcast Insights, updated October 1, 2020, https://www.podcastinsights.com/start-a-podcast.

99 *"While I'm prepping":* Jesse Thorn, email communication, October 18, 2019.

100 *"To sound casual":* Fountain, interview.

100 *set up a template:* Podcast Production Company, "Producing a Podcast Part 1: Pre-Production," September 18, 2018, https://www.thepodcastproductioncompany.com/blog/2017/12/18/podcast-pre-production-what-to-do-before-hitting-record.

101 *It's not the "what":* Alison MacAdam, "Want Razor-Sharp Focus in Your Audio Stories? This Group Activity Can Help," NPR Training, September 24, 2018, https://training.npr.org/2018/09/24/focus-audio-stories-exercise-with-your-newsroom.

101 *"One of the first lessons":* Kenny Malone, email communication, November 5, 2020.

101 *Below is a list:* This list is adapted from Alison MacAdam, "From Pitch to Story: These 32 Questions Can Help Editors Guide Reporters," NPR Training, February 25, 2015, https://training.npr.org/2015/02/25/guiding-reporters-questions-an-audio-editor-should-ask.

102 *What are your dream ingredients?:* MacAdam, "Beyond the 5 W's."

102 *Now, imagine the desired effect:* This list is adapted from NPR Training, "Project Blueprint," accessed September 3, 2019, https://training.npr.org/wp-content/uploads/2018/05/2018-Project-Blueprint-SLW.pdf.

103 *"We would have weekly":* Sami Yenigun, interview with author, December 10, 2019.

103 *some questions to help:* Except as noted, this list is adapted from MacAdam, "From Pitch to Story."

103 *your reading will probably:* Jessica Deahl, "15 Principles of Show Booking," NPR Training, June 4, 2015, https://training.npr.org/2015/06/04/15-principles-of-show-booking.

103 *What scenes and sounds:* MacAdam, "Journey from Print."

104 *Do you have the time:* Alison MacAdam, "What Makes a Good Pitch? NPR Editors Weigh In," NPR Training, January 24, 2017, https://training.npr.org/2017/01/24/what-makes-a-good-pitch-npr-editors-weigh-in.

104 *What challenges:* Andrea de Leon, "Front-End Editing: The 'Secret Ingredient' of Great Audio Storytelling," NPR Training, May 19, 2016, https://training.npr.org/2016/05/19/front-end-editing-the-secret-ingredient-of-great-audio-storytelling.

104 *What would help:* NPR Training, "Project Blueprint."

104 *What's not going:* MacAdam, "Want Razor-Sharp Focus."

106 *start sketching:* Details in this section are from MacAdam, "Journey from Print"; and NPR Training, "Project Blueprint."

106 *Before your story's even:* Eric Athas, "This Headline Process Can Make Your Stories Better," NPR Training, October 23, 2015, https://training.npr.org/2015/10/23/headline-process-can-make-stories-better.

106 *two to three max:* de Leon, "Front-End Editing."

107　*story structures:* See Robert Smith, "You Asked: How Do You Tell a Story in 3 Acts?," NPR Training, November 10, 2017, https://training.npr.org/2017/11/10/you-asked-how-do-you-tell-a-story-in-3-acts; and MacAdam, "Want Razor-Sharp Focus."

107　*The best reporters:* Adapted from de Leon, "Front-End Editing."

107　*some basic story structures:* Details in this list are from Alison MacAdam, "Understanding Story Structure with the 'Three Little Pigs,'" NPR Training, March 24, 2015, https://training.npr.org/2015/03/24/understanding-story-structure-with-the-three-little-pigs; and Smith, "You Asked: How."

109　*"I think one of the best":* Yenigun, interview.

109　*Our NPR One platform:* Alison MacAdam, "How Audio Stories Begin," NPR Training, July 26, 2016, https://training.npr.org/2016/07/26/how-audio-stories-begin.

109　*Bottom Line:* Jill Olmsted, *Tools for Podcasting* (Washington, DC: American University, 2019), 76, http://toolsforpodcasting.openbooks.wpengine.com.

110　*listen to the intros:* Olmsted, *Tools for Podcasting,* 75.

111　*"Finding stories is the hardest":* Fountain, interview.

112　*Just always make sure:* Alison MacAdam, "Radio Intros: 7 Engagement Tips to Keep Listeners from Hitting the Skip Button," NPR Training, March 5, 2015, https://training.npr.org/2015/03/05/radio-intros-7-tips-to-keep-listeners-from-turning-off-the-radio.

112　*"Imagine your audio story":* Ramtin Arablouei, email communication, November 10, 2020.

113　*"The smallest tweak":* Yenigun, interview.

113　*"For a conversational show":* Jessica Reedy, interview with author, February 4, 2020.

113　*"One of the things":* Gene Demby, email communication, February 11, 2019.

114　*"Music isn't a magical power.":* Arablouei, email.

114　*"You shouldn't use":* Fountain, interview.

114　*music should add emotional dimension:* Details are from Jeffrey Pierre, "Everything You Need to Know About Using Music in Your Podcast," NPR, February 16, 2020, https://www.npr.org/2020/02/13/805858075/everything-you-need-to-know-about-using-music-in-your-podcast.

114　*"For instance, what types":* Argin Hutchins, email communication, November 12, 2020.

114　*"Never be obvious,":* Arablouei, email.

114　*"Sound design and music":* Rund Abdelfatah, email communication, October 29, 2020.

114　*"It's often good":* Fountain, interview.

114　*it shouldn't be distractingly complex,:* Pierre, "Everything You Need."

114　*"Have fun.":* Arablouei, email.

116　*"We try to write":* Fountain, interview.

116　*But there are norms:* Alison MacAdam, "What Does a Radio Script Look Like?" NPR Training, March 9, 2015, https://training.npr.org/2015/03/09/what-does-a-radio-script-look-like.

118　*Figure roughly five to six hundred words:* MacAdam, "Journey from Print."

118　*"Longer is not better":* Fountain, interview.

118　*make your speaking lines stand out:* MacAdam, "What Does a Radio."

119　*If you always open:* Olmsted, *Tools,* 71.

119　*Write out words:* MacAdam, "What Does a Radio."

119　*Don't leave the best for last:* Charney, "How to Hook."

119　*Put your outro to work:* Olmsted, *Tools,* 82.

119　*the old "call to action":* Jon Levy, "Everything You Need to Know to Start Your Own Podcast, According to the Pros," *Forbes,* February 28, 2018, https://www.forbes.com/sites/jonlevy/2018/02/28/everything-you-need-to-know-to-start-your-own-podcast-according-to-the-pros/#373f9de7792e.

120　*Hearing numbers is far harder:* MacAdam, "Journey from Print."

120　*Write the way you talk:* MacAdam.

120　*"If you are aiming":* Madeline K. Sofia, PhD, email communication, October 30, 2020.

120　*"Definitely go after things":* Yenigun, interview.

121　*"My practical advice on writing":* McEvers, interview.

CHAPTER 9: COLLECTING AUDIO LIKE A PRO

139 *As humans we use the sounds:* Kevin Wait, "Audio Truth Killers: An Approach to Collecting Better Sound," NPR Training, November 13, 2015, https://training.npr.org/2015/11/13/webinar-avoiding-audio-truth-killers-a-guide-to-getting-good-sound.

139 *the soundscape you create:* Rob Byers, "Put Your Audio to the Test: Know When to Use It or Lose It," NPR Training, January 17, 2017, https://training.npr.org/2017/01/17/put-your-audio-to-the-test-know-when-to-use-it-or-lose-it.

139 *your podcast's credibility:* Wait, "Audio Truth Killers."

140 *What sounds could help:* NPR Training, "Get Great Sound!" and "Field Recording Checklist," accessed September 5, 2019, https://training.npr.org/wp-content/uploads/2017/06/Field-Recording-Checklist.pdf.

140 *What's your wish list:* Rob Byers, "Audio Production FAQ: Headphones, Levels, Mics, and More," NPR Training, May 19, 2017, https://training.npr.org/2017/05/19/audio-production-faq-headphones-levels-mics.

140 *Start a list:* NPR, "Starting Your Podcast: A Guide for Students," November 15, 2018, https://www.npr.org/2018/11/15/662070097/starting-your-podcast-a-guide-for-students.

140 *a basic approach might be:* Ross Winn, "How to Start a Podcast: A Complete Step-by-Step Tutorial (2019 Guide)," Podcast Insights, updated October 1, 2020, https://www.podcastinsights.com/start-a-podcast; Colin Gray, "Podcast Software: The Complete Guide, From Plan to Edit," The Podcast Host, February 7, 2019, https://www.thepodcasthost.com/general/podcast-software.

140 *there's a mic for each person:* The Podcast Production Company, "Producing a Podcast Part 2: Production," September 25, 2018, https://www.thepodcastproductioncompany.com/blog/2018/9/25/producingapodcast-part2.

140 *If you're holding:* Cindy Carpien, "Read This Before You Record Ambience in the Field," NPR Training, January 17, 2015, https://training.npr.org/2015/01/17/read-this-before-you-record-ambience-in-the-field.

140 *Suppose in a public space:* Unless otherwise noted, the details in this section are from Yowei Shaw and Jeff Towne, "Voice Recording in the Home Studio," Transom, May 22, 2013, https://transom.org/2013/voice-recording-in-the-home-studio; Rob Byers, "The Ear Training Guide for Audio Producers," NPR Training, January 31, 2017, https://training.npr.org/2017/01/31/the-ear-training-guide-for-audio-producers; Podcast Production Company, "Producing a Podcast Part 2"; and NPR Training, "Get Great Sound!"

141 *Field Equipment:* NPR Training. "Get Great Sound!" and "Field Recording Checklist," NPR Training, accessed September 5, 2019, https://training.npr.org/wp-content/uploads/2017/06/Field-Recording-Checklist.pdf

142 *"Audio quality can":* Guy Raz, interview, October 29, 2020.

143 *Another option she suggests:* Yowei Shaw, interview with author, December 12, 2019.

143 *Some low-level background:* NPR, "Starting Your Podcast."

143 *In a home:* Rob Rosenthal, "Before the First Question: How to Prepare for an Audio Interview," NPR Training, October 8, 2015, https://training.npr.org/2015/10/08/before-the-first-question-how-to-prepare-for-an-audio-interview.

143 *Try inside a car:* Byers, "Audio Production FAQ"; Byers, "Ear Training Guide."

143 *run a test that mimics:* The Podcast Production Company, "5 Mistakes That Make Your Podcast Sound Amateurish," October 3, 2017, https://www.thepodcastproductioncompany.com/blog/2017/10/3/5-mistakes-that-make-your-podcast-sound-amateurish.

143 *bringing a buddy:* Podcast Production Company, "Producing a Podcast Part 2."

143 *go over your script:* Jill Olmsted, *Tools for Podcasting* (Washington, DC: American University, 2019), 91, http://toolsforpodcasting.openbooks.wpengine.com.

143 *But beware of the dreaded:* Podcast Production Company, "Producing a Podcast Part 2."

144 *Charge all batteries:* Byers, "Ear Training Guide."

144 *bring a stopwatch:* Podcast Production Company, "Producing a Podcast Part 2."

144 *For location work:* Rosenthal, "Before the First Question."

144   *Whether it's opposite:* Rosenthal.

144   *Audio makers have to hear:* Byers, "Audio Production FAQ."

144   *had to turn the volume:* Rob Byers, "The Producer's Handbook to Mixing Audio Stories," NPR Training, October 31, 2018, https://training.npr.org/2018/10/31/mixing.

145   *If you're recording:* Byers, "Audio Production FAQ."

145   *Now, do a little mic tutorial:* Byers, "Ear Training Guide."

145   *Next do a test:* The Podcast Production Company, "Producing a Podcast Part 1: Pre-Production," September 18, 2018, https://www.the podcastproductioncompany .com/blog/2017/12/18/podcast-pre-production-what-to-do-before-hitting-record.

145   *For sibilance:* Byers, "Ear Training Guide."

145   *To minimize time editing out:* Byers.

145   *If so, flip on:* Shaw and Towne, "Voice Recording."

145   *or your recorder's:* Rob Byers, "Ask the Engineer: Don't Fear the Filter," Air, January 31, 2015, https://airmedia.org/tools/ask-engineer-dont-fear-filter.

145   *"slate the tape":* Rosenthal, "Before the First Question."

145   *say their own name:* Alison MacAdam, "Active Sound: How to Find It, Record It, and Use It," NPR Training, September 29, 2015, https://training.npr.org/2015/09/29/active-sound-how-to-find-it-record-it-and-use-it.

145   *Don't be afraid:* Discover Pods, "How to Start a

Podcast (The Complete Guide)," July 2, 2020, https://discoverpods.com/start-a-podcast.

146   *Do these things while:* The details in this list are from Wait, "Audio Truth Killers"; and Byers, "Ear Training Guide."

149   *You can use it:* Unless otherwise noted, details in this section are from MacAdam, "Active Sound."

149   *"You can ask people:* Nick Fountain, interview with author, February 27, 2020.

149   *And keep in mind these tips:* This list is excerpted from NPR Training, "Get Great Sound!"

150   *Ambient sound is:* Carpien, "Read This Before."

150   *use it under your vocal tracks:* Byers, "Audio Production FAQ."

150   *Get one minute* minimum: Byers, "Ear Training Guide."

150   *To give yourself:* Carpien, "Read This Before."

150   *Narration can help:* Alison MacAdam, "You Asked: How Can I Get Better at Standups?" NPR Training, March 15, 2017, https://training.npr.org/2017/03/15/you-asked-how-can-i-get-better-at-standups.

151   *Then add spotty internet:* Gray, "Podcast Software."

151   *see if you:* Olmsted, *Tools*, 58.

151   *One method, a tape sync:* Alison MacAdam, "'Butt Cut What?' A Glossary of Audio Production Terms and Definitions," NPR Training, June 1, 2015, https://training.npr.org/2015/06/01/butt-cut-what-a-glossary-of-production-terms.

151   *If both parties have:* Sam Mallery, "My First Experience Recording a 'Double Ender' Podcast" (blog), September 7, 2016, http://www.sam-mallery.com/2016/09/my-first-experience-recording-a-double-ender-podcast.

151   *For optimal mic position:* NPR, "NPR's Guide to Sending Audio," August 15, 2017, https://www.npr.org/2017/08/15/496888150/nprs-guide-to-sending-audio.

151   *your interviewee has the software/an account:* Olmsted, *Tools*, 58–59.

151   *They should use a headset or earbud mic:* Byers, "Ear Training Guide."

151   *If the quality's really bad:* Wait, "Audio Truth Killers."

151   *You can also ask:* Alison MacAdam, "The Journey from Print to Radio Storytelling: A Guide for Navigating a New Landscape," NPR Training, December 6, 2017, https://training.npr.org/2017/12/06/the-journey-from-print-to-radio-storytelling-a-guide-for-navigating-a-new-landscape.

151   *You could even record scene-description:* MacAdam, "You Asked: How Can."

151   *listen back to your tape:* NPR Training, "Get Great Sound!"

151   *take some pix or video:* Linda Lutton, "How to Inject 'Documentary Flair' into Your Story," NPR Training, November 17, 2015, https://training.npr.org/2015/11/17/how-to-inject-documentary-flair-into-your-story.

152   *Ten Commandments of Recording:* MacAdam, "Active Sound."

153 *"Get a lot of ambi":* Fountain, interview.

CHAPTER 10: ACING THE INTERVIEW

155 *an interview's got to be:* Jennifer Miller, "Have We Hit Peak Podcast?," *New York Times*, July 18, 2019, https://www.nytimes.com/2019/07/18/style/why-are-there-so-many-podcasts.html.

155 *to expand your audience:* Ross Winn, "How to Start a Podcast: A Complete Step-by-Step Tutorial (2019 Guide)," Podcast Insights, updated October 1, 2020, https://www.podcastinsights.com/start-a-podcast.

156 *"Terry Gross is a brilliant genius":* Jesse Thorn, email communication, October 18, 2019.

156 *to help them relax:* Alison MacAdam, "The Journey from Print to Radio Storytelling: A Guide for Navigating a New Landscape," NPR Training, December 6, 2017, https://training.npr.org/2017/12/06/the-journey-from-print-to-radio-storytelling-a-guide-for-navigating-a-new-landscape.

156 *NPR publishes its standards of journalism:* NPR, *NPR Ethics Handbook*, n.d., accessed September 13, 2019, https://www.npr.org/ethics; the quote is from "Respect" in "These Are the Standards of Our Journalism."

156 *That's not a good use:* Sally Herships, "The Art of the Preinterview," Transom, October 25, 2016, https://transom.org/2016/art-preinterview.

156 *Enter: the preinterview:* Jessica Deahl, "15 Principles of Show Booking," NPR

Training, June 4, 2015, https://training.npr.org/2015/06/04/15-principles-of-show-booking.

157 *"We do a ton":* Kelly McEvers, interview with author, June 8, 2020.

157 *Before you record anything:* NPR, "Starting Your Podcast: A Guide for Students," November 15, 2018, https://www.npr.org/2018/11/15/662070097/starting-your-podcast-a-guide-for-students.

157 *You never know:* Deahl, "15 Principles."

158 *Your preinterview should:* Deahl.

158 *While you want:* Unless otherwise noted, details in the rest of this section are from Herships, "Art of the Preinterview," and Deahl, "15 Principles."

158 *"We're sort of in":* McEvers, interview.

159 *get their name right:* Deahl, "15 Principles."

159 *start sounding stilted:* Herships, "Art of the Preinterview."

159 *"I often tell prospective":* Deahl, "15 Principles."

159 Scope out the technical side: Deahl.

160 *Try to get everything:* MacAdam, "Journey from Print."

160 *"For a half-hour show":* Sami Yenigun, interview with author, December 10, 2019.

160 *"Audie Cornish is astonishingly":* Thorn, email.

160 *"The kind of supercharged secret":* Guy Raz, interview with author, October 29, 2020.

161 *"If I find media":* Thorn, email.

161 *You want them:* NPR, "Starting Your Podcast."

162 *And set your levels:* Rob Rosenthal, "Before the First Question: How to Prepare for an Audio Interview," NPR Training, October 8, 2015, https://training.npr.org/2015/10/08/before-the-first-question-how-to-prepare-for-an-audio-interview.

162 *Bring your interview questions:* Rosenthal.

162 *"I think Ira Glass":* Thorn, email.

162 *Make the person feel comfortable:* Rosenthal, "Before the First Question."

162 *"I try to put them":* Thorn, email.

163 *let the person know:* Rosenthal, "Before the First Question."

163 *slate the tape:* Rosenthal.

163 *ask your interviewee:* NPR, "Starting Your Podcast."

163 *ask them to describe:* MacAdam, "Journey from Print."

163 *"I listen when they talk":* Thorn, email.

164 *"We really like when":* Nick Fountain, interview with author, February 27, 2020.

164 *It's another to lead:* MacAdam, "Journey from Print."

165 *"Susan Orlean, who writes":* Thorn, email.

165 *Try to get at:* Linda Lutton, "How to Inject 'Documentary Flair' into Your Story," NPR Training, November 17, 2015, https://

training.npr.org/2015/11/17/how-to-inject-documentary-flair-into-your-story.

165 *"There's nothing wrong"*: Raz, interview.

165 *"If the interview"*: Thorn, email.

166 *"Sometimes when you're"*: Yowei Shaw, interview with author, December 12, 2019.

167 *you want your podcast*: Jill Olmsted, *Tools for Podcasting* (Washington, DC: American University, 2019), 74, http://toolsforpodcasting.openbooks.wpengine.com.

168 *"I interviewed Betty Davis"*: Thorn, email.

168 *Just let your guest*: MacAdam, "Journey from Print."

168 *Say thank you*: Deahl, "15 Principles."

168 *"Note the things"*: Rund Abdelfatah, email communication, October 29, 2020.

168 *"Be curious"*: Thorn, email.

CHAPTER 11: IT'S ALL IN THE MIX

171 *It's about cutting*: Colin Gray, "Podcast Software: The Complete Guide, From Plan to Edit," The Podcast Host, February 7, 2019, https://www.thepodcasthost.com/general/podcast-software.

171 *The goal of both*: Kevin Wait, "Audio Truth Killers: An Approach to Collecting Better Sound," NPR Training, November 13, 2015, https://training.npr.org/2015/11/13/webinar-avoiding-audio-truth-killers-a-guide-to-getting-good-sound.

172 *"People think we"*: Jessica Reedy, interview with author, February 4, 2020.

172 *Glaring errors and*: The Podcast Production Company, "5 Mistakes That Make Your Podcast Sound Amateurish," October 3, 2017, The Podcast Production Company.

172 *Crackly distortion*: Rob Byers, "The Ear Training Guide for Audio Producers," NPR Training, January 31, 2017, https://training.npr.org/2017/01/31/the-ear-training-guide-for-audio-producers.

172 *this might be a stage*: Jon Levy, "Everything You Need to Know to Start Your Own Podcast, According to the Pros," *Forbes*, February 28, 2018, https://www.forbes.com/sites/jonlevy/2018/02/28/everything-you-need-to-know-to-start-your-own-podcast-according-to-the-pros.

172 *producers strive for*: Rob Byers, "Put Your Audio to the Test: Know When to Use It or Lose It," NPR Training, January 17, 2017, https://training.npr.org/2017/01/17/put-your-audio-to-the-test-know-when-to-use-it-or-lose-it; and Wait, "Audio Truth Killers."

173 *They know that their*: Wait, "Audio Truth Killers."

173 *Use your headphones*: Rob Byers, "Audio Production FAQ: Headphones, Levels, Mics, and More," NPR Training, May 19, 2017, https://training.npr.org/2017/05/19/audio-production-faq-headphones-levels-mics.

173 *Ideally, listen as many ways*: Rob Byers, "The Producer's Handbook to Mixing Audio Stories," NPR Training, October 31, 2018, https://training.npr.org/2018/10/31/mixing; and Kevin Wait, "Rock and Roll Mixing Tricks for Journalists," NPR Training, October 23, 2019, https://training.npr.org/2015/10/23/rock-and-roll-mixing-tricks-for-journalists.

173 *Make a hit list of major*: Podcast Production Company, "5 Mistakes"; and Matthew McLean, "How Much Editing Should I Do in My Podcast?," The Podcast Host, September 15, 2016, https://www.thepodcasthost.com/editing-production/much-editing-should-i-do-in-my-podcast.

173 *Create time-saving templates*: Ross Winn, "How to Start a Podcast: A Complete Step-by-Step Tutorial (2019 Guide)," Podcast Insights, updated October 1, 2020, https://www.podcastinsights.com/start-a-podcast; Byers, "Producer's Handbook."

173 *After you fix one thing*: Byers, "Producer's Handbook."

174 *fatigue can set in*: Wait, "Rock and Roll."

174 *sleep on it*: Reedy, interview.

174 *Here is an eight-step walkthrough*: This section is adapted from Rob Byers, "How to Mix: 8 Steps to Master the Art of Mixing Audio Stories," NPR Training, October 31, 2018, https://training.npr.org/2018/10/31/mixing-diy. Unless otherwise noted, details are also from Byers, "Producer's Handbook," and Byers "Ear Training Guide."

175 *Audio editing software:* Details in this list are from Byers, "Producer's Handbook."

176 *To check levels:* Wait, "Rock and Roll."

176 *"Some of it is":* Reedy, interview.

177 *help you eliminate:* Jeff Towne, "Real World EQ," Transom, March 11, 2003, https://transom.org/2003/real-world-eq.

177 *Low-pass filters might:* Towne.

179 *and natural:* Reedy, interview.

179 *or breaths upcut:* Rob Byers, "Do You Have the Ears of an Audio Producer?," NPR Training, January 30, 2017, https://training.npr.org/2017/01/30/quiz-do-you-have-the-ears-of-an-audio-producer.

179 *insert a teeny pause:* Reedy, interview.

180 *If you can't solve:* Byers, "Do You Have the Ears."

181 *"Trade your ears":* Yowei Shaw, interview with author, December 12, 2019.

CHAPTER 12: SHAPING THE STORY

183 *"The primary job":* Sami Yenigun, interview with author, December 10, 2019.

183 *So, take a look at:* Unless otherwise noted, details are from Rob Rosenthal, "Imagining the Story," Transom, October 25, 2011, https://transom.org/2011/rob-rosenthal-imagining-the-story.

183 *"Be open to the story":* Rund Abdelfatah, email communication, October 29, 2020.

184 *Based on the tape:* Chris Joyce, "Campfire Tales: The Essentials of Writing for Radio," NPR Training, March 20, 2015, https://training.npr.org/2015/03/20/campfire-tales-the-essentials-of-writing-for-radio.

184 *Have you looked:* Alison MacAdam, "From Pitch to Story: These 32 Questions Can Help Editors Guide Reporters," NPR Training, February 25, 2015, https://training.npr.org/2015/02/25/guiding-reporters-questions-an-audio-editor-should-ask.

184 *Does it have enough:* NPR Training, "Project Blueprint," accessed September 3, 2019, https://training.npr.org/wp-content/uploads/2018/05/2018-Project-Blueprint-SLW.pdf.

184 *"I used to tear":* Liana Simstrom, interview with author, November 7, 2019.

185 *ask yourself if:* Alison MacAdam, "Beyond the 5 W's: What Should You Ask Before Starting a Story?," NPR Training, December 13, 2016, https://training.npr.org/2016/12/13/beyond-the-5ws-what-should-you-ask-before-starting-a-story.

185 *"We had a situation":* Jessica Reedy, interview with author, February 4, 2020.

185 *Beware of using sound untruthfully:* Kevin Wait, "Audio Truth Killers: An Approach to Collecting Better Sound," NPR Training, November 13, 2015, https://training.npr.org/2015/11/13/webinar-avoiding-audio-truth-killers-a-guide-to-getting-good-sound.

185 *CBS got busted doing that:* Wait.

185 *It's fine to combine or select:* Alison MacAdam, "Active Sound: How to Find It, Record It and Use It," NPR Training, September 29, 2015, https://training.npr.org/2015/09/29/active-sound-how-to-find-it-record-it-and-use-it.

185 *"A conversation may":* Yenigun, interview.

186 *time markers:* The Podcast Production Company, "Producing a Podcast Part 1: Pre-Production," September 18, 2018, https://www.thepodcastproductioncompany.com/blog/2017/12/18/podcast-pre-production-what-to-do-before-hitting-record.

186 *Definitely clean up:* The Podcast Production Company, "Producing a Podcast Part 3: Post-Production," October 2, 2018, https://www.thepodcastproductioncompany.com/blog/2018/2/10/podcastpostproduction.

186 *"Sometimes at PCHH when they talk":* Reedy, interview.

187 *"There's a really good":* Yenigun, interview.

188 *Include who says what:* NPR, "Starting Your Podcast: A Guide for Students," November 15, 2018, https://www.npr.org/2018/11/15/662070097/starting-your-podcast-a-guide-for-students.

188 *Include timing and production directions:* Alison MacAdam, "What Does a Radio Script Look Like?," NPR Training, March 9, 2015, https://training.npr.org/2015/03/09/what-does-a-radio-script-look-like.

188 *If there's any chance:* MacAdam, "Active Sound."

188 *To hold interest:* MacAdam.

188 *Let your actualities:* Joyce, "Campfire Tales."

189 *"I would listen":* Yenigun, interview.

189 *let's just think in terms:* NPR Training, "Project Blueprint."

189 *If your podcast's dialogue-driven:* Podcast Production Company, "Producing a Podcast Part 3."

189 *But while you work:* Jeff Pierre and Lauren Migaki, "Everything You Need to Know About Using Music in Your Podcast," NPR, February 16, 2020, https://www.npr.org/transcripts/805858075.

189 *We sometimes call this:* Unless otherwise noted, details in this section are from Alison MacAdam, "How to Edit with Your Ears," NPR Training, November 13, 2015, https://training.npr.org/2015/11/13/how-to-edit-with-your-ears.

189 *Or your interviewee:* Alison MacAdam, "The Journey from Print to Radio Storytelling: A Guide for Navigating a New Landscape," NPR Training, December 6, 2017, https://training.npr.org/2017/12/06/the-journey-from-print-to-radio-storytelling-a-guide-for-navigating-a-new-landscape.

189 *"Typically, I do a rough":* Reedy, interview.

190 *"We usually go through":* Simstrom, interview.

190 *"Does this conversation":* Yenigun, interview.

190 *without giving away:* AlisonMacAdam, "Radio Intros: 5 Examples of Success," NPR Training, January 10, 2017, https://training.npr.org/2017/01/10/radio-intros-5-examples-of-success.

191 *sentences not punchy:* Joyce, "Campfire Tales."

191 *Stronger signposting or transitions:* Alison MacAdam, "Vocabulary for an Audio Editor: 15 Things to Say…Over and Over . . . ," NPR Training, May 14, 2015, https://training.npr.org/2015/05/14/vocabulary-for-an-editor-15-things-to-say-over-and-over.

191 *Figure out which facts:* Alison MacAdam, "'Once Upon a Time' and Other Devices for Starting Your Story," NPR Training, February 18, 2015, https://training.npr.org/2015/02/18/beginnings-where-do-i-start-my-audio-story.

191 *Ask someone else:* MacAdam.

191 *"We've become diligent":* Gene Demby, email communication, February 11, 2019.

192 *This time, follow:* MacAdam, "How to Edit."

192 *Is the writing skating:* MacAdam.

192 *Set up those sections:* Reedy, interview.

192 *Will your audience know:* MacAdam, "Radio Intros."

192 *Are there twists*: Robert Smith, "Understanding Story Structure in 4 Drawings," NPR Training, March 2, 2016, https://training.npr.org/2016/03/02/understanding-story-structure-in-4-drawings.

192 *Sometimes adding a rhythm:* Pierre and Migaki, "Everything You Need."

192 *If you're using music:* Michael May, "Score! Best Practices for Using Music in Audio Storytelling," NPR Training, July 5, 2016, https://training.npr.org/2016/07/05/score-best-practices-for-using-music-in-audio-storytelling.

192 *Does every scene:* MacAdam, "From Pitch to Story."

193 *"We first note big-picture stuff":* Yenigun, interview.

193 "The only person": Sam Sanders, email communication, November 9, 2020.

193 *"For episodes where":* Jessica Reedy quotes from Reedy, interview.

194 *"When we first started Embedded":* Kelly McEvers, interview with author, June 8, 2020.

194 *"When I was an intern":* Reedy, interview.

195 *If you aren't sure:* Russell Lewis, "Russell Lewis's Guide to Fact Checking," NPR Training, October 7, 2015, https://training.npr.org/2015/10/07/russell-lewis-guide-to-fact-checking.

195 *business and school names:* NPR, "The NPR Accuracy Checklist," NPR Training, n.d., accessed September 13, 2019, https://training.npr.org/wp-content/uploads/2015/03/The-NPR-Accuracy-Checklist1.pdf.

195 *our* NPR Ethics Handbook *can:* NPR, *NPR Ethics Handbook*, n.d., accessed September 13, 2019, https://www.npr.org/ethics.

195 *"As everybody gets":* Reedy, interview.

195 *"I've heard many audio":* Shaw, interview.

196 *"I'm not trying to say":* McEvers, interview.

CHAPTER 13: ME, MY PLATFORM, AND I

202 *"My model of promotion ":* J. C. Howard, email communication, November 6, 2020.

203 *Talk their talk:* Ilise Benun, "'Your Self Promotion Is Not About You'—What This Really Means," Marketing Mentor, July 9, 2016, https://www.marketing-mentor.com/blogs/news/your-self-promotion-is-not-about-you-what-this-really-means.

203 *It's not about what you do:* Benun.

203 *"Think give, not get":* Sara Horowitz, with Toni Sciarra Poynter, *The Freelancer's Bible* (New York: Workman Publishing Company, 2012), 207.

204 *Have freebies:* Castos, "How to Promote a Podcast: The 2020 Ultimate Guide," updated June 22, 2020, https://castos.com/how-to-promote-a-podcast.

204 *just one idea or request:* Lisa Mullis, "6 Tips to Build (or Reboot) Your Email List," Marketing Mentor, May 1, 2017, https://www.marketing-mentor.com/blogs/news/6-tips-to-build-or-reboot-your-email-list.

204 *Be someone who asks:* Castos, "How to Promote a Podcast."

204 *get their permission:* Ilise Benun, "When You Add Someone to Your Email List, Say This . . . ," Marketing Mentor, July 21, 2019, https://www.marketing-mentor.com/blogs/news/want-to-add-someone-to-your-email-list-say-this.

205 *It's a smart way:* Castos, "How to Promote Your Podcast to Your E-mail List," updated July 9, 2020, https://castos.com/promote-your-podcast-to-your-email-list; Frank Racioppi, "Why Your Podcast Definitely Needs a Website," Discover Pods, February 11, 2020, https://discoverpods.com/podcast-needs-website.

205 *What if you've only got time:* Ilise Benun, "Email Newsletter vs. Blog: What's the Difference?," Marketing Mentor, October 14, 2018, https://www.marketing-mentor.com/blogs/news/email-newsletter-vs-blog-whats-the-difference.

205 *Be sure to announce:* Castos, "How to Promote Your Podcast."

206 *"We have a newsletter":* Liana Simstrom, interview with author, November 7, 2019.

207 *stuff you might develop:* Racioppi, "Why Your Podcast."

207 *Potential sponsors, too:* Meagan Francis, "Are You Ready to Make Real Money?," *Podcast Business Journal*, December 3, 2019, https://podcastbusinessjournal.com/are-you-ready-to-make-real-money.

207 *"[Our] podcast relied":* J. C. Howard, email.

208 *Having a web presence:* RSS.com, "9 Effective SEO Tips for Podcasts," n.d., accessed May 25, 2020, https://rss.com/blog/nine-seo-tips-for-podcasts.

208 *regular activity:* Castos, "How to Promote a Podcast."

208 *But audio files:* Colin Gray, "The Best Podcast Hosting Services: Where to Host Your Podcast," The Podcast Host, September 16, 2019, https://www.thepodcasthost.com/websites-hosting/best-podcast-hosting.

208 *what professionals:* Ben Krueger, "Podcast Promotion Playbook: The Top 3 Ways to Promote Your Podcast," Cashflow Podcasting, July 30, 2019, https://cashflowpodcasting.com/podcast-promotion.

208 *make a list of podcasters:* Kristen Meinzer, *So You Want to Start a Podcast* (New York: William Morrow, 2019), chap. 35.

209 *follow them on social media:* Wenbin Fang, "How to Promote Podcasts: 21 Ways of Promoting Podcasts—Tips from 269 Indie Podcaster Interviews," Listen Notes, Podcast Academy, August 1, 2019, https://www.listennotes.com/podcast-academy/how-to-promote-podcasts-21-ways-of-promoting-14.

209 *Be sure to thank them:* Meinzer, *So You Want*, chap. 37.

209 *guest—hosting or interviewing:* Fang, "How to Promote Podcasts."

209 *Once you're ready to fully take on:* Unless otherwise noted, details in this section are from Allen Kratz, "20 Strategic Networking Steps for Your Next Business Conference," https://www.marketing-mentor.com/blogs/news/how-to-optimize-strategic-networking-at-your-next-business-conference; Castos, "How to Promote a Podcast"; and Meinzer, *So You Want*, chap. 37.

209 *Have business cards:* Fang, "How to Promote Podcasts."

211 "The most important thing": Shankar Vedantam, email communication, October 27, 2020.

CHAPTER 14: COUNTDOWN TO LAUNCH

213 *Is this podcast the one:* Matty Staudt, "8 Mistakes to Avoid When You Launch," *Podcast Business Journal*, November 13, 2019, https://podcast businessjournal.com/8-mistakes-to-avoid-when-you-launch.

214 *the guidelines we at NPR suggest:* Alison MacAdam, "Six Ways to Run a Listening Session," NPR Training, February 16, 2016, https://training.npr.org/2016/02/16/six-ways-to-run-a-listening-session.

214 *"making a lot of bad things":* Yowei Shaw, interview with author, December 12, 2019.

214 *"The key is to keep":* Rund Abdelfatah, email communication, October 29, 2020.

215 "There is no such thing": Sam Sanders, email communication, November 9, 2020.

215 *Picture the person:* Werk It: The Podcast, "How to Market Your Show," WNYC Studios, January 23, 2019, https://www.wnycstudios.org/podcasts/werkit/articles/how-market-your-show.

215 *review the show, share it, follow it:* Castos, "How to Promote a Podcast: The 2020 Ultimate Guide," updated June 22, 2020, https://castos.com/how-to-promote-a-podcast.

216 *insert ads in previous episodes:* Meagan Francis, "Real Money Can Be Made Podcasting," *Podcast Business Journal*, November 25, 2019, https://podcast businessjournal.com/real-money-can-be-made-podcasting.

216 *edited and uploaded:* Jill Olmsted, *Tools for Podcasting* (Washington, DC: American University, 2019), 39, http://toolsforpodcasting.openbooks.wpengine.com.

217 *"Pretend an elevator door":* Stephanie Federico and Colin Dwyer, "How to Write Great Headlines That Keep Readers Engaged: 5 Tips (and Examples)," NPR Training, October 25, 2015, https://training.npr.org/2015/10/25/the-checklist-for-writing-good-headlines.

217 *Brainstorm with or:* Eric Athas, "This Headline Process Can Make Your Stories Better," NPR Training, October 23, 2015, https://training.npr.org/2015/10/23/headline-process-can-make-stories-better.

217 *Definitely number them:* Kristen Meinzer, *So You Want to Start a Podcast* (New York: William Morrow, 2019), chap. 30.

220 *take a few of those:* This is adapted from Alison MacAdam, "From Pitch to Story: These 32 Questions Can Help Editors Guide Reporters," NPR Training, February 25, 2015, https://training.npr.org/2015/02/25/guiding-reporters-questions-an-audio-editor-should-ask.

221 *How might people:* NPR Training, *Project Blueprint*, accessed September 3, 2019, https://training.npr.org/wp-content/uploads/2018/05/2018-Project-Blueprint-SLW.pdf.

221 *add ways:* Meinzer, *So You Want.*

221 *you're improving (optimizing):* Mike McEvoy, "SEO Titles, SEO Descriptions, Meta Tags, Meta Data Explained," Web Presence Solutions, October 2, 2019, https://www.webpresencesolutions.net/metadata-meta-tags-web-page-titles-page-descriptions-explained.

221 *phrases and terms related:* Meinzer, *So You Want.*

221 *And it's smart:* Werk It, "How to Market."

222 *this is a brand statement:* Discover Pods, "How to Start a Podcast (The Complete Guide)," July 2, 2020, https://discoverpods.com/start-a-podcast.

222 *You might find:* Meinzer, *So You Want*, chap. 29.

222 *If you've got design chops:* Olmsted, *Tools*, 41–43.

222 *some general guidelines:* Unless otherwise noted, details in this list are from Matthew McLean, "How to Make Great Podcast Cover Art (aka Your Podcast Logo)," The Podcast Host, February 12, 2020, https://www.thepodcasthost.com/promotion/how-to-create-your-podcast-cover-art; and Georgia Grey, "How to Create Amazing Podcast Cover Art: A Complete Guide," Spreaker (blog), August 17, 2016, https://blog.spreaker.com/9-steps-making-great-podcast-cover-art.

222 *check your podcast name:* Olmsted, *Tools*, 37.

223 *Publishing free transcripts:* Olmsted, 110–17.

223 *It makes your content:* RSS. com, "How to Transcribe Podcast Audio—the Tools to Use, and Why You Should Do It," n.d., accessed May 25, 2020, https://rss.com/blog/ how-to-transcribe-podcast-audio.

224 *(including you!):* Join the Party Podcast, "The Podcaster's Guide to Transcribing Audio," Bello Collective, March 19, 2018, https://bellocollective.com/ the-podcasters-guide-to-transcribing-audio-2121f9e7992f.

224 *Transcriptions are smart marketing:* RSS.com, "How to Transcribe."

224 *Some transcription services:* Join the Party, "Podcaster's Guide"; Olmsted, *Tools*, 110–17.

224 *See if your podcast:* Ross Winn, "How to Start a Podcast: A Complete Step-by-Step Tutorial (2019 Guide)," Podcast Insights, updated October 1, 2020, https://www.podcastinsights .com/start-a-podcast.

224 *Set up a style guide:* Join the Party, "Podcaster's Guide."

224 *Show notes can:* Castos, "How to Write Better Podcast Show Notes (With 3 Templates)," updated March 17, 2020, https://castos.com/ podcast-show-notes.

224 *you could link:* Buzzsprout, "Monetize Your Podcast: 9 Ways to Make Money Podcasting," April 21, 2020, https://www.buzzsprout.com/ blog/monetize-podcast.

224 *advertiser or sponsor links:* Olmsted, *Tools*, 109.

225 *Search engines "notice":* RSS.com, "9 Effective SEO Tips for Podcasts," n.d.,
accessed May 25, 2020, https://rss.com/blog/ nine-seo-tips-for-podcasts.

225 *be ready with your:* Werk It, "How to Market."

225 *Other ideas:* Castos, "How to Promote a Podcast on Facebook," updated September 1, 2020, https:// castos.com/promote-a-podcast-on-facebook.

225 *create a schedule:* Werk It, "How to Market."

226 *Make sure to announce:* Sarah Rhea Werner, "A Step-by-Step Walkthrough of My Podcast Process," *Forbes*, December 31, 2016, https:// www.forbes.com/sites/ sarahrheawerner/2016/12/31/ a-step-by-step-walkthrough-of-my-podcast-process/ ?sh=6192c9f613bf.

226 *someone writing a review:* Werk It, "How to Market."

226 *includes your podcast title:* Olmsted, *Tools*, 120.

226 *And always:* Matthew McLean, "How to Do Podcast Sponsorship (& Keep Your Audience!)," The Podcast Host, June 3, 2019, https:// www.thepodcasthost.com/ monetisation/how-to-do-podcast-sponsorship.

226 *Other ideas:* T. Brian Jones, "The Zengineering Podcast Electronic Press Kit," Medium, November 3, 2017, https://medium.com/ zengineering-podcast/ the-zengineering-podcast-electronic-press-kit-199b9cf69000.

226 *listener reviews:* McLean, "How to Do Podcast."

226 *Downloadable logos:* Jones, "Zengineering Podcast."

226 *You can also draw:* McLean, "How to Do Podcast."

228 *some marketing habits:* Unless otherwise noted, details in this list are from Meinzer, *So You Want*, chap. 35.

229 *Drill down in:* Werk It, "How to Market."

CHAPTER 15: LET THE POD GO FORTH

231 *podcast aggregators or podcatchers:* Castos, "How to Promote a Podcast: The 2020 Ultimate Guide," updated June 22, 2020, https://castos.com/ how-to-promote-a-podcast.

231 *created your episode as a WAV:* Kristen Meinzer, *So You Want to Start a Podcast* (New York: William Morrow, 2019), chap. 31.

232 *info you provide:* Meinzer.

232 *A feed validator:* For more, see Jill Olmsted, *Tools for Podcasting* (Washington, DC: American University, 2019), 108, http://toolsforpodcasting .openbooks.wpengine.com; and Daniel J. Lewis, "How to Fix Common Podcast RSS Feed Problems," The Audacity to Podcast, May 31, 2016, https://theaudacity topodcast.com/how-to-fix-common-podcast-rss-feed-problems-tap271.

233 *internet search engines:* Mike McEvoy, "SEO Titles, SEO Descriptions, Meta Tags, Meta Data Explained," Web Presence Solutions, October 2, 2019, https://www .webpresencesolutions .net/metadata-meta-tags-web-page-titles-page-descriptions-explained.

233 *What search words:* Wil Williams, "Mind Your Metadata: A Podcaster's Guide to Titles and Descriptions," Bello Collective, August 28, 2018, https://bellocollective .com/mind-your-metadata-a-podcasters-guide-to-titles-and-descriptions-479087734e6e.

233 *This is your chance to speak:* MOZ.com, "Meta Description," n.d., accessed May 25, 2020, https://moz.com/learn/seo/meta-description.

233 *right up front, as alluringly:* RSS.com, "9 Effective SEO Tips for Podcasts," n.d., accessed May 25, 2020, https://rss.com/blog/nine-seo-tips-for-podcasts.

233 *You can do tagging:* Aaron Dowd, "How to Tag a Podcast MP3 File," Simplecast, January 5, 2018, https://medium.com/simplecast/how-to-tag-your-mp3-files-9f0750e7c51a; and Matthew McLean, "Adding Cover Art & ID3 Tags to Your Episode with iTunes | Podcast Metadata," The Podcast Host, July 26, 2016, https://www.the podcasthost.com/websites-hosting/adding-cover-art-id3-tags-episode-itunes.

233 *Your episodes need a place:* Unless otherwise noted, the information in this section is from Colin Gray, "The Best Podcast Hosting Services: Where to Host Your Podcast," The Podcast Host, September 16, 2019 https://www.thepodcasthost.com/websites-hosting/best-podcast-hosting; and Brian Benton, "The 10 Best Podcast Hosting Services (for New & Experienced Podcasters)," Discover Pods, September 28,

2020, https://discoverpods .com/best-podcast-hosting-services.

233 *be a tech- and time-consuming process:* Meinzer, *So You Want*, chap. 31.

234 *you might be caught:* Olmsted, *Tools*, 104.

234 *Some hosts have:* Matthew McLean, "How to Podcast for Free (or as Little Money as Possible)," The Podcast Host, January 3, 2020, https://www.the podcasthost.com/planning/how-to-podcast-for-free.

234 *Hosts without a free option:* James Cridland, "Who's the Best Podcast Host—How to Choose," Podnews, August 5, 2019 (updated August 4, 2020), https://podnews.net/article/choosing-a-podcast-host.

234 *Pricing's generally tied:* Discover Pods, "How to Start a Podcast (The Complete Guide)," Discover Pods, July 2, 2020, https://discoverpods .com/start-podcast.

234 *If you're not that into tech:* Cridland, "Who's the Best."

235 *What about website:* The details in this item are from Cridland, "Who's the Best"; Matthew McLean, "Libsyn vs Blubrry: Where Should I Host My Podcast?," The Podcast Host, July 9, 2019, https://www.thepodcasthost.com/websites-hosting/libsyn-vs-blubrry; Benton, "10 Best Podcast"; and Olmsted, *Tools*, 109.

235 *Do they include episode numbers:* Cridland, "Who's the Best."

235 *what kinds of stats:* McLean, "Libsyn vs Blubrry."

235 *Are they IAB certified:* The details in this item are from Cridland, "Who's the Best"; and Meagan Francis, "Are You Ready to Make Real Money?," *Podcast Business Journal*, December 3, 2019, https://podcastbusinessjournal.com/are-you-ready-to-make-real-money.

235 *Can they grow with you:* Gray, "Best Podcast Hosting."

236 *Do they change your files:* Gray.

236 *Is (good) transcription offered:* Benton, "10 Best Podcast."

236 *How easy (or not) is it to leave:* Cridland, "Who's the Best."

236 *Here's a partial sampling:* Gray, "Best Podcast Hosting."

236 *If you're pretty sure:* Benton, "10 Best Podcast."

237 *Given how hard:* Olmsted, *Tools*, 106.

237 *known as syndicating:* Meinzer, *So You Want*, chap. 31.

237 *Check out online tutorials:* Meinzer.

CHAPTER 16: GROW FOR ME

242 *how a podcast is doing:* Unless otherwise noted, the details in this section are from Elizabeth Hines, "The Art of Measuring Podcast Success," Fronetics, May 14, 2018, https://www .fronetics.com/art-measuring-podcast-success; and Werk It: The Podcast, "You Can Grow Your Audience…Without Going Batsh*t Crazy," WNYC Studios, December 19, 2019, https://www.wnycstudios .org/podcasts/werkit/articles/you-can-grow-your-audience-without-going-batshit-crazy.

242 *Got an email list:* Castos, "How to Promote Your Podcast to Your Email List," updated July 9, 2020, https://castos.com/promote-your-podcast-to-your-email-list.

243 *"Sometimes the episode":* Sam Sanders, email communication, November 9, 2020.

243 *If someone sends you:* Kristen Meinzer, *So You Want to Start a Podcast* (New York: William Morrow, 2019), chap. 34.

243 *that routes automatically:* Meinzer, *So You Want,* chap. 20.

243 *We're doing a poll:* Olivia Seitz, "5 Patreon Reward Ideas You Can Offer Your Fans Today," Patreon, March 29, 2018, https://blog.patreon.com/patreon-reward-ideas.

243 *leave a review:* RSS.com, "9 Effective SEO Tips for Podcasts," n.d., accessed May 25, 2020, https://rss.com/blog/nine-seo-tips-for-podcasts; Meinzer, *So You Want,* chap. 34.

244 *And of course:* Meinzer, *So You Want,* chap. 34.

244 *"We released the show":* J. C. Howard, email communication, November 6, 2020.

244 *Kristin Hume, director of brand:* All quotes by Kristin Hume are from interview with author, June 11, 2020.

246 *Even if your budget's:* Werk It: The Podcast, "How to Market Your Show," WNYC Studios, January 23, 2019, https://www.wnycstudios.org/podcasts/werkit/articles/how-market-your-show.

246 *Tell them how much:* Sean Howard, "Advertising a Podcast, Part 3," Podnews, March 16, 2020, https://podnews.net/article/advertising-a-podcast-pt3.

246 *you exchange thirty seconds:* Werk It, "How to Market"; Meinzer, *So You Want,* chap. 35.

246 *Specific terms are:* Howard, "Advertising a Podcast, Part 3."

246 *Ads can be placed:* Podsights, "Which Podcast Ad Placement Converts the Best?," November 7, 2019, https://podsights.com/blog/placements; Howard, "Advertising a Podcast."

246 *You'll notice that:* Buzzsprout, "Monetize Your Podcast: 9 Ways to Make Money Podcasting," April 21, 2020, https://www.buzzsprout.com/blog/monetize-podcast.

246 *After family and friends':* Hume, interview.

246 *Spikes in downloads:* Howard, "Advertising a Podcast."

246 *Search out shows:* Meinzer, *So You Want,* chap. 35.

247 *an "episode drop":* Howard, "Advertising a Podcast."

248 *"If you have a community":* Hume, interview.

249 *"If you hear an ad":* Hume.

249 *"If you get no pleasure":* Manoush Zomorodi, email communication, November 2, 2020.

250 *"The first thing is":* Guy Raz, interview with author, October 29, 2020.

252 *Podcasts historically have:* Jill Olmsted, *Tools for Podcasting* (Washington, DC: American University, 2019), 30, http://toolsforpodcasting.openbooks.wpengine.com.

252 *donations (with a donation button:* Buzzsprout, "Monetize Your Podcast."; Frank Racioppi, "Why Your Podcast Definitely Needs a Website," Discover Pods, February 11, 2020, https://discoverpods.com/podcast-needs-website.

252 *pay-what-you-wish:* Olivia Seitz, "6 Business Models to Use on Patreon Today," Patreon, December 3, 2019, https://blog.patreon.com/6-membership-based-business-models-you-can-use-on-patreon-today.

252 *Patreon, a crowdfunding:* Olmsted, *Tools,* 31.

252 *Technically, a membership:* Anna Fitzgerald, "13 Best Membership Website Builders and Platforms in 2020," HubSpot, May 4, 2020, https://blog.hubspot.com/website/membership-website-builder.

252 *Start investigating:* Fitzgerald, "13 Best Membership."

252 *These strategies usually:* Gerri Detweiler, "Financing Your Podcast Business to the Next Level," *Podcast Business Journal*, November 21, 2019, https://podcastbusinessjournal.com/financing-your-podcast-business-to-the-next-level.

252 *make sure you can:* Buzzsprout, "Monetize Your Podcast."

253 *what your audience can afford:* Olivia Seitz, "19 Patreon Rewards for Podcasters to Offer Their Fans," Patreon, July 24, 2018, https://blog.patreon.com/19-patreon-rewards-for-podcasters-to-offer-their-fans.

253 *Donors thanked:* Meinzer, *So You Want,* chap. 32.

253 *Existing services or products:* Sujan Patel, "8 Ways Podcasters Can Profit from Their Shows," *Entrepreneur,* June 27, 2016, https://www.entrepreneur.com/article/277912.

253 *Bonus content*: Werk It, "How to Market."

253 *Joining the gang:* Seitz, "6 Business Models."

254 *Episode access:* Colin Gray, "How to Make Money with a Podcast: Monetisation 101," The Podcast Host, September 3, 2019, https://www.thepodcasthost.com/monetisation/podcast-monetisation; and Seitz, "19 Patreon Rewards."

254 *Ad-free access:* Meinzer, *So You Want,* chap. 32.

254 *Early-bird special:* Meinzer.

254 *Discounts*: Patel, "8 Ways Podcasters."

254 *Inside info:* Seitz, "5 Patreon Reward."

254 *Interaction with you:* Seitz, "6 Business Models."

254 *Make* them *the show:* Seitz, "19 Patreon Rewards."

254 *Ask for votes, input, opinions, feedback:* Seitz.

255 *Exclusive original content:* Seitz.

255 *Products and services:* Gray, "How to Make Money"; Racioppi, "Why Your Podcast."

255 *a live recording session:* Olmsted, *Tools,* 122.

255 *You, with one fan:* Gray, "How to Make Money."

255 *Teach what you know:* Seitz, "6 Business Models"; and Buzzsprout, "Monetize Your Podcast."

256 *Mugs, T-shirts, stickers:* Wenbin Fang, "How to Promote Podcasts: 21 Ways of Promoting Podcasts—Tips from 269 Indie Podcaster Interviews," Listen Notes, August 1, 2019, https://www.listennotes.com/podcast-academy/how-to-promote-podcasts-21-ways-of-promoting-14; Gray, "How to Make Money"; Racioppi, "Why Your Podcast"; Seitz, "19 Patreon Rewards."

256 *Some podcasts lend themselves:* Unless otherwise noted, details in this section are from Matthew McLean, "How to Do Podcast Sponsorship (& Keep Your Audience)," The Podcast Host, June 3, 2019, https://www.thepodcasthost.com/monetisation/how-to-do-podcast-sponsorship; and Gray, "How to Make Money."

256 *"clear and conspicuous" and has guidelines:* Federal Trade Commission, "The FTC's Endorsement Guides: What People Are Asking," September 2017, https://www.ftc.gov/tips-advice/business-center/guidance/ftcs-endorsement-guides-what-people-are-asking.

256 *A sponsor generally pays:* Meinzer, *So You Want,* chap. 32.

257 *Caveat: Be prepared:* Meinzer.

257 *Ads read by the host:* B. J. Keeton, "How to Monetize a Podcast," Elegant Themes, July 31, 2019, https://www.elegantthemes.com/blog/business/how-to-monetize-a-podcast.

257 *keep careful records:* Meinzer, *So You Want,* chap. 32.

258 *Think about what your target:* Dan Misener, "Inside Charles Schwab's "Audio Funnel," Pacific Content, November 14, 2019, https://blog.pacific-content.com/inside-charles-schwabs-audio-funnel-1d427541624f.

258 *Are you promoting:* Olmsted, *Tools,* 39.

258 *Give the episode number:* Castos, "How to Promote a Podcast: The 2020 Ultimate Guide," updated June 22, 2020, https://castos.com/how-to-promote-a-podcast.

258 *quality and schedule consistency:* Meagan Francis, "Real Money Can Be Made Podcasting," *Podcast Business Journal,* November 25, 2019, https://podcastbusinessjournal.com/real-money-can-be-made-podcasting.

GLOSSARY

262 *This glossary is largely based:* Alison MacAdam, "'Butt Cut What?' A Glossary of Audio Production Terms and Definitions," NPR Training, June 1, 2015, https://training.npr.org/2015/06/01/butt-cut-what-a-glossary-of-production-terms.

Acknowledgments

Thanks to agents Jane von Mehren and Lauren Sharp at Aevitas, to Matt Inman and the team at Ten Speed Press, and to everyone at NPR who helped bring this book into being, including but not limited to Anya Grundmann, Kristen Hartmann, Michael Lutzky, Neal Carruth, Ashley Messenger, Micah Ratner, Luke Medina, Daniel McCoy, Argin Hutchins, Kasia Podbielski, Keith Woods and Mathilde Piard. I'd hoped to sort of loom over the desks of my NPR podcasting colleagues until they gave me a nugget I could use in the book, but COVID-19 meant they instead had to endure repeated, entreating emails and phone calls. Thanks for responding, and for your invaluable input, Rund Abdelfatah, Ramtin Arablouei, Rob Byers, Jessica Deahl, Gene Demby, Nick Fountain, Cardiff de Alejo Garcia, Jessica Hansen, Linda Holmes, J. C. Howard, Kristin Hume, Mike Katzif, Danielle Kurtzleben, Susan Leland, Candice Lim, Andrew Limbong, Alison MacAdam, Kenny Malone, Kelly McEvers, Shereen Marisol Meraji, Steve Mulder, Guy Raz, Jessica Reedy, Sam Sanders, Sara Sarasohn, Yowei Shaw, Liana Simstrom, Madeline K. Sofia, Cara Tallo, Stephen Thompson, Jesse Thorn, Shankar Vedantam, Sami Yenigun and Manoush Zomorodi. Mostly, though, I need to thank my collaborating writer Toni Sciarra Poynter, who did the heavy lifting—pulling together sources, wrassling the outline into shape, beating the manuscript into submission. I often felt like I was watching someone deftly change a tire while standing a few feet away, holding the lug nuts in a hubcap. Toni's a star.

Index

Ten Speed Press and the Ten Speed Press colophon are
registered trademarks of Penguin Random House LLC. Portions
of this work are drawn from NPR training materials including
NPR Training and *NPR Ethics Handbook*.

Library of Congress Control Number: 2021931530

Hardcover ISBN: 978-0-593-13908-0
eBook ISBN: 978-0-593-13909-7

Printed in the United States

Illustrations by John Mata
Acquiring editor: Matthew Inman | Production editor:
    Kimmy Tejasindhu
Designer: Isabelle Gioffredi | Art director: Betsy Stromberg |
    Production designers: Mari Gill and Faith Hague
Production manager: Dan Myers
Copyeditor(s): Jeff Campbell | Proofreader(s): Jennifer McClain |
    Indexer: Ken DellaPenta
Publicist: David Hawk | Marketer: Daniel Wikey

10 9 8 7 6 5 4 3 2 1

First Edition